Concerto

The Story of
Clara Schumann

Clara Schumann

Concerto

The Story of
Clara Schumann

by

Bertita Harding

GEORGE G. HARRAP & CO. LTD
LONDON TORONTO WELLINGTON SYDNEY

THE AUTHOR is exceptionally indebted to the distinguished publishing firm of Breitkopf and Härtel, Leipzig, for the privilege of quoting from the vast store of Schumann and Brahms correspondence, without which this book would have lacked authenticity and the very breath of life.

With equal generosity the Österreichische Staatsdruckerei, of Vienna, has permitted the citing of long passages from the pen of Austria's poet laureate, Franz Grillparzer.

For the above immeasurable help, my warmest thanks!

BERTITA HARDING

First published in Great Britain 1962
by GEORGE G. HARRAP & Co. LTD
182 High Holborn, London, W.C.1

Printed in Great Britain by
Lowe and Brydone (Printers) Ltd., London, N.W.10

TO

JACK HARDING

unforgotten

In 1801

an unknown woman named Caroline wrote
to the philosopher Wilhelm August von
Schlegel:

". . . Oh, my friend, I repeat to you incessantly how short is life, and that nothing
exists so truly as a work of art. Criticism
perishes, human generations die out, sys-
tems change, but when one day the world
goes up in flames like a scrap of paper it
will be the works of art that glow the long-
est before they return unto God, and
darkness descends. . . ."

Concerto

The Story of
Clara Schumann

CHAPTER 1 The erstwhile Lutheran theology student but now music master Friedrich Wieck, of Torgau in Saxony, was highly intelligent. Yet, in common with a great portion of mankind, he cherished the fallacy that passion is synonymous with love. At the age of almost thirty-one, when he might have known better, he married one of his pupils, the pretty nineteen-year-old Marianne Tromlitz, under the febrile conviction that without her he could not live.

Marianne came from the lace-making center of Plauen, on the White Elster River, and to see her in ripples of handmade bridal finery capped Friedrich's dream of earthly bliss. The wedding took place on May 23, 1816, and the couple moved to Leipzig, where both husband and wife formed a teaching partnership. Friedrich furthermore found employment in a pawnbroker's shop which permitted him a small private trade in used pianos.

Within seven years the marriage produced five children: Adelheid, Clara-Josephine, Alwin, Gustav, and Victor. Passion, at all events, had not been lacking. But love suffered early shipwreck. Despite professional compatibility and the bonds supposedly forged by the patter of little feet there were fierce quarrels in the Wieck household. In the eighth year of their union the couple separated. By this time the eldest girl had died and Clara-Josephine was not yet five. While awaiting the divorce (a shocking undertaking in the tradition-bound Europe of 1824) the mother was allowed to retain her brood. But when Friedrich presented proof that his wife was being courted by a musical colleague named Bargiel, the children came under paternal custody, except for the baby Victor, who was in delicate health. Once free, Marianne married Bargiel and moved with him to Berlin, where, soon after, the little Victor expired. The stern Friedrich Wieck looked upon this as just retribution inflicted by Heaven on his former wife. It helped him bear his own loss.

With the remaining children the embittered man continued residing in a building called Kupfer's Haus, located in the Salz-Gässchen (Small Salt Street), not far from his place of work. An old housekeeper, Johanna Strobel, took care of kitchen and nursery. So taciturn and absorbed in her duties was Johanna that only monosyllables issued from her lips. "Eat!" "Drink!" "Wash!" "Sleep!" As a result the children were slow in learning speech, though they early developed an ear for music due to their father's long hours at the piano, after their bedtime at night.

Clara-Josephine became Friedrich's favorite simply because, being older than her brothers, she could be turned into an object for his pedagogic theories. He loved music above all else, and he intended to make of his daughter a first-rate musician.

Clara Wieck, Pianist.

This was the vision. The dual name was shortened when, a few weeks after her fifth birthday, the small girl had her first keyboard lesson. "Clara" she would be called thenceforth, and nothing more. It was a name that carried meaning: the radiant one, destined for shining fame.

The child had talent. Friedrich liked to think that this had been inherited from him, but it could equally well have come from Marianne's family. There was a maternal grandfather, Johann Georg Tromlitz, who had gained some renown as a flutist, composer, and manufacturer of wind instruments. What Clara would owe exclusively to her father was his excellent teaching method, an exposition of which eventually was to be published by the firm of Leuckart, in Leipzig, under the title of *Klavier und Gesang: Didaktisches und Polemisches (Piano and Song: An Instructor's and Innovator's Views).*

Progress was handicapped at first by the girl's inability to speak and, indeed, to understand speech. Was she deaf? The alarmed father promptly put an end to individual lessons and brought Clara into contact with the older pupils at his school, whereupon a happy change occurred. Exposure to the outside world supplied what had been missing at home. From her new companions Clara learned to become vocal. Within a few weeks she was a normal little chatterbox, which in turn proved of benefit to her younger brothers.

Born on September 13, 1819, Clara was precocious, prematurely wise, pensive, methodical, prudent. September is a harvest month, belonging to the year's decline, with a touch of fall in the air. The small Clara seemed to reflect this in grotesque moods of grown-up solemnity when she was still of pre-school age. She also displayed a droll self-assurance and early need of approval. Contemporary infants gurgling in their cradles were the future Queen Victoria of England; her husband-to-be, Prince Albert of Saxe-Coburg-Gotha; Jacques Offenbach, James Russell Lowell, and a small girl named Mary Ann Evans, who would one day call herself George Eliot. In one way or another each of these was marked for distinction.

As for Clara Wieck, she knew from the first that she would become, or that it was planned for her to become, a concert artist. This realization, instilled before she learned to recite the alphabet, dominated her childhood as it would her later life. Whether it was implanted by her father or was of spontaneous origin, she was ruled by a true obsession. She felt her destiny to be marked out: her name meant Clarity—the Lucid One.

Friedrich Wieck fed her ambition. Under his piano method (based on a natural position of the hands, with loose wrist and fingers only slightly curved so as to avoid the "hammer touch" of other schools) she made rapid progress. At times Wieck resorted to the mechanical aids of Johann Bernhard Logier, inventor of the chiroplast (a glovelike device with metal splints to hold the wrist in place), though the ultimate benefit was doubtful. Wieck also paid special attention to the third and fourth fingers, structurally deficient in limberness. But above all he impressed upon Clara that no keyboard difficulty was insurmountable if attacked with industry and courage.

To study under Papa Wieck was never dull. His precepts included chromatic scales in all keys, plus the usual octave and arpeggio exercises. But there was more. "Piano playing," he preached, "must be a pleasure!" Thus he composed for his daughter, and for his outside pupils as well, short melodic pieces designed to develop technique while at the same time arousing in the student a sense of beauty and enjoyment.

He was a disciplinarian, but not to the utmost degree of "bend or break." Training and talent, he knew, were both essential in the shaping of a future artist, particularly in music. Though it was his ardent wish to turn his own daughter into a great pianist he would have desisted if he had discovered in her a lack of aptitude or of true ear. His effort then would have been directed toward the younger sons. And, if he failed here, there were still the many Wieck disciples among whom he might find his malleable clay.

In art the miracle does not work of itself. It must *be* worked to find fruition. A vivid example of this were the Mozart children—Wolfgang Amadeus and his older sister Marianne (Nannerl)—who, though enormously gifted, might never have been heard of but for the driving force of Leopold Mozart, their father. In providing that basic starting point, a home where music was cultivated, Leopold had opened the minds of his daughter and son to a world otherwise locked. Had the two children grown up on a farm, bucolically remote from the intellectual complexities of city life (and concertizing is an urban, not a rural, phenomenon), the boy Wolfgang Amadeus might playfully have carved himself a shepherd's fife on which to pipe an artless tune. But never could this reed have turned into a Magic Flute. In short, no artist of immortal stature is his own creation. At least one generation, and often more than one, must go before to lay and prepare the ground for the supreme flowering.

Friedrich Wieck was no sorcerer. He could not have forced an unmusical Clara into the pianist's mold. But he could instruct and drill her with severity until he obtained the sought-after response. "Yes . . . No . . . Maybe . . ." For the last two he had no use. Only the first would prompt him to go on.

With Clara the answer was an unequivocal affirmative. The five-year-old sat with aplomb atop the three cushions on the piano stool needed to bring her abreast the keyboard. Her tiny fingers obeyed deftly as, with dark eyes fixed on the paternal mentor, the child learned the first of the fundamental Wieck rules: "We *touch*. We do not *hit*." A corollary was to follow soon after: "Listen! There must be beauty in the sound." In time these cardinal principles were understood and applied by the child, both in *pianissimo* and *forte* passages. Not the least of Clara's qualities when she became a pianistic world figure would be the splendor of her tone production.

Her memory, from earliest days, was prodigious. Before she could read or write, her ear retained songs, minuets, études and sonatinas adapted by Papa Wieck to her elfin reach. She played in time and rhythm although she had not learned to count. When at the age of six she entered school and made the acquaintance of numbers she recognized these as graphic symbols for the tictac of her metronome. The strenuous curriculum to which she was subjected did not make of Clara a husky outdoor child. On coming home from school she received a daily music lesson from her father, and practiced for two hours after that. This left little time for active games and romps with her small brothers. Though healthy and high-spirited, she gave the impression of fragility, accentuated by her brunette coloring and the pronounced oval of her face. She had large almond-shaped eyes that could take on an expression of deep gravity. Her features were fine and elongated, somewhat Italian in cast. With crinoline, and hair done in the Biedermeier fashion of the age, she looked less like a petite girl than a diminutive woman. Far too early in life she had the grace and poise of a Dresden figurine.

From the day of her first music lesson Clara's father started a diary for her. Since she was unable to write, he took it upon himself to make the preliminary entries, in the first person singular, as though Clara were wielding the pen. In curt and unemotional terms he recorded the parental divorce, wasting no sympathy on the somewhat nebulous personality of Marianne Tromlitz, the former Frau Wieck. He also took great pains to underscore the dual job falling upon him, as a forsaken husband, left to act out the role of both mother and father to his children. Finally, he elucidated on his teaching methods, listing (still ostensibly in Clara's words) the repertoire that made up her initial year of study.

Apart from scales and short melodic exercises the tiny girl was playing compositions by Horr, Spohr, Kreutzer, Anthes, Arion, and Diabelli, apparently with such zest and abandon that she hummed and crowed the tunes while executing them. Papa Wieck encouraged this. To further the notion that piano-playing could be great fun he joined his daughter in performing four-handed waltzes and mazurkas, in which Clara was allowed to drum out a vigorous *oohm-ta-ta* bass.

At the age of six she began with finger-stretching exercises that would enable her to reach octaves, though as yet in a hit-or-miss grasshopper fashion. And shortly before her seventh birthday she joined her father and a neighborly string quartet in a parlor performance of Tobias Haslinger's *Concertino*.

Around this time Clara also visited her first theater. The play, *The Poor Poet*, by the German satirist August Friedrich Ferdinand von Kotzebue, proved beyond her comprehension, but she was impressed by a matinee idol of the day, the forty-two-year-old Ludwig Devrient. As for Kotzebue's work, it found little favor with the Saxon public, whose sensibilities were pricked by the dramatist's attack on the lachrymose *Weltschmerz* and other sentimental excesses of the Romantic Age.

Early nineteenth-century romanticism was the direct result of the social changes wrought, a generation back, by the French Revolution. Classic rigidity, the caste system, and every form of artifice had reached such extremes just prior to 1789 (people with perfectly good hair wore powdered wigs!) that literature and the arts had run dry with repetition. Painters, poets, playwrights, long fettered by the eighteenth-century concept that only the titled rich made fitting subjects for brush or pen, languished for lack of new ideas. With the fall of the Bastille, however, spiritual prison walls had also been demolished. Humanity discovered humanitarianism, and man recognized his image in the common man.

For the better part of fifty years the intellectual world would indulge in a back-to-nature spree. The animal kingdom, the simple peasant, the noble savage, all assumed unsuspected significance. With the surge of this rebirth Europe soon wallowed in a spurious emotionalism that was both unrealistic and grotesque. If creative artists heretofore had glorified only the mighty, the opposite was now the case. The disinherited had come into their own. Their misery, formerly unnoticed, now drew lyric apostrophes.

Commiseration spilled over geographic boundaries, eventually encompassing aboriginal life across the seven seas. Primitive existence acquired an odor of sanctity for no reason other than that it was primitive. Authors indulged in imaginary Robinson Crusoe expeditions to areas rarely traceable on a map, yet always depicted with fustian eloquence. Descriptive prose, interminable and deadly, was indeed in its apogee. Readers basked in such yarns as *Atala*, by the Vicomte François René de Chateaubriand; a dollop of bucolic pap called *Paul et Virginie*, by Bernardin de Saint-Pierre; and the farfetched fiction of an otherwise excellent diarist and political observer, Anne Louise Germaine Necker, Baroness (Madame) de Staël. In America, on the banks of the Susquehanna, James Fenimore Cooper almost simultaneously exalted the redskin in his *Leatherstocking Tales,* while Germany would see a spate of Tuareg and Bedouin sagas by Karl May, who, though he wrote in the first person and professed intimate acquaintance with his characters, pulled one Sahara tribesman after another out of his modest armchair-traveler's hat. Actually Karl May must be regarded as a late bloom in the florid jungles of romanticism, trailing into the limelight when the movement had entered its decline. His epic tracts would not fall into Clara Wieck's hands until she had left childhood well behind.

For the present, music dominated the small girl's life. By the end of 1827 Clara's sense of pitch was so well developed that she could turn her back to the piano and name any key struck by her father. She was also learning the basic elements of harmony. Without much effort she distinguished tonic chords from dominants, subdominants from sevenths, whether major or minor. This enabled her to improvise at will and to attempt her first childish compositions. The strength of her fingers had increased to the point where she was doing trills, and now Papa Wieck extended the daily practice period from two hours to three. Beyond this exaction he was never to go. Throughout his long and admirable pedagogical career (he stopped teaching at eighty-eight) Friedrich Wieck condemned the all-day practice marathons to which the more prominent academicians were addicted. He saw in mere bravura or brilliance of technique a corresponding loss of tonal quality and emotion. Again and again he impressed upon his pupils: "To dazzle is one thing; to give enjoyment, quite another."

He was proud of Clara's touch. Though a slim child, she had soft, chubby hands (no bones showing) which literally caressed the keys even when her play called for volume and verve. Beyond all else Papa Wieck wanted to preserve this *summum bonum.* His daughter's play must retain heart, and give the effect of strings stroked with silk or velvet. Above all, Clara must never suffer nervous exhaustion. He taught her the calm assurance and poise that went with a proper balance of mental and physical resources.

To encourage a spirit of adventure he allowed the girl to enter the warehouse where his supply of salable pianos was kept. She tried every instrument, scornfully dismissing upright and square models in favor of elegant ebony grands, especially when the latter bore the name

Andreas Stein of Vienna. So great was her enthusiasm for this trademark that, on her eighth birthday, a flawless new instrument was ordered for her directly from the Stein firm. Clara earned this reward by having played, four days earlier, Mozart's *Concerto in E-Flat Major* with the assistance of a chamber orchestra consisting of two violins, two violas, two horns, a cello, and a flute. The Wieck home had been thrown open to a group of guests for the occasion, and refreshments were served. Clara wore a ribbon in her perkily topknotted hair, small gold tassel earrings, and a new dress with huge sleeves puffed just below the shoulders. She was allowed to write her mother in Berlin, reporting the event. In her own words:

> Everything went quite well and I didn't get stuck. Only my cadenza wouldn't come off right away, where I had to repeat a chromatic scale three times, yet it didn't scare me at all.

A wistful footnote followed: "I hope to visit you soon and to play many four-handed pieces with you."

For the moment, however, there was no prospect of a reunion between the Wieck children and their mother. Stagecoach travel in those days was slow and full of hazards. Besides, Papa Wieck's activities were too manifold to permit overland jaunts that served no profitable end. As for sending Clara or her brothers in the care of a servant, that was out of the question.

He made the matter clear to the hapless Marianne: "Women who love their children should guard against giving grounds for divorce."

CHAPTER 2   The Leipzig in which Clara was growing up had only recently achieved a painful rebirth.

Scarcely fourteen years earlier the city, and all of Saxony, had been devastated by the clash of arms between Napoleon's forces returning from their Moscow defeat, and the dominated peoples of Austria, Germany, and Sweden, who joined Russia in trouncing the fallen conqueror on his long homeward retreat.

The great *Völkerschlacht* (Battle of the Nations) at Leipzig had opened on October 16, 1813, and lasted three days. A five-month-old baby named Richard Wagner lay in his cradle under the eaves of a house on Brühl Street, listening to the roar and thunder, while the as yet unmarried Marianne Tromlitz sighed with adolescent rapture and chagrin at the interruption of her piano lessons under the so admirable Herr Friedrich Wieck.

Leipzig was badly shattered at the time, and would require most of the following decade to rise from its ashes. Characteristically the music-loving community attended first to the repair of its concert halls and theaters. The noble Gewandhaus, frequented by Europe's leading artists since its founding in 1781, functioned again while Napoleon brooded on Elba. When the Corsican died on St. Helena, in 1821, Leipzig had already resumed its famous Easter Fair, to which Herr Wieck took his two-year-old daughter Clara to see the dancing bears and hear the chiming Glockenspiel. He also pointed to a dark, battle-scarred building, murmuring: "In a little while, with God's help, you will play the piano there, on the Gewandhaus stage."

The "little while" would cover seven years, and these were well employed. Soon after Clara had mastered her first scales, Wieck gathered family and friends to hear the child perform, knowing well the value of an audience in helping overcome self-consciousness. He followed the same principle with his other pupils. Periodically all of them appeared in recitals to which parents, acquaintances, and even long-suffering household servants were bidden.

"The artist who keeps his art a secret is of no use to anyone," declared the positivist pedagogue.

Friedrich Wieck was widely known by this time. Musical aspirants came to Leipzig from remote parts of Germany for the privilege of studying under him. Among these was a handsome youth named Robert Schumann, youngest of five children of a publisher in nearby Zwickau, Friedrich August Gottlob Schumann, and the latter's wife Johanna Christiane Schnabel.

Robert had been born on June 8, 1810, the same year as Chopin and the French lyric poet Alfred de Musset. The musical giant of the age, Beethoven, had turned thirty-nine, while Mendelssohn was a year old, and Schubert a boy of thirteen. The birth of another pianistic luminary, Liszt, lay only a year away.

When Robert Schumann was six, he lost his father. With the income from a small legacy his education was assured, including the eventual study of law. An obedient son, he followed his mother's wishes and enrolled at Leipzig University, but found the academic life unutterably boring. In part, the aspect of the city must be blamed for this. Leipzig was still in the process of rebuilding. Whole blocks lay devastated, streets unpaved, sidewalks littered with debris. He couldn't study there, wrote Robert to his mother; it was too depressing. She agreed to his moving to Heidelberg.

The beautiful university town on the Neckar River, Province of Baden, suited him much better. Here Robert fell in with fun-loving friends, among them a group of Bavarians who studied little but consumed vast quantities of beer. With these he spent less time in lecture halls than along the riverbanks or on excursion boats headed for neighboring pleasure spots. His was a restless spirit, responsive to outside stimuli and change.

He was highly musical, having learned his first notes from an archdeacon named Hans Doehner. The next teacher had been the local organist Johann Gottfried Kuntzsch, who urged Schumann *père* to introduce his son to Carl Maria von Weber, director of the Dresden Opera, and to Ignaz Moscheles at Carlsbad. Weber, wary of child prodigies, gave the boy a cool reception. The Czech Moscheles, on the other hand, was ravished and predicted a great future.

Robert's progress in music was hampered, nevertheless, by a strong literary bent, awakened through exposure to the treasures of his father's library and print shop. Thus the boy had gained early familiarity with the works of Shakespeare, Goethe, Byron, and a mystic poet-novelist named Jean Paul Richter. Inevitably he himself wrote verses while alternating with piano practice and the study of harmony.

At Heidelberg, instead of concentrating on his lawbooks, Robert launched a student newspaper in which philosophic articles and romantic novelettes alternated with theater and concert critiques. Most of the contributions were by his own pen, signed with a variety of pseudonyms. His split nature unquestionably was ruled by many demons.

When the beer-guzzling Bavarians proposed cutting classes in favor of travel, Robert responded eagerly. By stagecoach the party set out for Gotha, Hanau, and Frankfurt-am-Main. In the latter city they stopped at a lodging house flanked by a Roman Catholic church and the local insane asylum.

"If this be an omen," Robert wrote his shocked mother, "I don't know whether I shall one day turn monk or madman."

While sightseeing in Frankfurt he thought of a tune and felt an irresistible urge to try it out on somebody's piano. This would be difficult, since he knew no one in the big merchant metropolis. But a music shop near the business center soon attracted his eye. With an ingratiating smile he approached the owner, introducing himself as the private tutor of a talented young English lord who currently was visiting Germany.

Said Schumann, "My pupil plans to remain some time in your splendid city. He would like to rent a piano."

The proprietor fluttered solicitously. "His Lordship will want the best! A grand *piano-à-queue?*"

"An Andreas Stein, of course." In that day, Robert knew, nothing better was being built.

Several assistants stepped up, pointing to a prize instrument. "Perhaps His Lordship would care to come in person and have a try?"

"No, the decision has been left to me."

With an apologetic shrug Robert sat down and began to play. He played for three hours, astonishing and delighting the assembled personnel with his virtuosity, his gift for improvisation. Finally, having exhausted his inspiration, he bowed and walked off amid a roar of applause. The shop owner, accompanying him to the door, ventured a question:

"The piano—er—you find it good?"

"Excellent."

Then where was it to be sent?

Schumann lightly tapped the man's lapel. "I shall let you know." He winked significantly. "When His Lordship hears my opinion of this instrument we may not rent it, we may *buy*." He had put on his hat, but lifted it again. "You may compute the price in English pounds. Good-day!"

Departing, he left behind a happy dither of speculation. How many Frankfurt *thaler* to the pound? While this was being computed the carefree Schumann had reached his lodgings where his companions waited. They were off to Wiesbaden that day, with a Rhine journey ahead. Only at Rüdesheim, over a glass of vintage wine, did Robert feel a pang of conscience. He held too modest a view of his own talents to presume that a three-hour concert was sufficient to compensate the chagrin suffered by the piano dealer. In silent remorse he drank a toast to the justifiably enraged victim of his prank.

The wanderings ended soon after, with term examinations waiting at Heidelberg. Robert made a poor showing. Yet he still did not want to distress his mother by giving up the study of law. He started his second year with earnest resolutions to do better. By Michaelmas, however, the travel urge seized him again. The Christmas holidays were approaching, with eight weeks of freedom. The widow Schumann received a letter from her youngest son:

> Just listen to these enchanting names—Lago Maggiore, Milano, Brescia, Verona, Padua, Venezia—and you will write me: "My good Robert, a youth like you must kick up his heels so that his spiritual wings may function the better. This takes money. But it will help you see other worlds peopled by other men. You will learn French and Italian, which is worth spending a few coins" . . . .

Johanna Schumann's answer contained no such heartening words. Nevertheless, she let him have his way.

Italy put an end to Robert's prospective career as an attorney. Under the spell of that paradise of the arts he rebelled against further pursuit of a profession for which he knew himself unfitted. On returning he resigned from Heidelberg University and went for a second time to Leipzig, there to enroll in the music school of the noted Friedrich Wieck.

The year was 1828 and a number of changes had taken place in the world of cultural values. Franz Schubert lay ill in Vienna, of typhus (he would die on November 19, at the age of thirty-one). Beethoven had passed away the previous year, and Lord Byron shortly before that, fighting for Greece and liberty at Missolonghi. During the same interval, though hardly as compensation in kind, two births might be noted: that of Johann Strauss II, future composer of the "Beautiful Blue Danube," and the Russian novelist-to-be, Count Leo Tolstoy. At this time also, in the French town of Coupvray (Department of Seine-et-Marne), a nineteen-year-old youth named Louis Braille, blind since the age of three, was devising for himself an alphabet by means of pin-pricks, which one day would be put to universal use.

The Wieck household expanded, as Clara and her brothers acquired a kindly stepmother, Clementine Fechner, daughter of a Lutheran minister in Niederlausitz. Papa Wieck furthermore achieved an important triumph in winning for Clara her first professional engagement at the Gewandhaus, on October 20, 1828. The child would not appear alone on the program, the main attraction of which was an already established Austrian pianist, Ernestine Perthaler. The Perthaler repertoire falling short of Leipzig standards (in length, not quality), Wieck had succeeded in placing his master pupil Emilie Reichold and the nine-year-old Clara as supplementary artists. The two girls would render a piano duet, *Variations, Opus 94,* by Christian Kalkbrenner, with Clara executing the less arduous bass. It wasn't much. But the ambitious parent looked on the occasion as his daughter's debut.

Prior to the concert there occurred a mishap which almost prevented Clara's appearance. The Gewandhaus owned a fine brougham drawn by a pair of spanking palfreys, traditionally on hand to fetch performers to and from the concert hall. On her important night the small Clara was likewise to be accorded this honor. She waited, attired in her best frock and neatly buttoned lace mitts, when a concièrge called from the courtyard below:

"Carriage for Fräulein Clara!"

Papa Wieck having already left to supervise arrangements onstage, his daughter was to ride alone, chaperoned only by the Gewandhaus footman.

Proudly she descended the stairs, gaped at by awed neighbors. But now a shock awaited her. The well-known brougham with its polished lanterns was nowhere in sight. Instead, an aged barouche drawn by a tired nag waited in the shadows. A burly coachman helped Clara aboard before setting the vehicle in motion.

To her surprise the child found herself sitting beside another occupant, a girl in party clothes who was vaguely familiar, and yet did not speak and certainly was not Clara's duet partner Emilie Reichold. After rumbling on for a few blocks the carriage stopped again and a new passenger climbed in; some minutes later, another, and another. Now Clara noted the strange neighborhood through which she was being taken.

"This isn't the way to the Gewandhaus!" she cried, poking a finger in the driver's back.

"No, Miss," was the placid answer. "We're headed for the country dance at Eutritzch."

Frightened, Clara broke into tears. But now she heard shouts and the snapping of whips from somewhere in the rear. The Gewandhaus brougham had caught up and its uniformed lackey rushed forward to rescue the unwittingly kidnaped child-pianist. An explanation of the mishap followed. A ground-floor tenant at the Wieck address had a daughter likewise named Clara, who, on the same evening, was being hauled—in the company of other young participants—to the rustic frolic mentioned above. Hence the mix-up in carriages.

Backstage at the Gewandhaus a fretful Papa Wieck bit his nails. He was a punctual man who had taught his children to respect the clock. Clara's tardiness could mean only one thing: she had come to harm.

When the girl at last arrived, still shaken with sobs, he saw that her normal innocent self-confidence had gone by the boards. She trembled and could not compose herself. At this the stern pedagogue resorted to a ruse.

"Oh, didn't I tell you?" he extemporized. "Artists are always mistaken for other people, till *after* their debut!"

She took comfort in the logic of this. With a debut over, and critiques and portrait sketches in the papers, one became better known. Of course.

The concert took its course without grief. Clara played faultlessly and won her share in the final applause. She took a personal bow, and found her name mentioned in a music review the following day. Under the glow of this first brush with the limelight she sat down and composed a merry waltz for the housekeeper Johanna Strobel, who, more inarticulate than ever, wept in lieu of stuttering her thanks.

By the time Robert Schumann returned to Leipzig and took up his studies with Friedrich Wieck, the pre-adolescent Clara had played for Niccolo Paganini, the phenomenal violinist who was an annual headliner at the Gewandhaus. She had also been taken to Dresden for a number of private recitals organized by her father in the homes of wealthy business associates. These gatherings brought no material profit. But society folk and even persons linked to Saxon royalty attended these performances. Thus the name of Clara Wieck began to command attention.

She was a gangling eleven-year-old when her interest in Robert, now twenty, first awakened. It is uncertain whether Schumann remembered seeing her two years earlier during his initial Leipzig stay. In any case, Clara could be no more in his eyes than a precocious child, whereas Robert appeared to her the apogee of male beauty.

They met daily henceforth since, to keep close contact with his teacher, the young man became a paying lodger in a rear room of the Wieck flat, with windows looking out on the Reichstrasse. The front lay in the Grimmagasse, and bore the number 36. One reason for Robert's serious application was to prove to his mother, and to the guardian Herr Rudel who administered his funds, that he had done right in choosing music for a career.

Wieck had enormous faith in the youth's talent. In a long letter to Johanna Schumann, dated August 9, 1830, the teacher stated:

> . . . I herewith promise that your son Robert, with his talent and imagination, shall in three years' time be turned by me into one of the greatest now living pianists, more spirited and warm than Moscheles and more grandiose than Hummel. For proof I cite my own eleven-year-old daughter, whom I am just beginning to present to the world. As for the study of composition, I feel sure that our Cantor Weinlich will, for the time being, suffice. . . .

Christian Theodor Weinlich, cantor at the St. Thomas School in Leipzig, had also for a pupil the seventeen-year-old Richard Wagner.

The Wagner family being poor, Richard could not aspire to instrumental lessons under the prominent Herr Wieck; in part this may have led him to forego an interpretative career in favor of creative musicianship.

Soon after, though for a different reason, Robert Schumann was to arrive at the same decision. Bent on recovering the time lost at Heidelberg (pianists did not usually begin at twenty!) he overtaxed his hands in practice. Worse than that, he tried to achieve flexibility by tying back alternate fingers to his left and right wrist, respectively, which ended with serious nerve inflammation and permanent damage to his right hand. The promise made by Friedrich Wieck was thus never fulfilled, a defeat the proud mentor would not be able to forgive.

Clara meanwhile was progressing steadily. On November 8, 1830, she appeared as soloist with the Gewandhaus orchestra, playing the *Rondo Brillant, Opus 101,* by Kalkbrenner. This was followed by some Herz *Variations,* and a four-piano number of Czerny's in which she was assisted by three orchestra members. To wind up she offered some unpublished paraphrases on a theme of her own. The urge to compose, though it would not dominate her life, was nevertheless a notable part of Clara's talent.

A second visit to Dresden over the Christmas holidays won for the child additional laurels. Again Clara played before the aristocracy and twice in the concert hall of the Hôtel de Pologne. Not only was she now a paid artist, but the recipient of tribute in the form of jewelry. The time had also come for envy to raise its baiting voice. Some disgruntled fellow musicians circulated a rumor that Clara was not eleven but sixteen years old, and that she could neither read nor write her own name. Furthermore, she had never possessed a doll, and she was kept a virtual prisoner by her father, who made her sit at the piano for twelve hours a day.

To the untruth of such statements Robert Schumann could bear witness. Living with the Wiecks under one roof, he saw that Clara's musical education was indeed rigorous. But there remained ample time for normal schooling and childish play.

If Clara's interest in toys faded early it was supplanted by a tender love for birds, puppies, kittens, and other pets whom she mothered with a passionate abandon. Hers was an irrepressible temperament. Innumerable times she danced through the paternal flat, crashing into the forbidden sanctum where Robert sat over his books, and disrupting his concentration with a giddy chant:

"I am so happy—I am so happy!"

This when it was an altogether ordinary day like any other ordinary day, with nothing special to be happy about!

There lay here an early manifestation of a blessed truth. Genius—and who could doubt that in this child dwelled genius!—is rarely sad. The gifts of Heaven are a fount of joy, and they are seldom wasted on the misanthrope. Mere knowledge may be grim, but wisdom has a radiance.

This radiance enveloped Clara. Contemporaries and later biographers compared her sunny nature to that of the young Mozart. Certainly she possessed the Salzburg prodigy's disarming candor. Hers was the same ebullience shown by the six-year-old Wolfgang Amadeus Mozart, who at Castle Schoenbrunn, on hearing his clavichord performance praised by the Archduchess Maria Antonia Josepha Johanna of Habsburg (later Marie Antoinette of France), informed that pretty princess: "When I grow up I want to marry you!"

The bouncing Clara said no such thing to Robert. Yet, as he shooed her exasperatedly from his room, a not unsimilar Mozartian sentiment was taking form within her.

With the innocence of her not quite concluded childhood, and the temerity of the coming changeling years, she loved him.

CHAPTER 3   Robert Schumann was by no means unresponsive to feminine charm. But his susceptibility dwindled when he was confronted with the wiles of a gawky eleven-year-old. He frankly looked upon the adoring Clara as a confounded nuisance.

There were other and more mature young ladies on the student roster of Friedrich Wieck whom Robert liked far better. Also, two girls from his native Zwickau (identified only as Liddy and Nanny) disputed his favors between them in a rivalry he did nothing to quell since he wrote poetry to them both.

But the end of 1830 saw a sharp decline in these romantic interests. Following the damage he had done to his right hand Robert fell into moods of darkest melancholy which caused him to distrust his ability to redeem himself as a composer. In one of his more despondent moments he considered running off to America, or to Russia, where he had an uncle living at Tver, on the Volga. The uncle was a total stranger to him, but a cholera epidemic raged at Tver just then, and Robert thought he would like to catch it.

While he was thus engaged in battle against himself, the sanguine Clara continued to make steady progress. At the age of twelve she composed her first song, with the title "Swans Come Gliding." She was now studying music theory and counterpoint, which prepared her for an introduction to the works of Johann Sebastian Bach. Inevitably her growing self-assurance led to displays of sauciness and cheek. Thus, on a Dresden visit with her father, Clara was invited to the home of a certain Count Kospoth, whose wife ranked among Germany's best amateur pianists. Would Fräulein Wieck consent to play a duet, after dinner, with her hostess?

"Sure," was the impertinent answer, "if Countess Kospoth really can play. . . ."

This sort of thing needed curbing, and Papa Wieck lost no time taking his cocksure daughter in hand. He punctured her pride with withering criticism. Who did she, a mere beginner, think she was? Her technique lacked finish, her style was immature; instead of boasting of her prowess she might do well to observe and learn from others. He went on in this vein until the girl fled weeping to Schumann's door.

"Papa is furious with me," she wailed. "He threatens to stop giving me lessons. I am to learn housekeeping and cookery. . . ."

At such times Robert relented and allowed Clara the run of his study. When the storm had blown over he showed her what he was working on: his *Abegg Variations, Opus 1* (the title derived from the opening notes A-B-E-G-G-), in the Hummel-Moscheles tradition, and his "Butterfly Themes" called *Papillons, Opus 2,* somewhat reminiscent of Schubert. She was enchanted. "I will play your works in all my concerts," she promised, unconsciously patronizing. It was a promise she meant, and which she would keep through the rest of her life.

In 1831 Clara took up the study of French. Her father was planning an autumn tour for her which would include Paris and Berlin. During August, however, the girl fell ill with measles and there was coincidently an outbreak of cholera in Berlin. This delayed the trip and also modified the itinerary to include Weimar, where Clara was received by the eighty-three-year-old Goethe on October 1, at midday. In playing for the great man she required a cushion, fetched by Goethe from an adjoining room, to elevate the piano seat. After her performance the poet remarked: "This fragile maid has the strength of six boys!"

The comment was inspired by Clara's execution of the appallingly difficult Chopin *Variations, Opus 2,* considered "impossible" by most pianists of the day. In addition to this triumph in Goethe's presence Friedrich Wieck could now look upon his daughter, at twelve, as a published composer. An album of four polonaises by her hand was being offered for sale in leading music stores.

Another Weimar event was recorded in Clara's diary. Being invited one evening to play before the grand-ducal court, she found herself suddenly joined at the piano by her princely host, who pulled up a chair so that he could watch her fingers at close range. When Clara had finished her scheduled program, the Grand Duke kept her at the keyboard for another hour, during which she paraphrased old tunes or improvised new ones at will. It is noteworthy that the Weimar days took the young girl out of herself as nothing before had ever done. Though she was manifestly the center of attention she did not feel this to be so. The presence of Goethe had overawed her. She came away flaunting not the panegyrical reviews that acclaimed her achievements but the signature of Germany's giant of letters in her book of autographs.

The tour brought disappointments as well. At Gotha, where an appreciative public awaited her, Clara suffered her first platform upset. This occurred when a lady (the concert was in a private mansion) summoned a footman and ordered a cup of tea; on receiving the beverage she slurped it noisily while clattering with saucer and spoon.

On the makeshift podium Clara's concentration was disrupted. With tremendous effort she tried to ignore the disturbance but could not. Playing from notes, she lost her place in the score and broke down. It was the first time in her short life that the fearless child experienced failure.

The shock was terrible. Although she herself could not be blamed— the stupid woman in the audience was at fault—Clara discovered the frailty that spirit no less than flesh is heir to. Her superlative composure had faltered. It was a sobering experience.

Happily, the concert did not end on that dismal note. After a moment of panic Clara regained control. Calmly she smoothed the pages before her and played on. She finished the program with her already customary aplomb.

Friedrich Wieck, for his part, knew how to exploit the incident of the lady and the teacup. Here was a valuable object lesson. Whatever the provocation, sooner or later every performing artist fell victim to a mental blackout. In a sense it was almost necessary for this to happen, so as to awaken and develop the gift of improvisation. The more so as a new fashion was taking hold in France, where Chopin and Liszt dazzled their hearers by playing exclusively from memory. If this vogue became general, Clara must be prepared. Only the extemporizing musician could defend himself against a lapse in his retentive faculties, as must the resourceful actor who lost a line midway in a play.

"*Think* what you are doing," Wieck had long insisted to those of his pupils who prepared also for opera. "So long as the action on stage makes sense, you can forget a literal text by supplying phrases of similar meaning. Mechanical recollection is treacherous. Don't memorize. *Remember!*"

The advice held for concert artists as well. Clara paid heed, and decided to do both: memorize *and* remember. The Gotha experience thus was turned into a boon. Silly tea-drinking females, opined Herr Wieck, cropped up in concert halls to teach the virtuoso how to combat amnesia. Thenceforth Clara would be prepared.

On this same tour the travelers touched Hesse-Cassel, where lived Wieck's friend and colleague Ludwig Spohr. The latter operated a music school in addition to being a creative artist whom critics referred to as "the best among the second-best composers." Frau Spohr, the harpist Dorette Schneider, also enjoyed considerable renown. In short, Wieck requested an audition for his daughter at the Spohrs', to obtain their unvarnished views regarding her future handling.

After hearing the girl play, Spohr and his wife grew voluble in their praise. Privately, while Clara feasted in another room on cake and hot chocolate, Wieck heard his child referred to as another Emilie Belleville Oury or a Leopoldine Blahetka, pianists of the first magnitude in the current music world. What impressed the Spohrs especially was the fact that Clara appeared to be no hothouse plant, subjected to forced growth. Everything about her was natural, spontaneous, full of *brio* and delight.

This happy experience was followed by a letdown in Frankfurt. Here local musicians, jealously competing among themselves, banded together against any invasion by outsiders, particularly of the "infant prodigy" type. One of Clara's bookings was canceled due to an alleged error in dates. While Wieck negotiated for a new contract he learned that Frankfurt audiences tolerated only Mozart and Beethoven programs, whereas the pivot of Clara's present repertoire was Chopin.

Still hoping to surmount these obstacles, Wieck discussed the matter in a letter to Schumann, at home. Robert's answer contained some literary flashes, but no practical help:

> People are like a herd of cattle, looking up when there is a streak of lightning, then going back to placid grazing. Such lightning bolts have been Schubert, Paganini, Chopin, and now Clara. . . . You cannot imagine how I long for your return, and hers!

Schumann also reported on domestic affairs, particularly regarding the other Wieck children. Alwin was making progress on the violin, while Gustav appeared painfully unmusical. Then there was Clara's half-brother Clemens, born of her father's second marriage; in Robert's words the baby was "the funniest, most charming and stubborn chap, with a very sonorous voice. . . ."

The letter finished with a remark about Robert's *Sonata in A-Flat*, which would be ready for publication within a fortnight.

On January 25, 1832, Wieck succeeded at last in presenting his daughter to a Frankfurt audience. The diary concedes, by his own pen, that Clara played *"con amore, herrlich wie noch nie"* ("with passion, magnificently as never before"). But the public grudged applause. Only the orchestra members, with whom she appeared as soloist, showed approbation by gently tapping their music tripods.

An engagement followed in the university town of Darmstadt, and then at Mainz on the Rhine, before the four-day stagecoach ride to France. All the while, Clara was training for the supreme test in Paris: the playing of a full evening's program entirely from memory. The challenge excited her. The effect admittedly would be more impressive and pleasing to the eye. The added concentration required for such a feat was amply rewarded by audience reaction.

Another innovation, currently introduced by Franz Liszt, filled Clara with impatient curiosity. In Germany, pianists sat on stage (usually atop the prompter's box) with their backs to the public. The handsome Liszt, conscious of his blond mane and fine profile, changed this unflattering custom. In Parisian concert halls he turned the piano sideways, its graceful curve to the footlights, its keyboard at a right angle. This allowed him to sit away from dead center, in profile, and at the best possible advantage.

Friedrich Wieck pursed his lips in contempt for such foreign frivolities, which were likewise derided in the German press. But Clara saw an indisputable improvement in the Liszt maneuver; though it might not matter how an artist sat, if only he played well, aesthetically there was a difference. Few people were at their best in a flat rear view. Male pianists, owing to the concealing dangle of their swallow-tailed coats, enjoyed a decided advantage over their female colleagues. The latter were never quite free from the haunting fear that a seam might rip or a placket gape in the midst of a spectacular cadenza. Ah, to sit *en silhouette* surely spelled deliverance to all lady pianists from this dread.

Clara and her father reached Paris on February 15 and took lodgings at the Hôtel Bergère in Montmartre. Exhausted from the trip, they were also discountenanced by the inadequacy of their Leipzig-taught French. Also, since Clara was as yet unknown beyond German borders, no engagements awaited her. It was Wieck's hope to win auditions for his daughter with such Paris residents as Herz, Hiller, Kalkbrenner, and Chopin, whose works she had been mastering since early childhood. If but one of these famed men took a liking to Clara, introductions to some leading impresario would follow.

Right off, a courtesy call at the home of Chopin was decided upon. The twenty-three-year-old Pole received the visitors with warmth. He listened attentively to Clara's playing, marveling at the mastery with which she rendered some of his most difficult compositions. In conclusion he promised to introduce his guests to the Paris musical élite, including Hector Berlioz, Vincenzo Bellini, and the current lion of the opera world, Jakob Liebmann Beer (known professionally as Giacomo Meyerbeer).

A social evening soon followed at the residence of Friedrich Kalkbrenner, where Chopin played before a gathering of some four hundred people crowded into three not very spacious rooms. At a second reception in the home of Princess Vandamore, Chopin stepped aside and turned the piano over to Clara. The latter rendered a fair account of herself, considering the fact that the salon of the Princess was a distracting amateur museum, cluttered with tapestries, paintings, porcelains, stuffed birds, and bric-a-brac. In addition the totally unmusical hostess had an abominable piano that creaked and gave forth gruesome dissonances. This could well account for Chopin's ready surrender of the spotlight to the unsuspecting Fräulein Wieck.

But there were other disturbing factors. A nonprofessional lady volunteered (and couldn't be refused) to sing. She did so, and extremely well, in Italian. Next a Spaniard showed up in native costume, with guitar in hand. This fellow circulated among the guests, shamelessly ogling the women. Finally he leaped on a chair and strummed his instrument with breath-taking virtuosity. So bewitched were the listeners by his flamenco rhythms that no one was interested in further piano numbers. Quietly Papa Wieck and his daughter made their exit.

That same week they encountered a more suitable atmosphere at the villa of Madame Bonfils, a distinguished art patron. Here Clara played before a music critic from *Le Constitutionel,* who wrote a flattering article about her for his paper. This resulted in a professional engagement for her at the Paris City Hall, on April 9. Announcements were distributed and ticket sales began in mid-March.

While practicing for this event Clara learned of the death at Weimar, on March 22, 1832, of her patriarchal friend, Johann Wolfgang von Goethe. Though her contact with the great man had been too brief to allow a sense of personal loss, she became aware through the reaction of press and public that this was an event of worldwide significance. Her child's mind, nevertheless, dismissed solemn thoughts as quickly as they appeared. She was by now on marvelously companionable terms with Chopin, Mendelssohn, and Hiller, three Paris cronies with a fondness for revelry. With refreshing frequency these three were known to turn from musical preoccupations to a boisterous round of leapfrog.

As April—and Clara's concert—drew near, Paris grew suddenly empty. A cholera epidemic had broken out and people were leaving the capital in droves. The City Hall closed its doors, and Wieck received word that the recital was canceled. Regretfully he made ready to take Clara back home, when a chance meeting with the expatriate music dealer Franz Stoepel caused him to reconsider. Stoepel ran a small music academy.

"The concert can be held at my school," he suggested with earnest good will. "It would be fine for public morale, and might stop the panic."

Having up to now spent a great deal of money without pocketing any earnings, Friedrich Wieck agreed to take a chance. Clara played at the Stoepel school before a much smaller audience than had been promised at the City Hall. In compensation there was among the listeners, however, an important personality, the Hamburg-born opera star Wilhelmine Schroeder-Devrient. Lastly, Clara acquitted herself with merit. The applause was thunderous, even if the box office returns were meager.

When it was over, people dispersed without ceremony. No one shook hands or paused to chat, as the cholera bacillus was thought to be transmissible through respiratory channels and by skin contact. With smiles and nods of gratitude the Wiecks took their leave.

They hurried back to Montmartre where their luggage waited. By crowded stagecoach they set out for Metz and the border town of Sarreguemines. Before crossing into Germany they were held a week in quarantine. When no symptoms of plague appeared they received permission to continue their journey.

On arrival at Frankfurt, Clara promptly fell ill. Her condition, alarming at first, disclosed itself as extreme fatigue. After forty-eight hours of uninterrupted sleep she was again sound as a bell. The last lap of travel led through Hanau, Erfurt, and Merseburg. At noon on May 1 Leipzig was reached, where Clara's stepmother, the younger children, and the lodger Robert Schumann waited.

Within minutes it seemed as though father and daughter had never left home. Clara had scarcely put away her wraps and bonnet when it was time for *Mittagessen*, the midday meal. While helping to set the table she discovered that the steel knives were spotted and in need of scouring. In a trice she fetched the crock of emery powder and a cork. The gifted fingers that had been held admiringly by Chopin and Meyerbeer resumed with humbleness their customary household tasks.

With humbleness, yes, but also with a difference. It was Schumann who observed a new lightness and grace in Clara's movements, and the faintest trace of a French accent in her speech.

She would lose the accent presently. But never the lightness and the grace.

3

CHAPTER 4   The adolescent years were upon Clara. She became subject to abrupt changes of mood, from radiant joy to glum despair. At times she was listless and, when spoken to, gave no answer. This offended her stepmother, a good woman who took such discourtesy to heart. Even the patient Robert lost his patience; he too was a diary-keeper, hence his sentiments are known:

> Clara is stubborn, and a cry-baby. Her father has to scold her, but she has him under her slipper. She is dominating like Beethoven's Leonora [in *Fidelio*] but then again she can plead and wheedle like a child. . . .

This reversion to childish ways occurred almost daily and caused Schumann particular irritation. He complained on another page:

> I joined my friends at Brand's restaurant. Herr Wieck was pleasant; Clara, infantile and silly.

Again, after a visit to the zoo: "Clara acted fatuous and frightened." But two days later he revealed a decided confusion in his own feelings, to wit:

> Stayed home and did some more composing on my *Intermezzi*. I want to dedicate them to Clara.

As yet there was no hint of love between them, but each felt the other's life impinging on his own. There were few daily happenings in which they did not share. Schumann had during this period started publication of a musical journal, containing articles by himself and others on the cultural life of Leipzig. To please Wieck he also reported the latter's travels. Helpfully Clara brought forth her Paris program, adding some verbal commentary:

34

"At the Princess Vandamore's I was introduced as *Madamigella*—that's Italian for *Mademoiselle*, and much nicer than *Signorina* Clara Wieck."

Robert snorted. "*Madamigella* Clara Wieck! Don't you know that you aren't anybody so long as you need a title before your name? Does anyone speak of *Mister* Shakespeare? Do we not say Goethe, Paganini, Liszt?"

She understood. With greatness came simplification. The measure of her unimportance was still apparent in her press clippings, all of which referred to "the little Fräulein Clara Wieck."

For the present a busy spring and summer lay ahead. Due to her father's overburdened teaching schedule Clara was enjoined to start her brother Alwin on the piano. In addition she continued her counterpoint lessons with a Professor Dorn, and prepared two concerts booked for July at the Gewandhaus. Wieck wanted to startle Leipzig by being the first to present a German pianist who played in the new French fashion, without score. He would also have liked to seat Clara *en profile*, but this the tradition-bound Gewandhaus management would not agree to.

The two concerts, taking place during a spell of sultry weather, went exceedingly well. People were puzzled, to be sure, at seeing Clara come on stage unburdened by an armful of volumes. Their astonishment mounted on hearing her run through an ambitious program of Pixis, Chopin, Herz, Hummel, Bériot, and Moscheles. A few quibblers were not lacking who pointed out that such difficult numbers were made easier by keeping one's eyes on the keys, hence the French trick of doing without notes. For Clara, however, the real value of memory playing had disclosed itself once and for all. With a piano free of clutter, and the disturbing rustle of page-turning eliminated, she found herself able to polish and refine her technique. All her attention could now be given to accent, nuance, expression.

Later in the summer, on her thirteenth birthday, she was allowed to have a party with neighborhood children present. In the course of a game, which involved the paying of forfeits, Clara was ordered to the piano to perform a small *Scherzo*. So thoroughly had she reverted to the carefree friskiness of childhood that she bungled several times and never did get through her piece.

"Well," was her excuse, "I shouldn't really have to do this on my *birthday!*"

By now her name was on the list of artists booked for the winter subscription concerts at the Gewandhaus. The season began early, with Clara scheduled for September 30. Her program included the *Concerto in C-Minor* by the Prague composer Ignaz Moscheles, teacher and friend of Felix Mendelssohn Bartholdy. Moscheles made his home in London but he was currently in Leipzig on a visit. Hence Clara faced the challenge of playing the thirty-eight-year-old virtuoso's masterpieces under his critical eye. Paradoxically she accomplished this feat with greater dispatch and glory than had been the case at the children's party a fortnight earlier.

A short concert tour through Saxony followed in November, including Schumann's home town of Zwickau. On this occasion Clara played the opening movement of a symphony on which Robert was still working. The effect proved disheartening. Not even in Zwickau, where relatives and friends sat in the audience, was there more than a lukewarm response. The discouraged composer put his symphony aside. It was never published.

The tour nonetheless was marked by a moment of significance. Clara met Schumann's mother, whose heart instantly opened to her. Frau Schumann took the girl into her arms and said in a low voice: "When you grow up you must marry my Robert!"

It seemed a farfetched and preposterous thought since the irrepressible adolescent and the pensive youth, almost ten years her senior, got on each other's nerves and were for the most part at daggers drawn. But the words left an impression upon Clara. Curiosity and a new speculative feeling seized her when hereafter she looked on her father's lodger. To grow up and marry Robert! The idea pleased her. Yes, indeed, it pleased her very much.

For the present, however, she came down with scarlet fever and had to be taken home. She spent Christmas in bed and was barely convalescing when, early in 1833, her half-brother Clemens died at the age of three, of the same illness. The family grieved deeply over this loss. As the disease took on an epidemic character in Leipzig it was decided to remove the older boys, Alwin and Gustav, to Dresden, where Wieck enrolled them in a boarding school run by the Masonic Order.

After her recovery Clara found herself fired with new ambition. She begged to be given singing lessons, to which her father readily acceded. Her voice was as yet unformed, but clear and true of pitch. Above all, hers was a temperament that needed a vocal outlet. Like a forest bird she burst into song out of sheer vitality and natural ebullience. From the same source sprang a new urge toward composing. She wrote in quick successsion a series of piano numbers; a song, "To Alexis," a mixed chorale, and the finale to her *Rondo in A-Minor*. In addition, she boldly started a concerto and an overture. In all these efforts there was marked technical excellence, though, as with feminine composers of far greater maturity, the themes were conventional and imitative. Even so great an artist as Clara Schumann was destined to become could not alter a long accepted axiom: in music, women reached high peaks as interpretive performers rather than creators.

Inevitably Clara's intense preoccupation with musical studies, and the time spent on concert tours, caused her to fall behind in her normal schooling. Her acquaintance with mathematics, grammar, history, and allied subjects would remain hopelessly fragmentary. On the other hand there was the compensation of living in a city so culturally active as Leipzig. Poets, novelists, philosophers, and artists in every field came to this Mecca of the Muses, and Friedrich Wieck saw to it that his daughter met them all. As a result, though her textbook knowledge was skimpy, Clara absorbed much worldly wisdom through constant and intimate contact with people of genius.

In the spring of 1833 Robert Schumann tired of his back room in the Wieck flat, and moved to a summer cottage called *Riedel's Garten,* on the outskirts of town. This change initiated a new phase in his relationship with Clara. The young man and the childish minx, who so teased and annoyed him, suddenly missed each other. To fill the void they started writing letters.

At first their missives were quite formal. Clara wrote "Dear Herr Schumann" while he addressed her by her Christian name but refrained from employing the familiar "thou" (which would have been permissible in view of his considerable seniority). Soon this was not enough. They resorted to another means of communication, namely the choosing of a specified hour each day when they would sit at the piano and play a prearranged tune.

"Our ghostly doubles *(Doppelgänger)* will then meet," wrote Schumann, "somewhere midway in the distance that separates us, perhaps by the little side door of the St. Thomas Church. If you don't live up to this pact, I shall apply my angriest concentration to make a string snap in your piano tomorrow noon!"

The pact was lived up to. It would continue in force through the years when other and sadder separations were their lot. For the present Clara took up the *Doppelgänger* symbol, derived by Schumann from the fantastic tales of Ernst Theodor Amadeus Hoffmann, and wove it into one of her compositions. She sent this to Robert, with apologies for its imperfections. He in turn transcribed her melodic theme into a group of *Impromptus*, to be published as his *Opus 5*. It is significant that less than a dozen years earlier Franz Schubert had been obsessed by Heinrich Heine's poem on the same subject, and made of it one of his most haunting Lieder. The Heine lyrics were profoundly moving:

> *Still ist die Nacht, es ruhen die Gassen,*
> *in diesem Hause wohnte mein Schatz;*
> *sie hat schon längst die Stadt verlassen;*
> *doch steht noch das Haus auf demselben Platz.*
>
> *Da steht auch ein Mensch, und starrt in die Höhe,*
> *und ringt die Hände vor Schmerzensgewalt;*
> *mir graust es, wenn ich sein Antlitz sehe,*
> *der Mond zeigt mir meine eig'ne Gestalt.*
>
> *Du Doppelgänger, du bleicher Geselle,*
> *was äffst du nach mein Liebesleid,*
> *das mich gequält auf dieser Stelle*
> *so manche Nacht, in alter Zeit?**

It is doubtful that Clara knew these lines, though she had met the exiled Heine in Paris among the intimates of Meyerbeer and Chopin. On the other hand Schubert was no stranger, in his music at least. The Vienna composer who at the age of eighteen had already written one hundred and forty-four songs (sometimes finishing as many as eight in one day) was the creator of *Der Erlkönig*, which Franz Liszt had

---

* Still is the night, the streets lie quiet—
in yonder house, there, dwelled my love.
She left this town long since, the house remains—
and someone stands now, staring upward,
wringing his hands in deepest sorrow . . .

I shudder when I look upon his face
for in the moonlight I behold it is my own!

Thou double of my soul, pale ghost,
why dost thou mock love's agony
that tortured me upon this very spot
so many a sad night, and so long ago?

transcribed into a sensational concert fantasia. It had been Friedrich Wieck's ambition to coach Clara in this bravura number, prior to an eventual Austrian tour. But Schubert was never to hear her.

When not absorbed in music and letter-writing, Clara had girlish preoccupations typical of her time. During the long bout with scarlet fever she learned to embroider and sew, a pastime which delighted her. Then, through her father, she met another piano student named Emilie List, a daughter of the United States Consul in Leipzig. Between the two girls (Emilie was one year older) a warm friendship developed, which for Clara had a beneficial and broadening influence. The much-traveled diplomat's child, at home on oceans and distant continents, opened new perspectives to Clara's provincial mind. Also, the infinite small confidences that sprouted between girlhood chums served to palliate the sorrow of Schumann's absence, and certainly to keep it from becoming unwholesomely morbid.

Robert was less pleased. He complained repeatedly of Clara's lack of promptness in replying to his notes. However, since his handwriting was abominable, the reproaches often missed their target. Clara simply could not make out what he was talking about.

On January 10, 1834, when she was fifteen and a half years old, her confirmation day dawned. She underwent this ceremony in the company of Emilie, both girls wearing white dresses with silk sashes, and their hair in beribboned topknots. Friedrich Wieck commemorated the occasion by penning in Clara's diary:

> My daughter!
> Your independence now approaches, which is of the utmost importance. I have devoted almost ten years of my life to your education and development; consider, then, your obligations. Train your mind toward a noble, unselfish career, for the benefit of humanity, and always uphold virtue as the true religion. When you are misunderstood, maligned, or envied, do not falter in your principles. This is no easy charge, but herein lies real goodness. I shall remain your counselor and helpful friend, Friedrich Wieck.

The words marked indeed a point of transition. The Papa Wieck of childhood days had vanished. In his shoes walked thenceforth a preceptor who treated Clara as an adult, if not at times as an impersonal colleague. The Galatea he was creating must acquire distance, not proximity. She must fall prey to no human attachment, no binding loyalties. Not even his own.

CHAPTER 5 In underscoring the importance of consecration to the artistic life Friedrich Wieck was thinking of Schumann. He had observed his daughter's growing attachment to the absent young man, and the frequency of the postman's visits. This disturbed him acutely. Though he was fond of Robert, he did not want him (or anyone else, perhaps) for a son-in-law. From the beginning it had been his dream to turn Clara into the greatest woman pianist of the century. In such a glorious design there was no room for marriage.

Wieck was too intelligent a pedagogue, however, to thwart the incipient romance by direct means. His strategy was made to seem quite casual. At his music academy there was a moderately talented student named Ernestine von Fricken, the daughter of a wealthy Austrian baron. Ernestine, three years older than Clara and much prettier, dwelled in unsatisfactory lodgings and repeatedly mentioned giving up music and returning home. In order not to lose her, and to bar Schumann (who was coming back before autumn) from his former rooms, Wieck took the young baroness for a boarder. Clara, on the other hand, was sent to Dresden for a period of training under a prominent voice coach, Aloys Miksch. When Robert reappeared in Leipzig he had no choice but to seek quarters elsewhere. He did this good-naturedly, never suspecting his well-loved teacher of intended malice. As before, he spent many leisure hours at the Wiecks' where, in the absence of Clara, he cast an approving eye on the well-developed and more mature Ernestine. He found less and less time for correspondence. Friedrich Wieck was pleased.

In July of 1834 Clara was called home briefly to attend the christening of her new-born half-sister Caecilie. To her astonishment Ernestine and Robert stood as godparents to the baby, while Clara's stepmother Clementine made veiled references to the pair's forthcoming engagement. Unquestionably Ernestine was cool and aloof toward her former friend and school companion, while Robert appeared distinctly ill at ease.

After a week of forlorn disillusionment Clara was back in Dresden, where she must yet complete a course in composition with the exacting Professor Karl Gottlieb Reissiger before her exile ended. Friedrich Wieck meanwhile fanned the romance under his roof by every possible means. Now that his own daughter was not involved, he praised Schumann to the skies, always within Ernestine's hearing, while at the same time pointing out to Robert the advantages of winning so well-connected a young lady for his wife.

"Marrying into such a family will do wonders for your new review!" said Herr Wieck.

This was true. During April of that year Schumann had revised his paper into an enlarged magazine called *Neue Zeitschrift für Musik (New Musical Review)*, the success of which would depend on a steadily widening circulation. Ernestine, whose mother had been born Countess Zettwitz, could well bring him the added prestige of circles in which up to now he had found no entrée.

In the midst of these happy speculations Baron von Fricken appeared upon the scene. From certain hints in his daughter's letters the nobleman grasped that something untoward might be afoot. He came to have a look at Ernestine's suitor, and found the latter wanting. With promptness and dispatch the lovers were separated.

A secret and heartbroken correspondence followed which kept love's flame burning brightly. But soon Ernestine shocked Robert with an awkward disclosure: she was an illegitimate child, the fruit of a maternal indiscretion. Baron von Fricken was only an adoptive father who, unless she made a brilliant aristocratic marriage, would spare her not a penny of his fortune. This confession did not mean that Ernestine relinquished her love. On the contrary, she pleaded with Robert not to let her poverty and obscure origin stand in the way of happiness.

His reaction to the news was one of bitterness. He could not forgive the girl for waiting so long before revealing her secret. It made him fear future silences regarding other matters that might come up. His vision of marriage was a relationship ruled by candor and clearest

faith. Clara, he thought suddenly. Clarity, the light and limpid one . . .
How could he have been so disloyal to his first true dream?

On further reflection Robert did not overlook a second factor which
spoke for a rupture with Ernestine. He was self-supporting, but not
rich. A bride with even a modest dowry would permit his life to go
on as at present, with time left over from his duties as a journalist for
what he now considered his real career: that of composer. A disowned
and disinherited Ernestine necessarily put an end to such prospects.
Robert would have to seek an additional job as office clerk, salesman,
or piano teacher to make ends meet. Nor could he count on Fräulein
von Fricken's musical talents as a source of supplementary income
since that young lady would never attain an instructor's certificate, let
alone achieve stature as a concert artist. In short, the more he thought
about Ernestine, the greater his admiration for Clara grew. By autumn
of 1835 the engagement to Ernestine was broken.

For some weeks Robert now shunned his old teacher's home, to
which Clara had meanwhile returned. He had a feeling of guilt and of
distrust toward himself and his emotions. He deemed it flippant and
ignoble to attempt resumption of his earlier friendship with Clara quite
as though nothing had happened. Far better to occupy himself with
an *avant garde* society he had founded, called *Die Davidsbündler*
(Union of Davids), the youthful members of which were sworn to
defend the modern trends in music against the torpid Goliath of tradition. He did however put in an appearance at Clara's sixteenth birthday, to which Mendelssohn (recently appointed director of the
Gewandhaus concerts) was invited.

Soon after, Chopin came through Leipzig following a visit with his
parents at Karlsbad. He called on Clara, found her absent, and waited
a full hour for her return. When she came, he insisted on hearing her
play, whereupon she introduced him to Schumann's *Sonata in F-Sharp
Minor*, which he praised highly. Chopin was in the initial stages of
tuberculosis and ready to give up concertizing. But he played a *Nocturne* for Clara, giving evidence once more of the feathery *pianissimo*
she remembered from Paris, and which no pianist was ever to surpass.

Clara was at this time steeped in composition. She had put the last
touches on a concerto-with-orchestra, which was to have its première
at her forthcoming Gewandhaus recital on November 9. The program
would include among other offerings a three-piano number by Bach,

in which Mendelssohn and a lesser known artist named Rackemann took part.

During these weeks of triumph Clara saw little of Robert. He walked in the shadows, prey to spells of melancholy. But on the occasion of the Gewandhaus engagement, when Clara's performance was greeted with shouts of "Bravo"—though her concerto received the condemnation of stony silence—he gave himself a jolt and called at her home. She received him joyfully, under her father's stern regard. Later that night she carried an oil lamp to light Robert's way downstairs and, on the bottom step, they kissed for the first time.

"I thought I would faint," she confessed to him many years later. "The lamp nearly dropped from my hand!"

What did drop, however, was the heavy blow of Wieck's wrath as he waited on the landing for Clara's return upstairs. He had not witnessed the kissing scene, but he had timed it. The long adieu in the lower hall told him all he needed to know. The lovers must be permanently parted.

Clara was sent to Dresden once again and placed under Professor Reissiger's supervision. But the latter and his wife were kindly souls, ill-suited to a watchdog role. Thus Schumann managed several weekend visits with his beloved, apart from keeping up a lively correspondence. Wieck learned of this through a colleague who accidentally saw Robert on a Dresden street. Posthaste he rushed to the Reissiger home and called Clara to account. Did she think that he, a hardworking paterfamilias who had sacrificed the best years of his life in the interest of her career, was going to let her throw herself away on the first Lothario who plied her with honeyed talk? Were her energies, already keyed to the sublime cause of music, to be dissipated in crude household tasks and the servile functions of wifehood and motherhood?

While he was at it the outraged father also gave the Reissigers a piece of his mind, denouncing them as traitors and declaring his friendship for them at an end. After an hour's verbal storm he packed his daughter into the Leipzig diligence and brought her home. On the way the paternal philippic continued, climaxing in the command that Clara restore to Schumann all his letters and exact her own in return, after which there was to be no further spoken or written word between them. Failing this, the enraged man threatened to put a bullet through Schumann on sight.

In panic, Clara acceded. Under Wieck's dictation she wrote a brief note to Robert, quoting the above terms and bidding him a formal farewell. A few days later she was taken by her father on her hitherto most extended concert tour.

It was no easy task for the lovelorn seventeen-year-old girl to summon the composure needed for a succession of platform appearances. Her repertoire had greatly expanded by this time. She was playing the most daring of bravura numbers, such as Sigismund Thalberg's *Caprice, Opus 15,* and his *Grand Concerto.*

Thalberg, only seven years older than Clara Wieck, was the current pianistic rage of Vienna. He had been born in Naples, the love child of a Baroness von Wetzlar and one of Austria's gayest princes, Leo Dietrichstein. Adored by his parents, the boy had been marked for a diplomatic career, but his tremendous musical gifts led to a sensational concert appearance at fourteen, which sealed his fate. Thalberg possessed an exceptional ability to play *legato* with almost singing effect, which caused Liszt to remark: "He is the only artist who can play the violin on the keyboard." In addition, Thalberg originated the feat of splitting a melody between both hands, each taking up a fragment thereof, and rounding the whole into a smooth arpeggio; it was a spectacular device, soon to be copied and abused the world over.

Another of Clara's parade pieces was Adolph von Henselt's *Variations on an Aria from Donizetti's "L'Elisir d'Amore."* Henselt, only twenty-two at this time, was obsessed with surpassing the octave. His compositions called for long fingers and an abnormal reach. The same was true of Liszt's many concert transcriptions, and of Chopin when in bravura mood. For balance, to offset such technical fireworks, Wieck wisely supplied Clara with a solid list of Bach fugues and Beethoven sonatas. It was not to be said that he planned to turn his daughter into a musical acrobat.

The present tour included East and West Prussia, Silesia, and Pomerania, with important cities like Königsberg, Danzig, Breslau, Stettin, and finally Berlin. In the latter metropolis Clara was allowed to see her mother, Frau Bargiel, who had left Leipzig thirteen years ago. Ordinarily Wieck would never have relented toward his divorced wife, but Clara's downhearted state called for some sort of palliation if the concert tour were not to end in a nervous breakdown. As it was, the girl played listlessly, without her usual happy verve. Wieck knew full well that she took little joy in programs that contained no Schumann composition for her to interpret and make known. On this point he remained, of course, adamant. If the works of that upstart needed publicizing, let someone other than Clara Wieck serve as handmaiden. A call on the Bargiels, meanwhile, might dispel the girl's lingering moodiness.

Wieck was right. Mother and daughter rejoiced in the reunion, which also acquainted Clara with a new set of half-brothers and sisters, the Bargiel children. The family lived in a modest sector of the city, obviously under economic stress. Bargiel's schoolteacher salary was small at best, and he worked overtime giving private lessons.

"His health is broken," whispered Frau Bargiel to her former husband. "To think of Clara's wonderful travels! As for us, we have never had a week's holiday."

"You made your bed, Marianne," replied Wieck, unmoved.

His coldness banished for her any shadow of regret. Despite their struggles, Bargiel was a good man and a most loving one. The children, too, though none was as talented as Clara, gave her no grief. She held her head up in pride.

"Yes, Friedrich. It is a bed I don't mind lying in."

They talked of Leipzig, now and long ago. Marianne asked about her sons Alwin and Gustav. Did they have Clara's ability?

Wieck welcomed the chance to score a point. "They would have it, if I dedicated myself to them as I have done with Clara. Her career has been built up at the expense of my other children."

With this the subject of Robert Schumann was ready to be broached. Alluding to that young man's as yet problematic future, and letting the Bargiel situation serve as grim illustration, Wieck posed the question whether Clara ought honestly to be allowed to have her way. Marianne fell silent. But it was not the silence of heartlessness and alienation. On the contrary. Between mother and daughter an exchange of glances took place that spoke more eloquently than words. Instantly Clara knew that here was someone to whom she could reveal her innermost soul. Here was an ally who would stand by her and by Robert.

While in Berlin, Wieck missed no chance to introduce his daughter into the highest circles. A concert at the Opera House brought in its train the usual invitations to the homes of the aristocracy, among which figured the palatial villa of a famous hostess, Bettina von Arnim, wife of the writer Achim (Louis Joachim) von Arnim, and coquettish friend of the late Goethe. Bettina had been born Elisabeth Brentano in 1785, at Frankfurt-am-Main. She did not like being fifty-two, but she made the best of it by veiling her fading charms in an aura of pseudo-intellectualism and wit. Her salon, presided over by an elder brother, the poet Clemens Brentano, was patronized by a diverting and colorful élite.

Friedrich Wieck sunned himself in the fashionable Bettina's presence, even to the degree of overlooking her chief defect, a biting tongue. Thus, after applauding Clara's concert and ostensibly giving a soirée in her honor, Bettina greeted the girl with: "My God, how awful for anybody so young to know so much!"

On seeing Clara presently surrounded by a covey of male guests who normally made up Frau von Arnim's personal retinue, the lady really showed her claws.

"I think it vain and presumptuous for a pianist to play from memory. How much more modest is that young Theodor Doehler who spreads his scores before him on the music rack."

If all was not gold that glittered, still less could genuine warmth be found in superficial hospitality. The more far-spread her travels, the lonelier Clara became. Her father jotted down the endless list of names and titles that littered her path to fame, but Clara counted only the days and hours that separated her from Robert.

CHAPTER 6 Before leaving Berlin for Hamburg, Clara had filled no fewer than eight concert engagements in the Prussian capital, one of these at the court of King Friedrich Wilhelm III. The latter, born in 1770, had fought against Napoleon at the decisive Battle of the Nations, at Leipzig. His lovely wife Luise (of Mecklenburg-Strelitz) had earlier, in 1807, attempted to charm the Corsican into abandoning German territory. This had happened on a baldachined and velvet-draped barge anchored in the Memel River, and the result was failure. Napoleon's susceptibility to beauty did not surpass his love of power. Mission unaccomplished, the patriotic Queen died three years later of a glandular ailment, at the age of thirty-four (her portraits show the lady always with a scarf draped lightly across her throat to hide a moderately defacing goiter).

The Wiecks also had contact with the incumbent conductor of the Berlin Opera, Gaspare Spontini, the crabbed elderly composer of such music dramas as *La Vestale, Fernand Cortez, Lalla Rookh* (later rewritten as *Nurmahal*), and *Agnes von Hohenstaufen*. Of these works only the first brought the author any substantial reward, though an earlier one-act opera *Milton* was likewise deserving of praise. The Italian-born Spontini had been originally trained for the priesthood, and his initial efforts were devoted exclusively to church music. This surely accounted for his lack of ease in worldly circles. He warned Clara against wasting her time on composition, and in particular, against opera:

"There's heartbreak in it, Signorina!"

Where music was concerned, however, Clara remained undaunted. She grieved over being separated from Robert, but as the tour progressed, her normal zest and ebullience took over. Young and healthy, she seldom felt the strain of travel. At Naumburg, only a short while back, she had been driven to the concert hall in a carriage which overturned. Bruised, her dress torn, and with a left wrist wrenched and swelling painfully, she filled her program commitment to perfection and even sang two of her own *Lieder* for encores.

The remainder of the trip included Bremen, Hanover, and Braunschweig (Brunswick). An old disease with a new name prevailed in these areas: the respiratory infection called influenza. Concerts and theater attractions were poorly attended. Such listeners as Clara did encounter sat swathed in wraps and mufflers, their sniffles and coughs furnishing a noisy obbligato to her play.

In May the travelers returned home, laden with gifts, earnings, and fame. Friedrich Wieck had no small share in these rewards, since he pocketed his daughter's fees (in payment for the years of training he had devoted to her). As to Clara's growing renown, a considerable reflection fell automatically upon the teacher in whose watchful care her talent unfolded. New pupils flocked to Leipzig from near and far to enroll at Wieck's prospering academy.

Schumann, of course, no longer studied with his old master. His days were taken up with publication of his music journal for which, lacking collaborators, he wrote under various pseudonyms like Florestan and Eusebius, as well as under his own name. His evenings and nights were given over to composition. In the spring of 1837 he finished his great *Sonata in F-Sharp Minor, Opus 11,* dedicated to Clara. As the lovers had no chance to meet or communicate with each other, Robert waylaid the Wieck housemaid and entrusted the manuscript to her. He received no acknowledgment since Clara dared not imperil her beloved by defying the parental ukase. But she played the sonata, night after night, while Schumann lingered in the shadows under her window; the time chosen was prior to the hour of eight in the evening, when Wieck returned from some late teaching assignment. As it was, Clara lived in constant dread lest her father and Robert collide in the darkness, with tragedy ensuing.

Altogether the situation in the Wieck home was not unlike that which would prevail, less than a decade later, in London's Wimpole Street, where lived the Barrett family. The gifted poetess Elizabeth Barrett, reduced to invalidism by the oppressive solicitude of her jealous father, likewise would be denied the love of Robert Browning until, in desperation, she eloped with him to Italy.

In Leipzig the deadlock was eased somewhat when, on August 2, 1837, Clara appeared locally in a concert to which no one could prevent Schumann's buying a ticket. While seated in the audience, he spied a friend, Ernst Adolf Becker, who served in the law courts of nearby Freiberg. Becker knew the Wiecks, whom he greeted backstage during intermission. Aware of this, Schumann scribbled a hasty note of undying love and devotion, which he begged Becker to slip into Clara's hand. The intermediary performed his task and promised future help as well. In consequence the lovers exchanged a quick succession of missives which led to their secret engagement, pledged on the fourteenth of the same month.

They could not meet. They could not talk. But each now had the other's promise, fortified by an exchange of modest gold rings. The latter could not be worn but were to be carried in concealment on their persons. In addition, Schumann had a plan. Clara's eighteenth birthday was only a month away. He intended to spend the intervening time in preparing and polishing an eloquently persuasive letter to the girl's father, requesting her hand in marriage. A year and a half had gone by since Wieck had turned on Robert. The young man had saved money in that time, besides coming into a small inheritance through the death of his mother. This did not embolden him to press for an immediate wedding but for an acknowledgment, within the family circle, of the betrothal.

Much revised and carefully weighed from every angle, the document was presented to Herr Wieck on the morning of September 13, just as Clara appeared at table for her birthday breakfast. Knowing well what the letter contained, she scanned her father's face expectantly. Wieck remained stony. He read the missive, then stuffed it into a coat pocket, finished his coffee, and said no more that day.

Schumann received no written reply but he was summoned for an interview with Wieck the following evening. An unpleasant scene took place. Not only did the older man dismiss Robert's financial guarantees as laughable, but he declared marriage to be the destruction of Clara's career. A betrothal, therefore, was out of the question. He would relent to the point of allowing the young people to see each other, though only in the presence of others, never alone. Correspond-

4

ence remained forbidden except for occasional postcards Clara might care to send while away on concert tours.

"Sorry, my friend," concluded Herr Wieck. "That is all."

Robert was shattered. Having no intention of accepting the tyrant's conditions, he communicated with Clara (through Becker) at once. She could not run away with him, he admitted, since she was under age and the law would tear them apart. But they must see each other and write and keep in closest contact until she was twenty-one. Then they would need no one's permission. They would marry and be off to lead a life of their own choosing.

It sounded brave and confident and easy. But the goal they set themselves turned out to be the hardest test of their young lives. For one thing, Friedrich Wieck now accelerated his daughter's career with a feverish intensity. Only a month after her unhappy eighteenth birthday he took Clara away from Leipzig on a concertizing odyssey that would last seven months.

The tour began in Dresden, where the Belgian violinist Henri Vieuxtemps, one year younger than Clara, competed on the same platform for audience attention. Next came Prague, a city of eminent musical understanding and culture. Here three successful concerts won encomiums not only for the performer herself but, perhaps more particularly, for the paternal teacher-impresario who had formed and launched her. In Prague, too, an obscure painter named Johann Schramm asked Clara to sit for a portrait, to which she readily agreed since she would thus have something to send back (furtively, of course) to Robert.

The Schramm portrait, in charcoal, eloquently underscores the girl's transition into womanhood. The gay winsomeness of childhood is gone. In its place a pensive sadness bears testimony to the subject's lovelorn state. For the rest, Clara's wide almond-shaped eyes retained their odalisque look, the oval face continued to evoke Mediterranean rather than Germanic origins, the figure had filled out, the hair—worn low instead of in the former saucy topknot—is reminiscent of a Raphael or Della Robbia madonna.

"Everyone says it is a good likeness," Clara confided in a note to Robert, "though I know myself that I am not beautiful."

In a strictly pictorial sense this was true. Hers was a pleasing personality, but too muted in coloring to draw attention. If it had not been for her extraordinary talent, she would have passed unnoticed through her time. It is possible that but for the enchantment exerted on him by her music Schumann himself might not have given her a second glance.

From Prague the travelers headed for Vienna, accompanied by the Wieck housemaid Nanny, who heretofore had served as frequent go-between for Robert and Clara. Nanny's present job was that of a combined valet and personal *fille de chambre* who must look after the wardrobe of her master Wieck and young mistress. Thanks to this arrangement it became feasible for Robert and Clara to correspond with each other since Nanny continued her good services in behalf of Cupid. Though Wieck eyed all mail received at rooming houses and hotels, the loyal maid went to the post office of every town along their route, and, employing a prearranged code word, obtained Robert's letters from the general delivery clerk.

Even so, the messages exchanged by the lovers were few and far between due to the slowness of mailcoach travel, and to Wieck's capricious changes of itinerary when schedules permitted the filling of some unexpected but profitable engagement on the way. Such digressions often cut down on time farther ahead, thereby preventing Nanny's post office calls. Thus two and three weeks went by without news, while Clara and Robert inevitably fell prey to doubts regarding the permanence of their love. On the other hand, both lovers followed the inspired practice of writing aggregate letters, with pages added diary-fashion each day, until a safe opportunity arrived for the exchange of these missives. In addition, they retained their secret pact of sitting down at the piano each day at an agreed hour, to play the same music and commune with each other in thought. Since Clara's travels presented the obstacle that she might be bouncing along in a stagecoach at all hours of the day, late evening was chosen for the tryst of souls.

In the drama that suddenly and so cruelly overshadowed her life Clara was the chief sufferer. She stood defenseless between the two hostile men, each of whom she loved in a special indestructible way, with two kinds of love as different as night and day. Despite Wieck's despotism and injustice she knew well that his very life was wrapped up in her own. He was her father, to whom she owed the high art of which she was priestess. Through him, furthermore, she had met Robert and romance and the deeper awakening of the heart. Schumann and Wieck could clash in open hate, each insensible to the inner motivations of the other. For Clara, things were not so clear-cut or absolute.

She grew in moral stature as a consequence of these tribulations. The conflict within her was a salubrious discipline even if it led at times (frequent times!) to unavoidable prevarication. Thus she was able to persuade her father that there was no harm in including Schumann compositions in her recitals, particularly the effective *Carnaval*, since this involved professional considerations rather than sentiment. Similarly she constantly strove to soften Robert's anger toward the older man with promises of winning Wieck's ultimate pardon and consent.

Inevitably the spiritual growth so engendered must redound to her artistic benefit. She played magnificently these days, commanding a repertoire of impressive proportions.

In the short years elapsed since her Leipzig debut Clara's programs included:

John Field: *Second Piano Concerto*
Christian Kalkbrenner: *Concerto, Opus 66*, with orchestra; *Variations on March from Rossini's Opera "Moses"*
Jacques Simon Herz: *Variations Brillantes, Opus 23*
Johann Peter Pixis: *Trio No. 3; Concerto, Opus 100; Variations, Opus 20*, with orchestra; *Trio No. 4; Fantasie Militaire, Opus 121*, with orchestra
Ignaz Moscheles: *Concerto in E-Flat Major; Homage à Handel; Concerto in G-Minor*
Frédéric François Chopin: *Variations, Opus 2*, on Mozart's "La ci darem la mano"; *Mazurkas* (complete); *Nocturnes* (complete); *Concerto in E-Minor; Etudes* (complete); *Rondo, Opus 16*
Johann Sebastian Bach: *Well-Tempered Clavier* (complete)
Ludwig van Beethoven: *Trio in C-Minor, Opus 1; Trio in B-Major, Opus 97; Phantasie*, with chorus; *Sonata in F-Minor, Opus 57* ("Appassionata"); *Sonata in A-Major, Opus 47*, for piano and violin ("Kreutzer Sonata")
Sigismond Thalberg: *Adagio* and *Rondo; Divertissement on Themes*

from Rossini's "Soirées Musicales"; Fantasy "Don Juan"; Variations on "L'Elisir d'Amore" by Donizetti; *Fantasies on Operas "Semiramide"* and *"Mosé in Egitto"* by Rossini; *Caprice, Opus* 15

Robert Schumann: *Paganini Studies, Opus 3; Toccata, Opus 7; Symphonic Etudes, Opus 12; Sonata in F-Sharp Minor, Opus 11; Carnaval, Opus 10; Allegro, Opus 8*

Felix Mendelssohn-Bartholdy: *Songs Without Words; Capriccio Brillant in A-Minor, Opus 22,* with orchestra; *Capriccio in A-Minor, Opus 33; Prelude, E-Minor*

Adolf von Henselt: *Concerto* (in manuscript); Lullaby, "Wenn ich ein Vöglein wär"

Her own compositions to date, signed Clara Wieck, also appeared in her programs of this period, to wit:

Variations, Opus 23 and *Opus 50; Concerto, Opus 7; Capriccio; Mazurka; Opus 3; Opus 5; Opus 9; Concert Variations, Opus 8; Quatre Polonaises; Romance Varie; Valse Romantique; Quatres Pièces Caracteristiques; Soirées Musicales; Scherzo; Polonaise in E-Flat.*

The impending Austrian sojourn would inspire Clara to amplify the list of her own works with: *Trois Romances* (dedicated to Robert Schumann) and *Souvenir de Vienne.* The latter compositions being not yet in print, she played them as encores and in free rhapsodic style, for she was becoming dazzled by the scintillating technique of Vienna's keyboard idols, Thalberg and Liszt. To compete, before Austrian audiences, with these two master showmen it was necessary for her to display at least an approximation of their pyrotechnic flair.

The daughter of Friedrich Wieck was ready. In Dresden and Berlin she had fearlessly tackled Thalberg's more spectacular bravura numbers, whereas now on tour she practiced Liszt's flamboyant transcriptions of Schubert's "Erlkönig," "Ave Maria," and "In Praise of Tears," as well as his *Divertissement on a Cavatina by Paccini.*

The Danube capital held no dread for her. She had the intrepid pluck of youth that knew as yet no funk. That winter of 1837 the acknowledged lions of Europe's pianistic world, Thalberg and Liszt, were at their peak. But the eighteen-year-old Clara felt herself a match for them.

CHAPTER 7   The nineteenth century was, as no other has been, a time of glory for pianists.

A simple explanation lay behind this: the invention of the pianoforte or hammerclavier, with its capacity for modulating volume and tone color, whether loud *(forte)* or soft *(piano)*, had metamorphosed the art of keyboard music. Heretofore the weak dry tinklings of harpsichord, clavecin, clavichord—as their ancestors, the harp and lyre—had won only a limited following. Of these instruments designed for plucking, the harp alone achieved a caressing sweetness if not a round fullness of tone. Almost as much might be said for the zither. Among the somewhat related percussion devices—the dulcimer, xylophone, South African and Latin American marimba, or Hungarian czymbalom—the mallet action could change from forceful to feeble without affecting the quality of sound. This was equally true of the harmonium or its cousins, the organ, calliope, accordion, concertina, and humble harmonica, all depending on air forced through reeds or tubes; the amount of air could be controlled, but never the rudimentary flatness of even the gentlest blast.

With the arrival of the hammerclavier a miracle was wrought. The fine and intricate structure of its multiple levers, felt-padded tampers, superior resonance, and pedal control made possible for the first time a personalized method of play. If up to now the keyboard artist needed only finger agility and endurance—two attainments within reach of the most unmusical—in future there was room and range for individuality. In Mozart's day one harpsichordist, provided he did not neglect his practice hours, resembled every other (also practicing) harpsichordist. If you had one in your home you did not visit concert

54

halls and pay admission to hear another. The modern piano changed all that. Now technique was not everything; mere keyboard gymnastics lost appeal. What had been only a watching audience turned into a listening one as differences among performers became manifest. In the sphere of strings it had long been customary to distinguish between fiddlers and violinists; similarly people now ceased mistaking a soulless keyboard thumper for a pianist.

It was Clara Wieck's great good fortune to have been born into an age of such musical apotheosis. True, during her span as a child prodigy no spiritual subtleties or intellectual refinements had been looked for in her playing. Audiences had come to see rather than hear. But as she developed, the wonder of her touch—silken at times, when not rhapsodic and passionate, or firm and serene—singled her out, an artist among artists.

When she arrived in Vienna, fame had already preceded her. After the first press notices appeared, Clara and her father were invited to court for presentation to the Emperor Ferdinand I (great-grandson of the matriarch Maria Theresa) and his wife Maria Anna of Sardinia (daughter of King Victor Emmauel I). An unusual situation prevailed among the ruling Habsburgs at that time. The sovereign being childless, a younger brother—Franz Karl—filled the role of crown prince. The latter, married to Princess Sophie of Bavaria, was father to Franz Joseph, future Austrian monarch of extraordinary longevity. At the time the Wiecks visited the Hofburg, Franz Joseph was seven years old, handsome, frisky, and thoroughly unmusical. While Clara performed for their majesties the lad squirmed briefly, then dragged a hobbyhorse across the parquetry and trotted off to his playroom.

A second court appearance followed, during which the Empress bestowed on her talented visitor a precious brooch. Clara was also proclaimed "Imperial and Royal Court Virtuosa," a purely nominal kudos which nevertheless carried considerable prestige when engraved on one's stationery and calling cards.

Some public concerts followed, as well as engagements in Graz and Budapest. Finally, Wieck and his daughter were invited into some of the homes of Vienna's intelligentsia. Here Clara met the Hungarian-born Nikolaus Niembsch von Strehlenau who, under the pen name of Nikolaus Lenau, was adding one more version of the Don Juan legend to literature's hoard (his text would be set to music, many years afterward, by Richard Strauss). Also absorbed in the Faust theme, Lenau at thirty-five already showed signs of the imaginative aberrations which thirteen years later would cause him to die insane. There is a price on genius.

A special joy for the Wiecks was an encounter with Austria's poet laureate Franz Grillparzer, now forty-six, who in 1825 had seen his drama *König Ottokar's Glück und Ende (The Rise and Fall of King Ottokar)* triumph at Vienna's Hofburg Palace Theater. In this epic work occurred the inspired lines that are recited by successive generations of Austrian schoolchildren, princes, peasants, cabbies and highest statesmen. The rare and gracious words are free of pomp or patriotic bombast, forming instead a lyric psalm to the beauty of a land much blessed. On hearing Grillparzer's paean to Austria there came to Clara's lips but one question: why had it never been set to music? She found the text most noble:

> *Schaut rings umher, wohin der Blick sich wendet*
> *Lacht's wie dem Bräutigam die Braut entgegen.*
> *Mit hellem Wiesengrün und Saatengold,*
> *Von Lein und Safran gelb und blau gestickt,*
> *Von Blumen süss durchwürzt und edlem Kraut,*
> *Schweift es in breitgestreckten Tälern hin—*
> *Ein voller Blumenstrauss, so weit es reicht,*
> *Vom Silberband der Donau rings umwunden—*
> *Hebt sich's empor zu Hügeln voller Wein,*
> *Wo auf und auf die goldne Traube hängt*
> *Und schwellend reift in Gottes Sonnenglanze;*
> *Der dunkle Wald voll Jagdlust krönt das Ganze.*
> *Und Gottes lauer Hauch schwebt drüber hin*
> *Und wärmt und reift und macht die Pulse schlagen,*
> *Wie nie ein Puls auf kalten Steppen schlägt.*
> *Drum ist der Österreicher froh und frank,*
> *Trägt seinen Fehl, trägt offen seine Freuden,*
> *Beneidet nicht, lässt lieber sich beneiden!*
> *Und was er tut, ist frohen Muts getan.**

---

* Do look about you: whither turns your gaze
The landscape smiles as bridegroom does to bride . . .
Pale green are meadows, golden is the seed,
While blossoms blue and saffron yellow
Sweetly mingle with the scent of herbs—
So stretches out the chain of valleys,
A flower swath as far as eye can see,

Like all poets, Grillparzer embroidered truth in the interest of ecstatic scansion. The peoples of the Danube basin were no more winsome or less cantankerous than humanity anywhere else, though the mildness of the sub-Alpine climate did induce in them an easy-going frame of mind, a cozy and distinctly Mediterranean *laissez-faire*. If this was evident in the Habsburg realm as a whole, the peak of *Gemüt-lichkeit-cum-Charme* reigned in Vienna. It reigned to a degree which the Germanic Wiecks found at first bewitching, then cloying, and finally exasperating.

For one thing, the easy sentimentality of the Viennese colored their taste in music. While opera held a high place in public esteem, this was nevertheless the capital of operetta. A great symphonic orchestra played Mozart and Beethoven, but to the outside world the city was forever synonymous with Johann Strauss. The serious virtuoso seeking laurels here must have the spectacular dexterity and showmanship of Liszt or Thalberg. Despite the deepened quality of modern pianistic interpretation made possible by the marvelous new instruments, Austrian audiences still reacted first with their eyes and then their ears. They wanted a good "show."

Clara Wieck commanded an excellent technique. But the very essence of her father's teaching method was the search for profundity of expression. Thus her keyboard feats, though superb, contained no element of acrobatics. By the same token her Vienna concerts might be sold out, without stirring the press to delirious reportage. She was regarded a fine pianist, even an extraordinary one considering her age, but nowhere in a class with the Thalberg-Liszt team.

Christmas came and went. The dreary rooming house where the Wiecks stayed did not lend itself to celebrating. For Clara it was sad

---

Laced by the Danube's silver ribbon
The land rises to vineyard heights
With gilded terraces of grapes
Grown opulent in Heaven's radiant sunning,
And with dark woods and hunting grounds
To crown the whole . . .
God's gentlest breath, it hovers there
All things to warm and ripen, quickening the pulse
As never pulse can throb on icy northern steppes.
Here lies the reason for the Austrian's open joy
In living, and his will to happiness, even in error;
He envies no one, rather lets himself be envied!
And when he acts, he is impelled by cheer. . . .

to have no tree or other decorations, and sadder to overhear her father muttering to the servant Nanny: "If my daughter marries that Schumann fellow I shall disown her even on my deathbed!"

The trembling Nanny gave no answer. All the same, on Christmas Eve she brought her young mistress a note from Robert, fetched from the post office that afternoon. It proved a bright spot in the gloomy holidays.

"Amid the thousands who acclaim you," wrote Robert (who believed Clara to be deluged with applause and money), "you will perhaps hear a voice calling you softly by name. It is mine, for I follow you everywhere, unseen. . . ."

She wept for joy, then went to the upright piano at one end of her cramped room. Her third Vienna concert was set for January 7, 1838, and the fourth for a week thereafter. She must practice.

During both concerts Grillparzer was in the audience, seemingly entranced by Clara's interpretation of Beethoven's *Sonata Appassionata*. He wrote a tribute to her which, in manuscript, she cherished as a talisman the rest of her life:

> *Ein Wundermann, der Welt, des Lebens satt,*
> *Schloss seine Zauber grollend ein*
> *Im festverwahrten, demantharten Schrein,*
> *Und warf den Schlüssel in das Meer und starb.*
> *Die Menschlein mühen sich geschäftig ab,*
> *Umsonst! kein Sperrzeug löst das harte Schloss*
> *Und seine Zauber schlafen, wie ihr Meister . . .*
> *Ein Schäferkind, am Strand des Meeres spielend,*
> *Sieht zu der hastig unberuf'nen Jagd.*
> *Sinnvoll-gedankenlos, wie Mädchen sind,*
> *Senkt sie die weissen Finger in die Flut,*
> *Und fasst, und hebt, und hat's. Es ist der Schlüssel!*
> *Auf springt sie, auf, mit höhern Herzensschlägen,*
> *Der Schrein blinkt wie aus Augen ihr entgegen.*
> *Der Schlüssel passt. Der Deckel fliegt. Die Geister,*
> *Sie steigen auf und senken dienend sich*
> *Der anmuthreichen, unschuldsvollen Herrin,*
> *Die sie mit weissen Fingern, spielend, lenkt.* °

° A sorcerer [Beethoven], wearied of living and the world,
Put under lock and key his magic
In a perdurable, diamond-hard coffer,
Then tossed the key into the sea, and died.

Grillparzer's lyric vision confirmed what Friedrich Wieck had long cherished as a supreme ambition: Clara was to become a Beethoven interpreter par excellence. Not in Vienna alone but throughout Europe the "bucolic child" would astound listeners with her mastery of the "sorcerer's" imponderable art.

During the spring Clara was to have appeared in Budapest but, the raging Danube having gushed across its banks and flooded much of central Hungary, she could go no farther than Pressburg (Bratislava). Such concerts as were now given brought no personal gain other than honorary, because pianists, singers, actors, and circus riders were all indiscriminately petitioned to perform at benefits, with revenues accruing to the flood victims. On April 3, 1838, Clara wrote to Robert:

> At Pressburg I had to give two concerts in four days, and the day after tomorrow the Emperor wants me to play again at the Hofburg. It will be my last recital in Vienna. You can see that I am exerting myself beyond my strength, I feel tired all the time, and so sick of piano-playing. . . . Yet, Heaven knows, the moment I am before an audience I get carried away with always the same enthusiasm!

These words gave testimony that in Clara too there glowed the spark of showmanship that had turned Thalberg and Liszt into stars of the first magnitude. She had no fear of footlights, no dread of people in the mass. Solitary, serene, confident, she could walk out on the most immense and barest stage, losing not a heartbeat. She loved an audience.

Inevitably a great affinity developed between her and Franz Liszt.

Weak humans tried with futile tools thereafter
To spring the sturdy and unyielding lock—
But witchcraft and witchman remained aloof . . .
'Twas then a young bucolic child,
Observing the impatient and so fruitless search,
Herself casually, yet deep in meditation, as is a girl,
Dipped her pale fingers into the green sea
And touched and gripped and lifted—ah, the key!
With beating heart she bounded to the coffer
Which stood, as if long yearning for that moment . . .
The key was right. The lock flew open. And the genii
Escaped, to bend at once prostrate
Before the guileless and beguiling mistress
Whose gentle touch induced them back to life. . . .

The phenomenal Hungarian who, on a concert tour himself, had made a special stop in Vienna in order to hear Clara play, was frankly dazzled. He had written, earlier, to the music dealer Hofmeister in Leipzig, employing the French he mastered best after his mother tongue:

> *. . . Une jeune personne sachant exécuter avec énergie, intelligence et précision des morceaux de ma façon est un phénomène excessivement rare à tout pays, et tout à fait introuvable je crois dans celui que j'habite à présent: Chopin et plusieurs autres artistes m'en ont déjà parlé. Je désire vivement de la connaître et malgré ma paresse de locomotion je ferai presque un voyage pour l'entendre. . . .*°

When they did meet with Liszt and Thalberg at a musical soirée in the latter's home, Wieck and his daughter were tremendously impressed. Both artists were admirable, but it was Liszt who left Clara searching for superlatives:

> . . . He is to be compared with absolutely no other pianist. He stands alone, unique. Though arousing astonishment and shock, he nevertheless is the most gracious of artists. As for his presence at the piano, it simply can't be described. . . . His passion knows no bounds.

For Friedrich Wieck the Austrian capital held an additional interest; this was the stronghold of the phenomenal teacher Carl Czerny, among whose prize pupils figured Thalberg and Liszt. At forty-seven (six years younger than Wieck) Czerny was hailed for his chromatic drill, applied to scales, thirds, fifths, sixths, octaves, and arpeggios. His textbook *Schule der Geläufigkeit (School of Velocity)* was respected the world over. To date, this work was his 299th publication; in the next twenty years he would produce an *Opus 1000*.

Wieck could not but look with jaundiced eye on such a rival, especially as Czerny had just launched his latest *Wunderkind*, an eight-

---

° (. . . A young person who can execute, with energy, intelligence and precision, compositions in my style is a phenomenon excessively rare in any country, and altogether inconceivable, I think, where I live at present. Chopin and several other artists have already told me much about her. It is my urgent wish to meet her and, despite my dislike of locomotion, I would almost set out on a journey just to hear her. . . .)

year-old boy of Polish extraction, Theodor Leschetizky. For some time to come the Leipzig pedagogue would fret over this competition in which his Clara, being older, was at a psychological disadvantage. It was only when Leschetizky at fifteen decided in favor of a teaching career (he was too shy and highstrung for the concert stage) that Papa Wieck relaxed.

The hospitable Thalberg evenings were repeated. Most of the guests being musical, a general complaisance prevailed about playing for one another. Invariably the fiery Liszt outshone the rest. He did this, be it noted, by snapping from two to five strings (bass or treble, no difference) per night.

"What instrument can stand up under him?" wrote Clara to her beloved Robert, adding dejectedly: "Since hearing and seeing Liszt's pyrotechnics I feel like a schoolgirl. My own playing bores me. I think I ought to stop touring altogether. . . ."

Her dismal mood did not last long. Shortly before the Vienna sojourn ended, Clara was summoned by the Emperor and Empress to be awarded a rare endorsement. She received a gold medal inscribed with her title of "Royal and Imperial Court Virtuosa," an unheard-of grace accorded by the Habsburgs to a foreigner and a Protestant.

Clara's first reaction was one of fright. Did this mean they would hold her here in Austria? Was her father involved in some machination to keep her from seeing Robert Schumann again?

But no. The favor bestowed by their majesties entailed no palace job. What it did furnish, as Friedrich Wieck readily recognized, was a helpful fillip to be exploited in the young girl's publicity. An etching of the medal and a properly expanded story of its presentation would look well in print.

"Marriage!" snorted the paternal impresario. "Housekeeping, babies—indeed!"

He envisioned other horizons.

Clara Wieck was only at the start of her far and glorious climb to fame.

CHAPTER 8 When the Wiecks first arrived in Vienna they had been received with skepticism and even a certain hostility. In part this was due to the nature of Clara's programs, which contained too much of Bach for Austrian tastes. By the end of her sojourn, however, the eighteen-year-old pianist had wrought a change among her listeners. An article in the *Neue Zeitschrift für Musik (New Musical Review)* for April 27, 1838, ranks Clara third in a tabulation of the four greatest keyboard virtuosos of the day, to wit: Franz Liszt, Sigismund Thalberg, Clara Wieck, Adolf von Henselt. A brilliant light was missing in this constellation—Chopin, who was already ill of tuberculosis and had retired from the concert stage; that same year, in October, the world learned of his departure via Barcelona for the island of Mallorca in the company of Aurore Dudevant, a cigar-smoking seductress known in literary circles as George Sand.

In the *Zeitschrift* article the four artists were classified in relation to certain characteristics. Liszt symbolized impassioned performance; Thalberg, refined sensualism in expression; Clara, irrepressible enthusiasm; Henselt, Germanic lyricism. Again, Liszt was considered diabolical; Thalberg, fascinating; Clara, ennobling; Henselt, exciting. Other and more pertinent professional qualities rated as follows:

Greatest purity of technique—Thalberg, Clara, Henselt, Liszt.
Ability for improvising—Liszt, Clara. None in the others.
Warmth of musical feeling—Liszt, Henselt, Clara, Thalberg.
Inborn (rather than acquired) artistry—Liszt, Clara.
Highest soaring spirit—Liszt.
Ease and sophistication—Thalberg.
Affectation and mannerisms—Henselt.

Uniqueness, modeled after no one else—Liszt.
Complete absorption—Clara.
Reading at first sight—Liszt, Thalberg, Clara.
Versatility (evidenced in program variety)—Clara, Liszt, Thalberg, Henselt.
Scholarliness—Thalberg, Henselt, Clara, Liszt.
Musical judgment—Liszt, Thalberg.
Beauty of touch—Thalberg, Henselt, Clara, Liszt.
Audacity—Liszt, Clara.
Ego—Liszt, Henselt.
Dependence on finger practice—Liszt, none; Thalberg and Clara, free exercises; Henselt, slavish pedantry.
"Objective" performance, without imprint of personality—none.
Use of metronome—none.
Most worthy of imitation by future artists—Thalberg, Clara.
Correct (note-perfect) playing—Thalberg, Clara, Henselt.
Proper concert preparation—Liszt, Thalberg, Clara.
No hair-tossing or grimacing—Thalberg, Clara.

In a closing assessment the four artists were further classified according to their music-cultural background. Liszt was considered the embodiment of the French-Romantic School; Thalberg, the Voluptuous-Italian; Henselt and Clara, the Sentimental-German.

Whatever the demerits of such arbitrary comparisons, it was a triumph for Friedrich Wieck to see his daughter mentioned on a par with the day's foremost pianists. Nor did the fact that she was referred to in print by her first name imply belittlement. It appeared rather an affectionate concession to her freshness and youth.

As teacher and father, Wieck could be well satisfied, the more so as yet another grace was conferred upon Clara almost at the moment of departure from Austria. She was made an honorary member of the Vienna Society of Music Friends, a distinction that carried considerable prestige. Wieck was already concentrating on ways of putting this to propaganda use.

For the present, however, there was Leipzig to be faced, and the problem of keeping Robert Schumann out of Clara's way. It was impossible for the young people not to meet in a town of such small size even if, as was not the case, the girl were docile and meek of character. Preferably Wieck would have liked prolonging the tour for a whole year, without going home. But Clara required rest and time to prepare a new repertoire; these needs could not be satisfied while being jostled in drafty post-chaises across the map of Europe. There remained, then, only one expedient to thwart the lovers. Wieck must continue his threat of causing Schumann bodily harm, not in a match of fisticuffs (Robert, broad-shouldered and athletic, would have been more than able to defend himself) but by pistol or gun. While it is unlikely that the level-headed musicmaster would ever have taken such drastic action, Clara had no way of knowing but that her beloved dwelled under constant menace of sudden death.

They saw each other nonetheless, even if they dared not speak. On errands in town, at a Gewandhaus recital, in theater audiences, or at the homes of friends (where Wieck, to be sure, played Cerberus), their eyes met and gave comforting assurance of a pledge unbroken. Then there was also Nanny, still serving faithfully as love's courier. Through the daily exchange of notes Robert and Clara unburdened their hearts and made plans, defying adversity.

One fact had to be faced, beyond question. Even if they contained themselves until Clara came of age, there was no hope for them in Leipzig. Wieck would find ways of preventing their marriage or, failing in this, of destroying their happiness by unrelenting schemes of vengeance.

Suddenly Robert had a bright idea. From Clara's descriptions, Vienna must be a pleasant place. With the friends and excellent professional contacts she had made there it might be well to choose Austria for their future home. He decided to move at once, so as to take root and establish himself (with his music journal and printing press) in anticipation of the time when Clara might be able to join him. "Our present life in Leipzig," he wrote disconsolately, "is unbearable!"

She agreed. In Vienna, far removed from Wieck's wrath, Robert was out of danger. He would compose and write his essays or critiques, while she spent the next three years concertizing and saving her earnings toward the day when she was legally free to decide her fate. She would then speed to Vienna, to her beloved, and happiness eternal.

This was the dream. And quite so, according to plan, they intended to carry it out.

Schumann departed for Austria in the fall of 1838, stopping en route in Dresden and Prague. He carried letters to Clara's Viennese friends, among them the Moravian journalist Joseph Fischhof, and an imperial

lady-in-waiting named Cibbini who composed music under the signature of Kotzeluch, her maiden name. Another person who might prove
helpful was an official in the Foreign Ministry, Vesque von Püttlingen,
himself an amateur pianist who had set the Grillparzer on Clara Wieck
to music. The important Thalberg circle could also be counted on to
further Robert's interests—if not for his own as yet obscure sake, then
for love of the young Clara they had so recently applauded.

The journey southward was not without hazards. To begin with,
the erstwhile Heidelberg student who had hated being chained to one
spot now found his taste for travel gone. In younger years Schumann
had heartily subscribed to the Goethe postulate, "*Wo Du nicht bist, da
ist das Glück. . . .*" ("Where thou art not, there is happiness"), namely
at the end of an ever unattainable rainbow. In more popular doggerel
the saw went:

> *Hier, da bin ich sowieso;*
> *schöner ist es anderswo!*°

Time was when his chronic ailment had been not homesickness but
wanderlust, the need to be off and gone, anywhere, nowhere. But
love had wrought a change, causing him to dread distance and separation. He wanted to be near his love, at anchor, safely in port, never to
set sail again. Yet there he was, bouncing along over the abominable
carriage route to Austria and growing lonelier by the minute.

As the journey wore on, his sentimental pangs were overshadowed
by the sheer discomfort of his position in the cramped coach. Only
with greatest effort could he wriggle a half inch or so to right or left
of the wedge assigned him between two portly fellow passengers.
Washington Irving in his *Tales of a Traveler* graphically described just
such a plight:

> There is a certain relief in change, even though it be from bad
> to worse; as I have found in traveling in a stagecoach, that it is
> often a comfort to shift one's position and be bruised in a new
> place. . . .

In Prague there was a short stop, utilized by Robert to pen a quick
note to his beloved. While so engaged he lost track of the time and

---

° Why prefer the here and now,
  since that is where I am anyhow?!

was left behind by the departing coach. Racing after it on foot, he failed to catch up, but managed to jump on the trestle of a second vehicle along the road. He gripped the doorknob and held on in panic as the double team of horses thundered ahead at a gallop. Suddenly, through an inadvertent twist of his hand, the latch gave way and the door flew open. Schumann swung out into space, but he continued to hold on until helpful arms reached out to pull him inside. In the course of this near-catastrophe he lost several heartbeats, a good measure of composure, and his cap.

In Vienna further misadventure awaited him. It became evident almost at once that Friedrich Wieck, guessing the young people's intentions, had likewise indulged in letter-writing. Aware that at the age of twenty-one Clara could leave him, the embittered father resolved to hinder Schumann's success wherever possible so that, on economic grounds, the marriage plans must fail.

Among others, Wieck warned the Austrian censor Count Sedlnitzky (in most of Europe there was no free press at the time) against Robert's journalistic activities. He painted the young man in sinister colors, describing him as a dangerous innovator not only in the world of music but of ideas as well.

The poison worked. When Schumann presented himself in Sedlnitzky's office to apply for a license for publication of his magazine he met with a scarcely veiled refusal. So many obstacles were put in his path—including objections to his being a foreigner and farfetched demands for proof of his editorial competence—that someone less idealistic and determined than Robert would have lost heart.

As it was, Vienna enchanted the nature-loving Saxon. He was thrilled by the city's beautiful surroundings, its circle of gently rising mountains, the dense woodlands, and the always enthralling sweep of the great Danube. Why should he not take root here, and find the means to build a happy future? If, as a foreigner, he could not set up his own print shop, he would seek a partnership with some local publisher like Tobias Haslinger.

Alas, Haslinger too had had a confidential note from Wieck. Schumann's proposal was thus coolly received, with counter offers that were not only unacceptable but downright insulting.

Still Robert's courage did not flag. In his next letter to Clara he assured her that if he could not prosper as a journalist he would win

Vienna with his music. To familiarize himself with local tastes and standards he attended several concerts and even a dance recital by the thirty-four-year old Stockholm-born Marie Sophie Taglioni, ballerina of the Paris Opera.

Of Taglioni he wrote to Leipzig:

> I cannot say that she dazzled me, but I was strangely transported. She does not excite as much as she becalms through a distinct naturalness. She makes the new seem familiar. That is her secret.

He also heard a coloratura, Jenny Lutzer of Prague (wife of the poet Franz Dingelstedt), and found her unbearable. Only twenty-two then, this singer was already noted for a cloying coyness which caused Schumann to snarl:

> I can't stand her curtsies, and that abashed humility she puts on after she has sung really well; because she certainly *can* sing, and she breathes for two. But I could never marry that kind of woman. . . .

Clara loved reading this, and gaining assurance that her adored Robert would not fall prey to another's wiles. She was herself meeting new people at this time. The young (barely sixteen) Pauline García, daughter of a famous Spanish singing family, had come to Leipzig on her first concert tour. She possessed an extraordinary mezzo-soprano with a three-octave range, from low C to F above high F. Even so, Pauline did not outshine her elder sister Felicità, divorced from the impresario Malibran and later married to the violinist Bériot. Until her recent death at Manchester, after being thrown and dragged by a horse, La Malibran had been regarded as the most sensational woman vocalist of the century. Her deep contralto with its additional register of soprano head tones was said to have been past belief. A brother of these two singers, Manuel García, was himself a basso and a professor at London Conservatory, where he taught Jenny Lind. He also dabbled in science and invented the laryngoscope, a complicated apparatus, mirror-equipped, for examining the throat.

Clara was greatly impressed by such remarkable statistics. But above all, on meeting the Paris-born Pauline backstage, she delighted in the latter's brunette beauty and *chic*. Mademoiselle García had two additional Christian names, Michelle Fernande, which only enhanced her glamour; she traveled currently in the company of her mother and the widowed brother-in-law Bériot. Unusual among singers, Pauline was also a good pianist, able to take over at the keyboard and perform an entire song recital in the event her accompanist broke down. She furthermore personified the French school of concertizing, by doing everything from memory. With such gifts the young lady's rise to fame was rapid. A year after the Leipzig visit she made her opera debut in London and was then engaged by the French littérateur Louis Viardot for his Théâtre Italien in Paris. Presently Monsieur Viardot was to think of a better way to keep his hold on such valuable property; he married the girl and directed her future tours as press agent and personal manager.

Another artist playing in Leipzig during the winter of 1838 was the Czech pianist Alexander Dreyschock, who, only a year older than Clara, overwhelmed audiences with the tremendous agility of his fingers. In a note to Schumann there were hard words by Clara:

> This Dreyschock from Prague has no soul, and his playing is terrible. He created a furor at the Gewandhaus, amazing everybody with his speed. Thalberg, however, is infinitely superior. . . .

The reference to Thalberg was pertinent, as he too had embarked on a tour of German cities and appeared at the Gewandhaus within a few days of Dreyschock. Indeed, on hearing Thalberg again, Clara suffered one of her periodic spells of discouragement.

> "I seem so insignificant to myself," she wrote Robert, "I could cry. If I just had the will to pull myself together, I could do much better. But I am handicapped by love. I cannot live, as my father wishes, *for art alone*. . . ."

In another reference to Thalberg she added:

> His touch is the most marvelous of all. He never has a mishap. . . . A magnificent pianist; though the most magnificent is Mendelssohn!

There was a reason deeper than mere critical appraisal for Clara's present preoccupation with her professional contemporaries. She was being groomed by her father for the most ambitious concert tour of her young career, culminating in another assault on Paris.

In laying these plans Friedrich Wieck had one eye on financial gain and the other on a craftier purpose, namely, to double the distance between his daughter and Schumann, preferably over a period long enough to ensure their estrangement. He discussed it one evening with his wife. Clara accidentally passed a half-open door just as her stepmother Clementine was saying: "The girl will forget him. She'll never stick it out."

Instantly Clara made for her writing desk. "Not stick it out? They don't know me," she confided to Robert in high dudgeon. "But they're going to. Me, not standing by my love!!"

She accepted the Paris trip now as a challenge. Gone were her doubts regarding her artistic insufficiencies. Suddenly it didn't matter very much how she made out alongside the pianistic luminaries of the day. Indeed, it might be the most excruciating of punishments for Papa Wieck if she played badly, thus discrediting him before the world. She knew his one weakness. He could not bear to be thought a mediocre teacher.

It was a maneuver worth pondering.

But she did not ponder it. Her heart and will were set on a nobler purpose: she must gird herself for the cruel battle against distance and time.

She must prove to herself and Robert that she was capable of undying devotion.

CHAPTER 9 Robert Schumann was discovering an aspect of Vienna that is known only to people who have lived there. To transitory visitors indulging in tourist pastimes the Danube metropolis is a city like all others, though with an added magic. But the resident sees the overgrown kraal, with its tribal groupings and internal jealousies and feuds. *Der Wiener Tratsch,* the murderous "Vienna gossip," has been for untold generations a source of macabre pleasure and dread. In late December of 1838 Clara received the following warning from her beloved:

> ... When you come to know Vienna in a sober frame of mind, and over a longer period, you will find many things lacking and others quite different from the way they appeared during your local professional triumphs. I don't want to put on paper some of the matters I see with my own eyes, or anything concerning the petty and mediocre people to be encountered—with their ignoble tongue-wagging; conceit and material gain dominate in most actions, the majority live superficially and their platitudes are frightening when directed at world affairs, humanity, art. Were I to cite names, some of your own acquaintances would figure prominently among them. But this is too bothersome for a letter. I merely want to warn you, so there will be no disappointment later. After all, we must seek happiness by our own fireside, and we shall find it; joy will live in our home, and honesty and truth. ...

Despite the closing note of hope it became daily more evident that Schumann would have a difficult time building a future in Austria. In part the malicious propaganda launched against him by Friedrich Wieck must be held responsible for this.

... Your father thinks that my compositions don't sell [Robert complained to Clara]. I have gone to the publisher to find out; he checked his books and saw that nearly 300 copies of *Carnaval* and *Phantasieen* were sold, and at least 350 *Kinderszenen.* These works were printed only six months ago. You can believe that I walked away from Härtel more than satisfied. . . .

It was his dream to compose something jointly with Clara. To this end they exchanged notations on various original themes, letting their fancy soar to daring heights, not fearing to tackle either a symphony or an opera. Robert insisted, over and again:

... It is important for us to publish something under both our names; this way people will see that we have not only one heart, but one soul. The idea enthralls me. When I sit at the piano I think only of you. Ah, if we could finish all the works we are projecting, what an eternity we would need! As for my own compositions, do not worry, Clara; you will live long enough to hear them spoken of and to see them triumph. . . .

They wrote each other daily, the faithful maid Nanny still serving as intermediary. But a morning dawned, early in 1839, when Nanny was trapped by Wieck as she returned from an unscheduled trip to the Leipzig post office.

"What have we here?" asked the glowering master, divesting the girl of a fat envelope. "Looks like some extra-heavy mail!"

Alas, the missives exchanged by Robert and Clara were invariably of great length. It took a good half hour of Herr Wieck's valuable time to peruse the present specimen, not only because of its bulk but also because of Schumann's almost illegible penmanship. When he had finished, the angered father reached a quick decision. Clara's departure for Paris must be advanced to an earlier date, and under no circumstances was Nanny to accompany her. Instead he would hire a French secretary-governess to take his own place during the trip and to keep Clara under close surveillance. He himself, for the first time, did not plan to go along. He wanted Clara to have a taste of what life would be like without a paternal impresario to handle baggage, book hotels, hire concert halls and—last but by no means least—negotiate for decent pianos everywhere (most available pianos in rented concert halls were in lamentable condition). If Schumann counted on marrying a money-making virtuoso, he, Wieck, had no further interest in managing his daughter's tours. It was best for Clara to find out right now what she would be up against.

The French travel companion proved a dour and straitlaced watchdog. For a week after leaving Leipzig on January 8, by the early morning diligence for Nuremberg, Clara found no chance for mailing even a postcard with news of her whereabouts. Nor did she know of a dependable address to give him, as the vigilant Mademoiselle was in charge of all tour data, with Clara expected to do only one thing: go on stage and play.

There remained another dilemma. Robert's letters would continue to arrive in Leipzig, possibly into Wieck's hands, revealing to him the plan of an ultimate elopement. True, the lovers had been using a code word for delivery. But Nanny knew that word, and it could be obtained from her by intimidation. Thus Wieck would gain time for setting up countermeasures so elaborate that they could never be surmounted. Clara already had an idea of what these measures might be: Wieck claimed to have heard that there was congenital insanity in Schumann's family. It was true that a sister of Robert had suffered a nervous breakdown, dying soon after in a state of mental incoherence. Wieck would have little difficulty obtaining an injunction against his daughter's marriage, on such grounds, even if she were of legal age.

Such were the thoughts that plagued Clara as she drove through Bavaria in a snowstorm so violent and prolonged that the stagecoach left the road and was bogged down in mountainous drifts. In Nuremberg two concerts had been booked, but the weather kept people from coming to the theater. This led to an argument between Mademoiselle and the local impresario regarding fees, which in turn gave Clara an opportunity to bribe an idle stagehand to put a letter in the mail. At least Robert would know that, for the present, all correspondence between them must cease.

At the next stop, Stuttgart, this pessimistic decision could be retracted as Clara remembered that her friend Emilie List lived now in Paris, at 43 Rue des Martyrs. Surely here was the perfect solution! She sent Robert the address, then unburdened her heart in a letter to Emilie. By the time Clara arrived in France a packet of missives from Schumann had piled up in the Rue des Martyrs.

In Paris the travelers stopped at the Hôtel Michodière, where by coincidence the singer Pauline García was also staying. This might prove helpful as no concerts were yet contracted for and, without her able father to break the ice, Clara expected to have a difficult time. Secretly she had counted on renewing her friendship with Chopin, through whom an entrée in the best professional circles would have been assured. But since his return from Mallorca the ailing Pole was being held, romantically sequestered, at a flower-banked villa in Nohant (Département d'Indre) by his matronly mistress George Sand.

All Paris buzzed with details of the nightmare lived by Chopin in the Balearic Isles. Palma de Mallorca, at sea level, had been too damp and oppressive for his health, whereupon Madame Sand had leased three convent cells in an abandoned Carthusian monastery on a mountain top at Valdemosa. Here matters soon took a dismal turn, for Chopin's beloved had brought along the children of her broken marriage, two undisciplined brats named Maurice and Solange. The idyl was further disrupted by bigoted Valdemosa villagers, who soon divined the irregular domestic situation of the visitors as well as took umbrage at Madame Sand's eccentric clothing (when she did not wear men's top hats, cravats, and tight-fitting trousers, the lady took long moonlight walks in filmy white veils, after the bairns and Chopin had gone to bed). When it was discovered in addition that none of the strangers appeared at Sunday Mass, open hostility broke out. No native servant girl would cook or wash or clean for the "sinful heretics," while farmers round about refused to sell them food. In panic Chopin urged departure, leaving his prized Pleyel piano behind. The small party sailed on the freighter Mallorquín which carried a load of pigs to Barcelona. Due to Chopin's increasing hemorrhages (people spoke in horror of tuberculosis as the "white plague") the ship's captain would not permit the travelers on deck. They spent the voyage in the hold amid the stench and squeals of the jampacked porkers.

No, Clara Wieck could not look to Chopin for help. Through Pauline García, however, a concert was arranged in the recital hall of the Érard music firm, at 13 Rue de Mail. Pauline and the violinist Bériot took part on the same program, and the ticket sale was gratifying. Since the earnings were split three ways. and the hall had to be paid for, Clara made little profit; but the reviews were good and gave rise to hopes that better engagements would follow.

At this point a strange problem presented itself. Paris, already world-famous for its sophistication and gayety, was still steeped in early nineteenth-century prudery, if not skittishness. After local critics jubilantly acknowledged the excellence of Mademoiselle Wieck's performance an eyebrow-raising comment spoiled the happy effect. The young artist, so reporters had learned, was touring *alone;* that is, in the company of a hired secretary. No mother, grandfather, brother, uncle, or cousin twice removed to watch over her virtue! It raised a punctilious quandary: could well-bred society (and who else bought concert tickets?) listen to a piano-player of feminine gender, who traipsed about the Continent inadequately chaperoned? Another triumph, Clara recognized, for Papa Wieck. Again it was brought home to her that without her father's guidance and protection her career would soon be at an end. It looked indeed as if, at the moment, it wasn't even going to get started.

To cap matters, Friedrich Wieck now wrote a letter to Emilie List, complaining bitterly of his daughter's folly and insubordination. "If you think anything of your former Leipzig teacher," he ranted, "you will deny Clara any comfort or aid."

Emilie thought something of Herr Wieck. She thought him an insufferable tyrant and a prig. It was too late to obey the letter's bidding, even had she wanted to; Clara was a daily guest at the List home, if only to escape the supervision of her bodyguard. But there was one service Emilie could render. She would "lend" Clara a dear family adjunct, her own Aunt Simonetta, for travel escort and *Anstands-Wauwau* (propriety watchdog or bow-wow).

"Will Aunt Simonetta agree?" asked Clara.

"Watch her! Auntie will do anything for a free ride on a carrousel."

There remained the problem of Mademoiselle who was in Herr Wieck's pay and could not therefore be fired by Clara.

Emilie had an answer. "We'll threaten to tell people she has false hair and a stuffed bosom. That's enough to make any woman clear out."

It was.

Within hours Clara's unhappy plight took an optimistic turn. Freed of the unwanted hireling, she "borrowed" Emilie's Aunt Simonetta with enthusiasm and set out in the latter's company to make the rounds of Paris impresarios. The effect was galvanic. Bookings materialized in flattering succession, and, when a portrait sketch of the somewhat formidable Simonetta appeared in the papers, there was a small flurry of requests for private lessons by the talented Fräulein Wieck. Clara began planning for a long stay, moving with the Lists (father, mother, and daughter) to a new town house, Rue Navarin 12.

"I am making plenty of money," she wrote Robert in April of 1839, "and can save quite a bit of it. In a little over a year I shall be yours."

His answer cast a veil of gloom over her cheer. Things were not going well for him in Vienna. He too was giving music lessons, but not at luxury fees commanded by a headlined performer. The sales of his recent compositions had subsided again, after a promising initial spurt, due to the untrammeled modernism of his melodic idiom. As for gaining a foothold in the journalistic field, Vienna offered too much opposition to a foreigner (and Protestant, to boot).

"I see no alternative," he told Clara, "but to return to Leipzig where my magazine flourished and I was economically well established. Unless you will gamble with me on emigrating to England after our marriage, where, with hard work, we are bound to make a success. . . ."

He touched on another and more serious subject. Since no reconciliation with Friedrich Wieck appeared likely, and an open battle was to be expected at the moment of Clara's attaining her majority, Schumann proposed obtaining a legal writ assuring her right to marry over any parental objection whatever. He had already drawn up an application to this end, which, duly notarized, was to be signed by Clara and returned to him. "Our struggles, my dearest," he urged upon her, "must soon come to an end."

She agreed with Robert, of course. But her heart was heavy. Despite her father's cruelty and intransigence she could not set aside completely her love for him. In her reply to Robert she begged for his consent to one more attempt on her part toward appeasement. On May 1, 1838, she wrote a long letter to Wieck, addressing him as "My beloved Father"; in part it ran as follows:

> Yes, there is passion in my love for Schumann, but not alone passion or infatuation; I love him because he is in my eyes the best of human beings, because I believe that no other man can love me so purely, so nobly, and can understand me as does he. . . . We would need nothing for our happiness beyond a small but sure income, and your blessing; without the latter I should be utterly miserable, I could have no peace, nor could Schumann—who is

so tenderhearted—be truly happy. And I, how could I live, cast from you, and knowing you unhappy! I couldn't stand it.

Dear Father, would you promise us your consent if Schumann can prove that he has an income of 1,000 *Thaler?* Two thousand *Thaler* would really be asking too much, this is possible only as time goes on. Give us hope, and we shall be happy, with Schumann gaining so much more courage to work toward winning me; I in turn promise you not to marry Schumann until we are certain of having no economic worries. . . . You can make us the most joyous of human beings, or the most despondent. . . . I beg you, answer me right away, as I suffer under this uncertainty; you will see that I shall not abandon my music; you think I do not love my art? Dear God, the only time I am able to forget my sorrow is at the piano. . . .

Robert backed up her financial claims by tabulating what they each owned in the way of savings:

Clara	4,000	*Thaler*
Schumann		
1. Government investments	1,000	"
2. On deposit in business of brother Karl . .	4,000	"
3. On deposit in business of brother Eduard .	3,540	"
4. Inheritance from Eduard, recently		
deceased	1,500	"
Total	14,040	*Thaler*
Paying interest of	560	"
Additional Schumann earnings per year . . .		
Through writings (journalistic)	624	*Thaler*
Music sales	100	"
Compositions ready for publication	100	"
Therefore total yearly income:	1,384	*Thaler*

The amount was approximately 1,100 American dollars at the time. Allowing for the fact that Clara intended to continue concertizing, and that both she and Robert planned to teach music and harmony, their economic prospects were by no means dreary. Living standards in that era were immeasurably less exorbitant than they would become a century later, hence the young couple had every reason to believe that they could at least materially make a go of marriage.

In June of that year Robert was twenty-nine years old, and in September Clara would become twenty. More than twelve months still lay ahead before they could proceed legally, without Wieck's approval. It seemed an unbearably long time. For this reason Schumann himself wrote one more letter of conciliation to his former teacher, requesting that the remaining period of trial be shortened to Easter of 1840. The answer was a note from Clara's stepmother Clementine, stating that her husband wished no contact whatever with his daughter's suitor.

But this was not all. Realizing that the young people's industry and thrift had weakened his economic arguments, Wieck now girded himself for a different sort of battle. He attacked Robert's character. Harking back to Heidelberg student days, it was easy to learn that Schumann once took part in the beer-drinking carousals of that university city. This was enough for warning Clara against entering wedlock with a drunkard. Furthermore Wieck remembered the engagement, engineered by himself, between Robert and Ernestine von Fricken. Had this pledge ever been formally dissolved? Most likely the flighty Romeo was not even free to woo Clara, and bent only on wasting her time.

Luckily both points had easy answers. From mutual friends and through personal observation Clara knew that her beloved led a life free from dissipation. As for his onetime ties with Ernestine, these had been long abrogated. The lady in question was well consoled with a more glamorous catch; she had married a Count von Zedwitz-Liebenstein.

CHAPTER 10   Sentiment aside, Clara suffered in other ways through the estrangement from her father. She sorely missed the man who coped so well with business dealings, itinerary problems, and the dissemination of intelligent publicity. But more than that she felt the lack of the brilliant teacher, for she did not consider herself a finished pianist. On June 27 of 1838 she confided to Robert a secret anxiety:

> Do you know what I long for, above all else? A music lesson from my father; I fear I am losing ground because there is no one now to tell me my mistakes, of which undoubtedly many have crept in when I study without supervision and get carried away by melody, thus failing to hear the sick notes. In this I owe Father a debt of gratitude, which I seldom accorded him—and then, ungraciously. Oh, how I would now value his criticism!

Schumann saw in this outburst a danger signal. He sensed that in the tug of war between her emotional need and the tremendous compulsion of her talent the balance might at any moment go against him. He himself had long ceased to be a musical performer and his energies were turned entirely to composition; he could not therefore supplant the preceptor she longed for. But he likewise could not further endure the drawn-out agony of doubt. Suddenly he had had enough of it. He did not want to wait another year before taking decisive action. Clara must make up her mind now, for or against him. Either they parted forever, or she allowed him to apply for legal consent to marry even ahead of her coming of age.

Faced with this alternative, she bowed to love. Schumann filed his petition in Leipzig, whither he had returned on July 16, and informed Clara that she would have to put in an appearance before the court sometime within the next two months. The die was cast.

Happiness and sorrow mingled now in bitter ratio. There were unavoidable confrontations between Clara and her father, in which the stern man ultimately faced defeat.

The opinion handed down from the judge's bench made much of the fact that this was not a case of a dependent adolescent requiring parental protection, but of a most capable and self-supporting young woman whose earnings had for years contributed to the economic well-being of her elders. In short, Fräulein Wieck was declared free to marry the man of her choice.

It was a victory with heartbreak, for Clara had yet to feel the whiplash of paternal revenge. Wieck, who had control of her bank deposits and savings, demanded that these be turned over to his younger children whose education, he averred, had been neglected at the high cost of Clara's training. Furthermore, her grand piano, music scores, jewelry, and other possessions still at home were likewise to be sacrificed in payment for the special devotion always shown her in the family circle. Apparently the irate father did not pause to consider that in nurturing Clara's talent he had himself been guided by sound profit motives. At an age when other little girls played with dolls his daughter had been exploited as a child prodigy, and for good pay. She owed him much, to be sure, but not as much as he was now bent on collecting.

Clara had been summoned to Leipzig for the court hearing, but she did not stay under the paternal roof. Lodging at the home of friends, she hoped, nevertheless, for a chance meeting with some member of her family. Might not a greeting at some street corner, a quiet talk in a public park, lead to a reconciliation? This was her secret purpose as she roamed daily through the town. But nothing happened. The Wieck house remained grimly shuttered, its occupants nowhere to be seen.

With the coming of winter, Clara recalled that her heavier clothing was all stored at home. Here at last was a pretext to ring her father's doorbell! A strange maid opened and asked the visitor's wishes. Timidly Clara mentioned coming for her warm coat. To this her stepmother gave answer, through the servant, that Fräulein Wieck was a stranger to this household and consequently could have no wardrobe here.

This was the end.

Deeply saddened, Clara left Leipzig for Berlin, where her mother, Frau Bargiel, received her with tender concern. The Bargiels lived in cramped quarters, but she was welcomed to stay with them until the final steps were completed for her marriage.

Friedrich Wieck had one more weapon. He could appeal the court's decision, if for no purpose other than to cause delay. The margin allowable for such an action extended till August of 1840, exactly one month before Clara's coming of age on September 13. Thus Schumann's desperate effort to expedite matters was again hamstrung by bureaucratic red tape.

Herr Wieck took all winter, spring, and summer to think things over. Rebelling against the torture of this deliberate suspense, Clara defiantly embarked on one more concert tour, the last under her father's name. In future, she promised herself and Robert, she would perform publicly as Clara Schumann.

Having taken this decision she nevertheless fell prey to occasional moments of despair. Too often her father had warned: "Once married, you will bog down in domesticity, and be artistically extinguished." Robert had a hard time bracing her. Did the famous coloratura Henriette Sonntag vanish from sight after her marriage to Count Rossi? Was La Pasta (Giuditta Negri) no longer heard in opera because she too had been led to the altar? For himself, he was full of confidence and good cheer. He wrote during this time one of his finest songs, *"Mondnacht"* ("Moonlit Night"), to the text of a poem by Joseph von Eichendorff:

> *Es war, als hätt' der Himmel*
> *Die Erde still geküsst,*
> *Dass sie im Blütenschimmer*
> *Von ihm nur träumen müsst'.*

> *Die Luft ging durch die Felder*
> *Die Ähren wogten sacht,*
> *Es rauschten leis die Wälder*
> *So sternklar war die Nacht.*

Und meine Seele spannte
Weit ihre Flügel aus,
Flog durch die stillen Lande,
Als flöge sie nach Haus. . . .°

Robert, too, knew that the time of aimless straying would soon be over. Even if Clara's father strained their patience to the allowed limit (and he was doing just that!) the outcome remained assured. By mid-September, Herr Wieck's consent or his disapproval would have lost all meaning.

Gradually Clara's pessimism also gave way to a lighter mood. She was having considerable success on tour despite a campaign of slander let loose upon her by Wieck and a venal press. Unsigned newspaper articles appeared, describing her as an ingrate daughter under the unwholesome dominance of a conscienceless seducer. Here and there she met with cold stares or pointed mutterings, but on the whole audiences were partial to the unhappy lovers.

In Hamburg a mishap occurred for which, however, even the malevolent Wieck could not be held responsible. Most concert halls furnished no bench or stool, but expected the performer to repose atop the prompter's box. This proved to be the case in the port city. Clara was halfway through her program when the makeshift seat beneath her began to sag. In desperate fear of its vanishing altogether, with herself tumbling into the depths under the stage, she struggled bravely to lighten her weight and at the same time keep on playing. Her number, a Thalberg *Caprice,* was badly garbled—what with her own confusion and the loud creaking of the worm-eaten box. But she finished her

---

° It seemed as if the Heavens
In silence kissed the Earth
And that in blossom-splendor
Her dreams were Heaven, thenceforth.

The fields were swept by breezes,
The grain swayed with delight,
The woodland whispered whisperings,
So star-clear was the night . . .

Wide now my soul did open
Her wings, to rise and roam
Across the soundless country
—for it was going home!

stint without audience or critics being seemingly the wiser. Hamburg, it appeared, was used to supplementary noises with its concert offerings.

During this period Clara also had a long-awaited experience, for she heard, at Berlin, her most competent rival, the twenty-nine-year-old French pianist Camilla Pleyel. She could not help falling prey to some moments of dread, for Pleyel was magnificent. Apart from her musical proficiency the Frenchwoman knew how to dress and to roll her pretty eyes coquettishly. Instruction in the latter two accomplishments had been notably absent from Clara's curriculum under Papa Wieck. Hence her diary notation after hearing La Belle Camilla: "She is much better than I. And how discouraged this makes me feel!"

But her dismay was temporary. The summer flew by and the time for wedding preparations drew near. In August it became clear that Wieck recognized the uselessness of filing an appeal. The span allowed him expired on the eleventh of the month. When he took no action, Robert and Clara, now thirty and twenty-one respectively (in the bride's case only four weeks were lacking), were free to marry.

The date chosen for the ceremony was September 12, the eve of Clara's birthday. Again she confided to her dairy: "A new life now begins, a beautiful life, a life wrapped up in him whom I love above all things and above myself. . . ."

So the year 1840 would close for her in rich fulfillment, despite two heavy shadows. The first of these, almost unbearable to one of Clara's emotional nature, had been the bitter legal contest with her father. The second was the belated news that one of her most admired professional idols, Niccolò Paganini, had died in Nice at fifty-seven, of phthisis of the larynx. To musicians everywhere Paganini's money-making ability had served as incentive and beacon of hope. The phenomenal violin wizard left his young son Achille a fortune of 80,000 pounds, at that time approximately 400,000 tax-free U.S. dollars. To be sure, not everyone shared Clara's unreserved enthusiasm for the great Italian. Paganini the man was said to be frugal and ungenerous. He disapproved of tipping, and doormen, valets, waiters and even bootblacks spoke of him as *Paga-Niente* ("Pay-Nothing").

An undertone of sadness notwithstanding, Clara took her marriage vows with a confident and grateful heart. So sure were she and Robert of embarking on a blissful future that they started a new diary (the nineteenth century teemed with eager diarists), to be kept jointly, with

each taking over the entries on alternate Sundays. Schumann wrote
on the frontispiece:

> This book which I open today [September 13, 1840] has a most
> intimate significance; it is to be a record of all that concerns us
> in our home life and marriage; our dreams and hopes are to find
> expression here, as well as those things we would tell each other
> but for which the spoken word may fail. . . .

Expatiating on the above theme, he let himself be carried away, filling several more pages with resolutions and noble sentiments that
ended with the motto (nothing could be more Saxon):

DILIGENCE, THRIFT, and FAITHFULNESS

It was a maxim with which Clara could not but be in fullest accord.

Due to Robert's resumed publishing activities the newlyweds were
obliged to live in Leipzig. This brought about immediate tensions
as awkward meetings with members of the Wieck household could not
be avoided. Secretly Clara saw in this circumstance a chance for
eventual reconciliation, though nothing in her father's attitude justified
such optimism. The angry man looked elsewhere when his daughter
and son-in-law walked toward him in the street, nor did his attitude
change on hearing within only a few months that Clara was an expectant mother.

"There you have the end of her career!" he complained to his wife
Clementine. "The reward for my wasted energies; an artist turned
diaper-washer. . . ."

Things were not really so bad as that. While Schumann, like most
bridegrooms, would have preferred a wife entirely wrapped up in the
concerns of her own fireside, he knew that Clara could not fit the norm.
To cut her off from her musical destiny was to destroy her very personality, her soul. To reduce her to a domestic drudge who thenceforth, and only in odd moments, might dawdle over some forgotten
ditty at the piano, meant the killing of that which he most loved—the
nobility and grandeur of her art. It was from this, her spiritual worth,
that his own creative forces would draw new impetus and inspiration.
He did not know it yet, but the best of his works were to be given life
after his marriage to Clara Wieck.

There were economic reasons as well to keep the young bride from
dropping an already established career. Schumann's journalistic activi-

ties sufficed to keep the household afloat, but it became more apparent daily that Leipzig was far from an ideal setting for their happiness. To move away would mean giving up the printing shop, jeopardized once before during Robert's experimental move to Vienna. Unless he and Clara risked their slight capital they must build up some reserves before attempting a change. In that Golden Age of Music, rejoiced in by mid-nineteenth-century Europe, few undertakings were financially more fruitful than a concert tour. It would have been sheer folly for Clara to turn her back on such a ready source of income.

Soon after returning from their honeymoon at Zwickau, Schumann's birthplace, she started practicing. She counted on Dresden, Berlin, and Frankfurt for her first public appearance under her married name, with Robert accompanying her as protector and impresario. But the early pregnancy put an end to these projects. Suffering from nausea, Clara did not dare to venture onstage, whether in Germany where she must sit on a prompter's box and risk plunging into a theater basement, or in France where playing *en profile* flagrantly emphasized her growing girth. For the present, then, she and Robert must bide their time and live within a modest budget, thereby allowing Papa Wieck to gloat over the mediocre course taken by his daughter's life.

On September 1, 1841, not quite a year after her wedding, Clara gave birth to a baby girl. Elsewhere in the world a child named Peter Ilyitch Tchaikowsky was taking his first steps, as were two other toddlers of future fame, Émile Zola and Auguste Rodin. One week later, near Prague, was born Anton Dvořák, intended by his father for a butcher's trade but drawn by Fate into less gory channels.

To Robert and Clara, thrilled with parenthood, the occasion seemed propitious for calling off the family feud. A touching announcement was sent by Schumann to his father-in-law. But the latter, whose intensified teaching activities caused him to spend more time in Dresden than in Leipzig of late, ignored the happy event. Nor did he attend the christening of his grandchild, who was named Marie after Wieck's own mother.

As for Robert, the year of the infant's birth stirred him to rampant lyric creation. He had discovered for himself a medium ideally suited to his talent, the *Lied*. This special song form was, by definition, a melody that gained its inspiration from an already existing poem, rather than vice-versa. Its most accurate classification was indeed the German

Kunstlied (art song) for which a poet and a composer were requisite, rather than a doggerel salesman and a tunesmith. Between the closing months of 1841 and the following summer Robert finished more than a hundred *Lieder* to texts by Adalbert von Chamisso, Heinrich Heine, Friedrich Rückert, Julius Mosen, Justinus Kerner, Robert Reinick, Joseph von Eichendorff, and Eduard Mörike.

In this period there appears a line among his notes for a critical essay on Mendelssohn: "The compulsions of genius are a cosmic rather than a personal force." Unwittingly he put thus into words the hidden pressures that were driving him. Did he suspect that for all who are cursed and blessed with the creative spark, time is forever and inexorably running out? How short the hour of awareness; how long the time for sleep!

Before his present surge of activity subsided, Robert was to find further incentive for artistic expression. By August of the following year Clara faced her second pregnancy. On April 25, 1843, she was delivered of another daughter, Elise. At Bergen, Norway, only six weeks later a not irrelevant event took place. This was the birth of Edvard Grieg, future pianist-composer who some decades hence would submit for Clara's approval an article on her husband's works, written by the admiring Norseman for an American magazine.

For the moment most of these works, and the article about them, were nonexistent. Schumann himself was in the throes of youthful effort, barely spreading his wings. But he had outstripped his recent *Lieder* period.

He was putting the finishing touches on an opera.

CHAPTER 11 Throughout the nineteenth century the lure of the music drama had many artists in its grip. The Italian Fortunio Giuseppe Verdi and the German Richard Wagner, both three years younger than Schumann, were still in their experimental phase of imitating such successful forerunners as Gaetano Donizetti and Giacomo Meyerbeer. Until they outgrew this unworthy slavishness their pseudo-creative efforts would of course remain valueless.

In 1839 Verdi had managed to obtain a hearing for his first opera, *Oberto,* at La Scala in Milan. The work won no applause but the then twenty-six-year-old composer was encouraged to undertake a trio of music comedies, on commission. He had finished the sketches for these when, in an influenza epidemic, his wife Margherita Barezzi and two small children died in the space of three months. For more than a year all courage and inspiration left him, but in 1842 he braced himself and wrote the tragedy of *Nabucco (Nebuchadnezzar),* word of which reached Leipzig music circles and prompted Robert Schumann to search through classical literature for some equally adaptable theme.

The young Wagner was at this time similarly occupied. After some puerile trifles ("The Marriage," "The Fairies," "The Snake Lady") he had fixed on Shakespeare's *Measure for Measure,* which, happily, exacted no payment of royalties. He turned this into a thing called *Das Liebesverbot (Forbidden Love)* and persuaded a band of jobless actors and musicians to go on tour with it. The company went bankrupt, whereupon Richard chose a theme from Roman history and wrapped it in a score of such sure-fire Meyerbeer imprint that its acceptance was assured; with this opera, called *Rienzi,* Wagner made his debut at the Dresden Court Theater in 1842.

By now Schumann could not resist the pull of buskin and sock. He was paging through Goethe's *Faust*, Byron's *Manfred, Childe Harold,* and *Don Juan*, and Thomas Moore's *Lalla Rookh*, analyzing their libretto possibilities. His choice fell on the last-named subject, unquestionably because of its exotic oriental nature. The narrative poem dealt with an Indian princess Lalla Rookh, who was being sent by caravan to Cashmere for her marriage to a despot she did not know. Along the route a poet, Feramorz, introduced himself and offered to dispel the lady's misgivings by reciting a string of Persian legends concerning a benevolent winged being of the spirit world, known as the Peri. So handsome was Feramorz, and so beguiling his speech, that the princess fell in love with him and grieved the more over her impending fate. But the poet now disclosed himself as her unknown betrothed, the Sultan of Bucharia, who—similarly worried about the kind of bride that was being shipped to him—had come in disguise for an advance look.

Whether so sugary a historiette was doomed to failure from the start, or whether Schumann's treatment of it lacked dramatic focus, the opera would not achieve immortality. Structurally Robert emphasized the mystic secondary element, namely the Persian tales within the tale. Thus Lalla and her lover Feramorz became only cardboard figures in a superficial framework.

The opera was titled *Paradise and the Peri*, whereby its "otherworld" quality was readily made manifest. Just how the activities of a female sprite called Peri could hold audience interest through several ponderous acts remained yet a question. The plot elaborated by Schumann suffered from monotony and repetition. That is, his Peri, cast out from Paradise because of some minor infraction, must offer the Supreme Deity some gift of atonement before being readmitted into the celestial company. The pattern of the action was thereby set, as was the expected conclusion that the Peri would undertake a number of useless feats until, just before the final curtain, one of her deeds at last was deemed acceptable. For the record, the peace offerings assembled by the penitent Peri were three: some drops of blood spilled by a hero dying for his country; the last sigh of a virgin who has nursed her lover through the plague; and the tears of a blaspheming sinner who has repented and promised thenceforth to do nothing but good. It is the sinner's tears that win the day.

Theatrically, this feeble anecdote might never have merited production. But Schumann composed for it so rich and inspired a score that the effect approached symphonic splendor. Not only did Leipzig give *Paradise and the Peri* a sold-out première, but Dresden clamored for a chance to see the work under auspices of the Saxon royal family.

And now Friedrich Wieck was heard from.

Aware that the name of Robert Schumann was suddenly on everybody's tongue, the publicity-minded pedagogue did an about-face. Was he not Robert's father-in-law? Perhaps it might be prudent, in view of Schumann's growing prestige, to let bygones be bygones and smoke a pipe of peace. The Dresden *Peri* performance was set for December 23, 1843. One week earlier the peppery Herr Wieck sent a placating note to Leipzig, in which he sought a rapprochement with his son-in-law but could not bring himself to employ the latter's Christian name:

> Dear Schumann,
> *Tempora mutantur et nos mutamur in eis.* [Times change and we change with the times.]
> We cannot, in view of Clara and the world at large, continue estranged. You are now yourself a father—is there need for explanations?
> In art we were always united; I was indeed your mentor, and my counsel led you to your present composer's career. I hardly need to assure you of my interest in your talent and in your beautiful and certain triumphs.
> You are awaited with joy in Dresden by
> > Your father,
> > Fr. Wieck

Robert could not help smiling at this extraordinary missive. But both he and Clara welcomed the opportunity it offered for ending the lamentably poisonous family feud. With Christmas only a few days away, the younger couple rushed to Dresden for the reconciliation to be celebrated in the expansive mood engendered by the festive season. Only now could Clara feel that her own happiness was fully blessed.

As Mendelssohn foresaw, but did not have the heart to tell Robert, the Dresden showing of *Paradise and the Peri* rated the praise of music critics but met with coolness on the part of theater lovers. If it survived at all it would be as an orchestral work of symphonic character. It was never to find a place in operatic repertoire.

Oddly, neither Robert nor Clara saw matters in this light. They were already going through their Shakespeare once more, and also eyeing Goethe's *Hermann und Dorothea,* with a new libretto in mind. In the intimate communion of marriage a subtle dominance was making itself felt; yielding to love's compulsion, Clara spent herself in wifely dedication to her husband's interests and to the care of the two babies.

The apartment they occupied at Number 5 Inselstrasse contained two grand pianos, in separate rooms, but there appeared less and less opportunity for the young wife to practice and keep herself musically in trim. With Robert submerged in study and creation, it would have been unthinkable to let the walls reverberate for three hours on end (the minimum daily period Clara was used to spending at the keyboard). Thus she relinquished her own spiritual need in deference to that of her beloved partner. This was the more remarkable as, at the time of their marriage, Clara was by far the more successful and widely acclaimed artist. Most of Robert's output, and certainly his public recognition, lay yet ahead of him. The prediction of Herr Wieck was therefore proving itself justified, even sooner than expected. As early as January of 1841, four months after the wedding, Clara wrote a sad small sentence on the diary page assigned to her for that week:

"If only the room partitions were not so thin! I fear my piano playing will deteriorate altogether. . . ."

All at once it seemed to her unreal, a dim hallucination, that someone named Clara Wieck should for years have figured on the international concert stage. Timidly she wondered whether Clara Schumann would ever catch up with that lost identity.

Through the joint diary Robert learned of these broodings and doubts. He realized his own selfishness in having allowed such discouragement to grip Clara's soul. With the help of Liszt, who happened to be passing through Leipzig on tour, a musical evening was promptly arranged at the Gewandhaus, with the three friends taking part. That is, Liszt played his own version of Mozart's *Don Giovanni,* Clara performed the *C-Major Sonata, Opus 53,* by Beethoven, and Schumann conducted the orchestra in a première of his new *Spring Symphony.*

So well received were these almost impromptu offerings that other and more ambitious programs followed even after Liszt's departure. Soon the news had spread to neighboring cities that Clara was being heard again. Requests began arriving from Weimar, Frankfurt, Berlin, and Vienna for booking dates to be filled in the coming autumn or winter. Gratifying though this was, the young Frau Schumann suffered pangs of remorse on discovering that the public clamor was directed at her person exclusively, without mention of her husband. She had decided to turn down all offers when Robert called attention to a recent rumor concerning the child-virtuoso Anton Gregorovich Rubinstein (born of Jewish parents at Wechwotynecz, Romania, in 1829), whose phenomenal brilliance was a threat to all living pianists.

"You must hear this boy," insisted Schumann, "and see for yourself what truth there is in all that talk. Besides, who rests, rusts."

She agreed. Yet it was less easy than formerly to pack a bag and leave home. Apart from sentimental considerations (she became tearful at the thought of being separated from husband and children), there were problems of a practical nature. A nursemaid would have to be engaged, besides a dependable cook to run the little household.

When the tour finally took shape, extending as far north as Hamburg, Robert decided to go along. While this pleased Clara it led also to a quandary neither of them had foreseen. What could possibly be the function of a man who waited idly in hotel rooms or self-consciously sat among his wife's listeners while she performed onstage?

"I'll take along my papers," he told himself confidently. "While Clara garners applause, I'll stick to my composing."

But things did not work out that way. The fuss and bother of travel robbed him of energy, concentration, peace. He belonged to the special breed of intellectuals who are at their best in the dew-freshness of morning, before wordly contact impinges upon the mind. While escorting Clara from stagecoach to hostelry, from concert hall to backstage dressing room, Robert's calm (essential for literary or musical labors) was constantly assailed and shattered. What brief periods of rest such a schedule afforded might banish the fatigue of performers, but it drove a creative artist to despair. Robert's decision was certainly a mistake.

The Schumanns were to discover this from the start of their first trip away from home. Yet they refused to face it. That is, they blamed specific conditions in provincial Germany for discomforts characteristic of even the best arranged tour. "Things will be easier in Russia," they told themselves, cheerfully planning to accept an invitation from Mos-

cow and St. Petersburg, the latter city including a command performance by Clara before the Tsar. In Russia they would be received like
royalty, with every luxury and attention. Robert saw himself enrich-
ing his idle hours in observation of Slavic dances and folklore, from
which to derive new inspiration for his work. No, the trip to Muscovy
was something they could not forgo.

Eager and hopeful, they started out in February of 1844, making a
short stop in Berlin. Here the Mendelssohns were their hosts. Frau
Mendelssohn (born Cécile Jeanrenaud of Frankfurt, daughter of a
French Protestant clergyman) presented Clara with a pair of charming fur cuffs to be slipped over dress or coat sleeves against the Russian
cold. So decorative were these cuffs that Clara wore them on all occasions, even on stage where drafts quite often chilled and stiffened her
wrists.

They continued by coach to the East Prussian town of Königsberg,
where there were two concert dates to fill. The border was crossed at
Tauroggen, whence travel proceeded by sleigh. Recitals followed at
Riga (Latvia) and Dorpat (Esthonia) with the added fillip of moving
from one city to the next through forest areas where bands of wolves
ran quietly beside the sleigh like an escort of hunting dogs. In these
Baltic provinces the Schumanns became acquainted with a form of
hospitality never before encountered. Hotels and lodging houses being primitive, the gentry and nobility of the area fetched mattresses,
sheets, coverlets, and quilts from their own homes, so as to pamper
their visitors. From their own kitchens and wine cellars they also sent
provender to supplement the dreary menu served by innkeepers of
that day. Despite these attentions Robert fell ill of influenza and was
forced to spend six days in bed, thus missing the lavish reunions and
parties with which his wife was fêted.

On March 1 they were able at last to travel on, reaching St. Petersburg the evening of the fourth. Through a mistake in timing their
arrival coincided with the presence of an Italian opera company,
starring their friend Pauline García. To see Pauline again was wonderful, but to have her absorb the music-loving public to the point of
leaving only a few stragglers for Clara's opening concert proved a strain
on amity. Fortunately the singing troupe soon left and Clara was able
to capture the errant crowd. She gave four concerts through the rest
of that month besides playing in private for Nicholas I and the imperial

court at the magnificent Winter Palace. Her program at this time included Mendelssohn's *Spring Song*, which entranced audiences and invariably brought cries of "Encore!" The Russians also for the first time heard compositions by Robert Schumann, especially the suite called *Kreisleriana* (inspired by a fictional character, the eccentric orchestra conductor in one of E.T.A. Hoffmann's novels).

April was spent in Moscow, again in competition with a rival event, the spectacular and long-drawn-out Easter celebration of the Russian Orthodox Church. Once more Clara's initial recital drew a poor attendance. But after Holy Week the Kremlin city bethought itself of the celebrity in its midst. Madame Schumann was hailed with warmly appreciative enthusiasm so that the month (with four sold-out concerts) ended in triumph.

And now a doleful truth dawned on Robert. Throughout the Russian journey he had filled a kind of pageboy role, trailing in the shadow of his wife's glory. Unquestionably Clara had made every effort to draw him likewise into the limelight. His compositions appeared nowadays on all her programs, while at receptions and during newspaper interviews she took pains to reveal the new romantic movement originated by him. But eyes and ears were fixed on her, the soloist, the star of her own show. Whether Robert waited backstage or lost himself in the milling audience, he was equally overlooked. Like it or not, he was reduced to being Herr Clara Schumann.

The situation threw him into darkest melancholy. This in turn destroyed any chance to utilize leisure hours on tour for his prime interest, musical creation. Had such "leisure hours" existed (another snare and delusion!) his discontent would have foiled all inspiration, for he saw himself as a figure of pity, if not ridicule.

Back in Leipzig the issue was brought into the open. Did Clara intend to continue with the vagabond life of a concert artist? If so, she must count on going off uncompanioned, since Robert felt himself unfitted for the job of luggage porter and valet. His work and his manly pride were equally at stake. So was the welfare of their children and, last, not least, their marriage.

Clara faced a quandary. The choice she must arrive at would exact from her a very considerable price. It was necessary for her to recognize that a performing artist is, intrinsically, inferior to a creator, and that therefore it was she who must not stand in Robert Schumann's way. Another aspect of their joint musical pursuits also came under scrutiny—her own spasmodic efforts at composition. She had written a great number of piano pieces, including a concerto with orchestra accompaniment, under her maiden name. But were her things sufficiently mature and weighty to merit survival? Had any woman, throughout the history of music, ever achieved something worthwhile as a composer? In short, ought she—as Clara Schumann—enter into competition against her husband in a field so eminently his own?

It happened that Nature answered these questions for her. A short time after her triumphant Russian sojourn Clara found herself again expectant. With a third baby on the way her thoughts would be absorbed by matters far removed from the pianoforte, whether in a creative or interpretive capacity.

Instead of concertizing she would be humming, once more, a nursery tune.

CHAPTER 12 The Russian experience taught Robert Schumann an invaluable lesson. Never again would he trail after his wife on tour as an awkward husbandly shadow. If in future they traveled together in professional pursuits it would be because he himself was likewise engaged as conductor for one of his own works. Not again, as had happened in St. Petersburg, did he intend to be approached by some fatuous admirer of Clara's with the words: "Ah, the fortunate Herr Schumann! Do tell us, are you also musical?"

In all justice, Clara herself did not want this to happen. The errors of the Russian trip must under no condition be repeated. If a choice had to be made between their two careers, Robert's was certainly the more important. Without composers, of what use were performers? She might have reversed the question but, her conscience knew, the answer was not quite the same. Every composer could, without being a virtuoso, play his own works. It was the interpretive artist, then, who rated as a lavish surplus, easily dispensed with. Such reflections, besides her newly impending motherhood, caused Clara to renounce what she had hitherto regarded her path of destiny: the life of a dedicated pianist.

The first of Friedrich Wieck's predictions had not waited long to come true.

"All I have taught you," the embittered father had said, "will be wasted. I can see you as a stagnating *Hausfrau,* absorbed in tending the porridge and the infant wash. . . ."

Herr Wieck was going to be right on yet another score, namely, Robert's health. The Russian atmosphere had had a mortifying effect on Schumann's ego. There had been at Moscow and St. Petersburg symptoms of extreme psychic depression which Clara at first dismissed as manifestations of boredom and bad temper. But headaches, fever, and dizziness accompanied these "spells," indicating that their cause was something deeper than mere doldrums. During intervals of abatement Robert also admitted now that in childhood and adolescence he had suffered similar seizures which, doctors speculated, might disappear with early marriage and a regulated sexual life. This explained Robert's impulsive engagement to Ernestine von Fricken after only the briefest acquaintance. The rupture of that romance and the subsequent long wait for Clara's hand had evidently aggravated the disorder to a point where, even with the physical and mental compatibility existing between husband and wife, the harm was not completely banished.

When they returned to Leipzig at the end of May there was an immediate improvement in Schumann's condition. The reunion with the children and a resumption of normal working hours in the peace of his study brought a surge of inspiration to the mind long hungering for new creative tasks. He plunged into composition of a music score for Goethe's *Faust*, laying aside two previous projects toward which a sightseeing tour of the Kremlin had impelled him: a dramatization of Napoleon's defeat at Moscow; and an operatic treatment of the story of Ivan Walikji, bellmaker to the Tsar Alexis Michailovitch (father of Peter the Great), whose masterpiece, the great bell of the Cathedral of the Assumption, failed to chime true due to a flaw in the pouring.

Early summer went by in unbroken activity. But by August, while finishing a choral passage of his *Faust*, Robert fell ill again. The doctor diagnosed nervous fatigue, plainly induced by overwork. Complete rest was ordered.

During this period Mendelssohn resigned his directorship of the Gewandhaus to answer a call from Birmingham. A general impression had prevailed that Schumann would be appointed to the vacant post. But as news of his broken health got about, applicants from various parts of Europe solicited hearings and the Gewandhaus board eventually made a choice. In Schumann's place a twenty-seven-year-old Dane, Wilhelm Niels Gade, received the appointment.

Though no slight was intended, Robert took the matter very much to heart.

"They should have asked me first," he complained illogically. Since he could not have accepted from his sickbed, the issue became academic at best. But there was no taking his mind off the imagined affront.

As Robert's depression deepened he cursed Leipzig and wished himself far from its "hostile" atmosphere. Sadly Clara wrote her father in Dresden, conceding humbly that the older man's prophetic warnings had proved partially founded. While not insane, Robert was in a seriously disturbed mental state.

It would have been in keeping with Wieck's nature to answer "I told you so!" But the grief that assailed him at thought of his daughter was sharper than any spite. Promptly he wrote back, urging the young family to move to Dresden. Here Schumann would be able to forget the innocent Herr Gade, against whom he harbored an unreasonable and hardly salutary grudge. Also, with Clara's accouchement drawing near, it would be well to have helpful relatives at hand. The Wiecks knew of a vacant apartment at Number 35 Waisenhausstrasse (Street of the Orphans) which could be readied for occupancy by mid-December.

Just before Christmas of 1844 the move had been accomplished. Robert meanwhile showed no signs of improvement. He suffered from insomnia and fits of panic for which there was no explanation. He was also weakened by various cold water cures and Sauna baths, popular among North-Europeans.

As far as Robert Schumann was concerned, the cold water cultists couldn't have been more wrong. Added to his other ills he was now saddled with a stubborn bronchial cough.

On March 11, 1845, the third Schumann child came into the world, again a girl, to be named Julie. Although Clara and her stepmother were not on cordial terms, it was comforting to have Clementine in attendance.

The new baby helped ease tensions. Clara's father, in particular, showed signs of mellowing. His former arbitrariness gave way to diffidence, if not an admission of outright error.

The cause was not hard to find. Ever since Clara's marriage the embittered music master had endeavored to turn one of his other children into a concert artist. With his sons Alwin and Gustav he was to achieve only mediocre results on either the piano or the violin. Inevitably they took up other and more practical professions, with their father's wry approval.

But the matter did not end there. Clara's half-sister Marie, born of Wieck's second union, would now be groomed for greatness. There appeared only one drawback: the girl was painfully untalented.

Wieck had forced the issue by presenting Marie prematurely in public, informing Clara at the same time (by letter) that her desertion was no longer felt. But Marie proved no replacement for her father's onetime prize pupil. Clara would have occasion to attend some of the girl's recitals, and to comment in her diary:

> . . . She lacks spirit, and her playing strikes me as mechanical and joyless, also feeble and without any real personal accent; she wants persistence. . . . True, as a child I too did not always like practicing, but the moment there was an audience I became seized by a verve; what worries me about Marie is her technical deficiency. One must consider that the public expects more of child performers than in my day; infant prodigies are on the increase everywhere and they acquit themselves eminently, which is not the case with Marie. She plays well but not excellently. . . .

As a matter of conscience Clara voiced the above opinion to her father, not only to spare him public ridicule but for the sake of the tortured Marie. Brilliant though Wieck's teaching methods might be, his creed—that artists were manufactured, not born—had proved pitifully wrong. His mind, however, remained locked to truth. Irritated by Clara's remonstrances, he pushed Marie the harder. He also now proclaimed another "discovery" among his pupils, an altogether hopeless young pianist named Minna Schulz. Of the latter's sorry debut Clara wrote:

> . . . It is impossible to describe what I suffered that evening. I felt such pity for my father in his nervousness and worry—an uncommon experience for him, and the like of which I surely never made him endure. . . .

Her distress intensified when she read the critical reviews. Disparagement was directed not so much at the unimportant Fräulein Schulz as against the culprit who had overpublicized her: Friedrich Wieck. The aging teacher (he was sixty-one) tasted his bitterest defeat.

7

Into this time of tensions fell the birth, on February 8, 1846, of the fourth Schumann child, a boy who was baptized Emil. The baby was delicate from the start, being afflicted with a glandular malfunction that was to slow his growth. Clara had scarcely recovered when a summons came from Leipzig, requesting that she perform her husband's *Concerto in A-Minor, Opus 54*, at a Gewandhaus première. She was in poor practice, but so generous an offer from Niels Gade (whom Robert, with his persecution mania, still considered an enemy) could not be turned down. Much was at stake. The *Concerto* was to Clara's eyes Schumann's finest pianistic effort to date. A Leipzig triumph ought to go a long way toward restoring his faith in mankind and himself.

Her judgment proved correct. The Gewandhaus evening went magnificently and Clara brought back a sheaf of press clippings to gladden the composer's heart. Immediately his inspiration surged anew. Ignoring medical warnings, he plunged into work on his *Second Symphony, Opus 61, in C-Major* and, on the side, set to music five poems by Robert Burns. These tasks out of the way, he turned again to an old obsession: opera. Among subjects that attracted him were Lord Byron's *Manfred,* Sir Thomas Malory's *Morte d'Arthur,* and a fourteenth-century legend about Geneviève de Brabant, recorded by Jacobus de Voragine.

In England the poet Alfred Tennyson (only one year older than Schumann) was currently absorbed with Arthurian themes, though the first of his *Idylls of the King* would not reach publication for more than a decade.

Robert's choice was ultimately influenced by Friedrich Hebbel's stageplay *Genoveva,* which the dramatist agreed to turn into a libretto for him. This proved more easily said than done. Unable to meet Schumann's musical requirements, Hebbel called an older writer, Ludwig Tieck, to his aid. A folklore expert, Tieck had furnished Richard Wagner with the Tannhäuser tale.

The two men set to work but still the script bogged down, possibly due to the subject's lack of operatic character. Now Schumann alone took over, finishing the libretto by himself and using the Hebbel title *Genoveva.* Before he started on the music, personal tragedy struck. The baby Emil, scarcely fifteen months old, died on May 22, 1847, of the congenital gland disturbance for which no remedy had been found.

It was the first loss experienced by the couple since their marriage.

Of the two saddened parents Clara bore the blow with greater stoicism; she had only just discovered herself one month along in a new pregnancy.

Another sorrow was faced in November of that same year—Mendelssohn's death at the age of thirty-eight. After a long stay in England, Felix was concertizing in Germany when his eldest (and favorite) sister, Fanny Hensel, fell fatally ill. Wealthy, cultured, urbane, the Mendelssohns (originally Mendel) were the Christianized descendants of a prominent Jewish banking family. The mother of Fanny and Felix had been a noted pianist, Lea Salomon-Bartholdy, while a paternal grandfather, Moses Mendelssohn, ranked as an orientalist and philosopher. Apart from such talents, the Mendelssohn tribe was known for the devotion among its members, and their capacity for friendship. On a human basis alone Felix was easily the most loved musician of his time, exceeding even the supreme charmer Liszt in popularity. But he who drew others to him, loved them the more. On learning of his sister's sudden end, Felix Mendelssohn suffered a paralytic stroke. Happily married, and with five children to enrich his days, he survived Fanny by only six months.

The Schumanns took the tidings much to heart. Robert in particular found solace only at work. He devoted most of the following year to his opera, completing the orchestration in August of 1848, but it would be almost two years before a Leipzig première could be arranged.

Genoveva was, alas, not destined for success. While opera libretti were notoriously weak in content, the plot in this case was overfamiliar and boring. As recorded in saga anthologies, Genoveva of Brabant was the virtuous wife of a German Palatine Prince at Trier. While her husband dashed off to the wars, Genoveva had been left under the surveillance of his majordomo, Golo, who—betraying his master— thrust unwanted attentions upon the lady. On being rejected, Golo maligned Genoveva on Prince Siegfried's return, claiming that her newborn child was engendered by the handsome young serf Drago. Siegfried thereupon ordered his wife and her baby killed, but the headsman, taking pity, allowed the intended victims to escape into the woods. For some time mother and son survived on roots, berries, and the milk of a doe. A year later, while hunting (in some versions a much longer time elapsed), Siegfried followed this doe and came upon his wife's hiding place. The truth about Golo's perfidy was now revealed, as well as the fact that Siegfried himself was father to Geno-veva's child. The story ended with a horrendous medieval turn: Golo was drawn and quartered within sight of the castle where the reunited family engaged in merry wassail.

Schumann had barely done with the above subject when Byron's *Manfred* attracted him again. But now new signs of overwork made themselves felt. His hearing failed. Then, of a sudden, a merciless ringing started in his ears, strident, incessant, turning the most casual outside noise, such as the buzz of a fly, into polyphonous discordant sounds.

Doctors warned once more that all musical activity must cease. Since the proximity of his piano made it difficult for the patient to obey instructions, a journey was advised. The family went to a nearby health resort called Maxen and leased a sunny cottage with a fine view of the surrounding country. All went well until one morning when Robert learned that a distant villa seen from his window was Der Sonnenstein, a famous insane asylum.

He was promptly seized with an attack of hypochondria. Maxen had to be abandoned. The holiday would be continued in a more cheerful setting, on the North Sea island of Norderney. Railroads were becoming generalized in Europe ever since France, in 1823, laid the first track from Lyons to Saint Étienne outside Paris. The Schumanns would avail themselves of this new means of transport.

The journey ended in Hamburg, whence the travelers must proceed by ship. In the port city Clara and Robert saw billboard notices announcing the presence in town of Jenny Lind, whom they had heard praised by Mendelssohn and Liszt. Tired though they were, this they could not miss: Jenny Lind as Donna Anna in Mozart's *Don Giovanni,* a role they had last heard interpreted by Wilhelmine Schroeder-Devrient.

The performance proved only moderately satisfying, due to the inferior quality of the orchestra. Jenny Lind, however, was a revelation. The twenty-six-year-old Swedish Nightingale, one year younger than Clara, stood on the threshold of a spectacular career that would take her from operatic triumphs in Europe to the remotest American hinterland, under the aegis of a circus promoter named Phineas Taylor Barnum.

With a voice of generous range (from D to E above high E) but no great volume, the Stockholm-born soprano combined such purity and sweetness of tone that listeners were left entranced. In addition, her personality was as beguiling as her coloratura. No arrogance, no tantrums, no pose or trickery marred her dealings with managers, fellow artists, or the admiring public. Withal, she was not beautiful, though her face gave the illusion of loveliness due to the tender expression of her eyes.

Clara and Robert congratulated the singer in her dressing room before retiring to their hotel and continuing to Norderney the next morning. July and August were spent on the Friesian island where the sunshine and bracing salt air wrought a miracle in Schumann. On returning to Dresden he finished his overture to *Manfred,* revised some scenes for *Faust,* published six *Lieder* and the *Concerto in A-Minor, Opus 129* (for cello). Between these major efforts he also read proof on manuscripts submitted to Breitkopf and Härtel just prior to the Norderney trip, among them a Christmas carol with text by Rückert, and the *Album für die Jugend (Youth Album)* written for his own children.

Again the pressure was on. Schumann labored, heedless of warnings, as though a limit were set on his time. His whole attitude changed from one of patient calm to that of frantic haste. His manner became that of a haunted man.

CHAPTER 13 While the Schumanns lived in a special walled-in world of music there had been changes taking place around them of which they hardly were aware.

After faint beginnings in the late eighteenth century, the age of mechanization was dawning, and with it a whole new concept of human rights. Throughout history the world's work had been performed by the muscle power of subjugated men, women, and children, aided in some degree by draft oxen, horse traction, and such burden carriers as the camel, elephant, donkey or mule. The chief solicitude of rulers, then, had always been to keep up a supply of human drudges.

With the discovery of steam power and its revolutionary effect on land transportation, shipping, mining (the pumping of water from flooded shafts), agriculture, and untold varieties of manufacture, the mass of mankind was for the first time liberated from degrading anonymity. If the greatness of ancient Rome rested on cheap human labor, modern civilization was being built with cheap mechanical power, thereby giving to man another standard of his dignity and worth. Freed from blind drudgery, human beings found time for education on a scale hitherto unknown. The universities, accessible only to the privileged few, were now overrun by throngs hungry for knowledge. The vast inchoate mass was learning to think for itself.

While government tyrannies were weakened by these developments there soon arose a new menace. Industrial autocrats sprouted, who, through personal cleverness and application, managed to enrich themselves and gain a stranglehold over the meek commonality from which labor was now recruited. The idea of wage standards being as yet unknown, employers could glean vast profits while paying out a slave's hire. Thus the old feudalism of lordly master and abject serf was reappearing in an economic guise to which new names must be applied. A scholarly Jew, Karl Marx, who did most of his study and research in the library of London's British Museum, found those names: the new aristocracy was Capital, and the new commoners were the Proletariat. Marx, born one year before Clara Schumann, did not advocate a class war between those two increasingly hostile elements, but he predicted it. The course of events, through his own century and that which was to follow, would seem very amply to have borne him out.

With the fall of the first Napoleon, who had dreamed of a united Europe under French rule, the same sort of reaction set in that had followed the French Revolution a generation earlier. That is, *ancien régime* diehards tried to turn back the clock by restoring the pre-storm status quo, both at the end of the eighteenth century and in the first quarter of the nineteenth. At the Congress of Vienna in 1815 the nations chose for their arbiter an Austrian statesman of rigidly feudal principles, Prince Clemens Lothar Wenzel von Metternich-Winneburg. The Corsican conqueror had vanished along with his vision of a compulsory but nonetheless progressive European federation. Under Metternich's advocacy the worm-eaten and discarded chessboard was set up again with every petty tyrant and helpless pawn back in place. All other factors being equal, this plunge into retrogression might have worked as it had through centuries long past. But something had been overlooked in Metternich's calculations: the mental makeup of modern, machine-age man.

The years following the Vienna Congress were marked by mounting outbursts of unrest that had nothing to do with political issues between rival nations but sprang strictly from social causes. From 1820 to 1830 public debate became the fashion, with much oratory expended on propagating the rights of the common man. In Britain this proved so effective that the Reform Bill of 1832 was passed, extending the franchise and fortifying the representative function of the Lower House of Parliament. Reports of this event brought valor to the Continent. In France the Orléans dynasty began to totter, while North Italians and Hungarians defied Habsburg rule, and the Poles in Posen rose against the Germans. At about this time a Pan-Slavic conference was even held at Prague, foreshadowing most of the territorial readjustments that were not to be realized until nearly a century later.

With the New Year bells of 1848 the death knell of Metternich's world was definitely sounded. For a brief period the Austrian realm saw itself without a sovereign until the dethroned Emperor's sister-in-law, Archduchess Sophie (born a Bavarian Wittelsbach), led the eldest of her four sons, Franz Joseph (aged eighteen), to the vacated Hofburg. The young man's grace and candor overcame popular ire and preserved Habsburg might for yet another spell, but it was the beginning of the end. In England the scandalous Hanoverians had given way to the enlightened rule of a princess named Victoria, and the tarnished shield of monarchy across the Channel regained its luster. But in France the day of royalty was ended with the expulsion of all Bourbon and Orléans adherents, and the proclamation of the Second Republic. Germany, too, had its quota of trembling crowned heads, among them King Friedrich August II of Saxony; in an armed crowd storming this monarch's palace there figured a revolutionary hothead named Richard Wagner, who thereby earned himself a prolonged exile from his native land.

Robert and Clara Schumann took as little notice of these events as they did of such remote happenings as the just ended war between Mexico and the United States after a conclusive battle in a place called Churubusco. They had never heard of an American president, James Knox Polk, currently in office at Washington, or of one Horace Greeley just elected to Congress, any more than they knew about a Mormon caravan moving that year across the plains west of the Mississippi, while the original Siamese Twins—Eng and Chang—awed carnival crowds from the Atlantic to the Pacific seaboard.

The year 1848, to Clara and Robert, was marked by only one important event: the birth, on January 20, of their fifth child, a son to be named Ludwig. With this the loss of the boy Emil was not blotted out but certainly assuaged. There existed in this marriage of artist souls a live and potent sensual bond that made fecundity inevitable. The growing nursery, therefore, was for husband and wife a source of infinite joy, linked in some mystic way to the holy fires of all creation.

Political upheavals notwithstanding, 1848 was a year replete with other signal events. Richard Wagner's fourth important opera, *Lohengrin*, received its world première, not in Dresden to be sure, since the composer was banished from his native region, but at Weimar under the baton of Franz Liszt. In France the Second Republic accepted for its president an ambitious forty-year-old Bonaparte, son of King Louis of Holland and Hortense Beauharnais, and nephew of the great Napoleon. This as yet insignificant tendril on the Corsican family tree was in four short years to dissolve the Assembly that had elected him and to proclaim himself Emperor (he would choose the name Napoleon III; a second Napoleon—better known as *L'Aiglon,* the King of Rome, or the Duke of Reichstadt—having died in Vienna sixteen years earlier). Finally, in 1848, there was born in Paris at 56 Rue Notre Dame de Lorette, the infant Paul Gauguin, whom France would one day count among her most prized painters.

For the Schumanns the year ended with a minor vexation in their circle of intimate friends. The glorious singer Schroeder-Devrient, admired by Robert and Clara, was breaking up with her husband (Herr von Doering) in order to marry another gentleman (Herr von Bock). As if this were not deplorable enough from a publicity angle, the lady, now forty-four, showed signs of losing her voice as a result of living at too high an emotional pitch.

"Since you plan marrying again," Clara counseled tactfully, "why don't you give up your career and concentrate on happiness?"

Defiantly Wilhelmine rejected any such suggestions. She would continue rejecting them ten years later when people left her recitals in pity and dismay. To Clara her friend's professional dilemma proved a valuable object lesson. It made her feel less poignantly her own renunciation of fame and personal fulfillment in favor of motherhood and— even more important—the furthering of her husband's genius.

Robert's musical output was tremendous at this time. He had finished *Genoveva* and started work on another opera, based on Lord Byron's drama *Manfred.* He likewise revised his *Faust* and readied more sheaves of *Lieder* for print. Clara exulted in this spasm of creative activity which ought, on the contrary, to have alarmed her. In her pride over his accomplishments she did not notice that her husband was growing daily more silent and withdrawn. If she came upon him at times when his eyes stared glassily into space and his lips pursed in an odd childlike pout, she tiptoed carefully away.

"Papa is concentrating," she told the children, urging them not to play under the window of their father's study.

But he was not always concentrating. Some of those periods of remoteness were mental blanks of variable duration from which the highstrung composer emerged with a sense of confusion and dread. If at night, in panic, he sought the arms of his wife she took this to be the always intense physical compatibility existing between them. Indeed, at the height of that feverishly productive summer of 1849, Clara's sixth child was born on July 16—a boy named Ferdinand. Her joy was immense. With such a father, surely much was to be expected from their rosy-cheeked young brood!

Schumann was at this time aware of certain anomalies in his condition, as could be inferred from a note in which he warned a former associate, the journalist Anton von Zuccalmaglio, whose visit had been announced:

> I shall be happy to receive you. But let me caution that I shall not say one word. I speak almost nothing at all, save in the evening when I am at the piano. . . .

Zuccalmaglio, who had had repeated contact with the expansive and always garrulous Richard Wagner, sensed something wrong. He took Clara aside to question her. Her answer was lighthearted, unperturbed.

"Isn't it wonderful to see him so transported by his art?" Some years earlier she had written similarly to Felix Mendelssohn: "My husband is all music at present, and not to be attracted by anything else—I love his being that way. . . ."

She herself was not inactive musically during this period. Apart from having taken on a number of piano pupils, she accepted occasional concert engagements that paid well and did not take her too long away from home. With the money thus earned she was able to hire adequate domestic help for a household that had grown far beyond her capacities. But this was not the prime factor that impelled her to cling, even so desultorily, to her virtuoso past. Apart from the hunger within her for artistic expression, she saw the need to bring Robert's compositions to public attention. Musically, Europe was approaching the end of an era. The classicism of Bach, Mozart, Gluck, Handel, Weber, and their allied contemporaries had reached a point of imitative repetition. Beethoven had known this and had succeeded, in the works of his third period, to break old molds. Schumann had taken up where Beethoven left off, avoiding set patterns and bringing a fresh romantic sweep to musical phraseology.

Wagner, after an initial slavish adherence to Meyerbeer, was doing the same for opera. His conventional *Rienzi* had no relation to the polyphonic liberation of *Tannhäuser, The Flying Dutchman, Lohengrin,* and the transcending masterworks that were to follow.

The same revolution and rebirth was taking place among sculptors, painters, writers, poets, in compliance with the mandate of the ancients, *"Aut renovaberis aut morias"* ("Renew thyself or perish"). Goethe, to be sure, had given to this dictum a more hopeful twist with his exhortation, *"Stirb und werde!"* ("Die, and live again!"), a comforting passport to immortality. Certainly without constant renewal, as exemplified by the physical world around him, man's soul must wither. In the midst of life he is then, indeed, dead.

Such spiritual injunctions were not easily accepted by the general public. Everywhere within the confines of civilization the vanguard thinker or artist ran up against a wall of prejudice. Italy wished poetry to abide by Dante rulings, France favored stage plays of the Molière school, while England and Holland and Spain wanted portraits to continue looking like Gainsboroughs or Rembrandts or Murillos. The mass mind is lazy and unwilling to break with habit.

The popularizing of so radical an innovator as Robert Schumann was thus fraught with difficulty. Music publishers hesitated long and argued much before printing compositions that might lie forever on their shelves. Performers, and particularly orchestral groups dependent on state subsidies, dared not depart from routine programs. The audience ruled. Listeners accustomed to easy tunefulness in the classics refused to follow a new voice that promised relief from the banal, the threadbare, the hackneyed. Any modification of the obvious, the fixed, was rejected as dissonance, which in truth it often and deliberately turned out to be, if only to escape from dreary prettiness.

When an artist of the stature of Clara Schumann championed the new order, the situation changed. People gave ear, they pondered, and made an effort to overcome their bias. This reaction was partly sentimental. Public sympathy responded to so open a display of wifely loyalty, though Clara's action was assuredly prompted by less mundane motives. She saw in Robert the flowering of a rare, predestined genius. It was her mission to provide the springboard from which his creations were to be flung in brilliant showers upon an as yet unenlightened world.

Her present prize number was his *Concerto in A-Minor, Opus 54,* composed between 1841 and 1845 but only now beginning to achieve recognition. Similarly his *C-Major Symphony, Opus 61*, was winning German adherents for the Schumann idiom. All the while, however, Clara's devotion blinded her to the threat inherent in her husband's frenzied working schedule. There were times when she found him in a trancelike state, unaware of her presence or of anything that went on around him. She misinterpreted this. What she took to be sublime absorption was far more likely a mental lacuna induced by fatigue. She thought him soaring on wings of inspiration, when he was plunging earthward, his brain a sudden vacuum.

A respite appeared in this stage of mounting crisis, with news from Ferdinand von Hiller, a friend of the Schumanns. Hiller had served for some time as conductor of the Düsseldorf Orchestra, a post he was giving up to head the conservatory at Cologne. A confirmed classicist himself, he nevertheless admired Robert and recommended him for the vacant Düsseldorf job.

Though her husband hesitated to accept, Clara saw merit in such a move. She was increasingly resentful of the poor reception with which Saxon audiences greeted Robert's operatic efforts while the exiled Wagner's *Lohengrin* won plaudits and praise. In her resentment Clara denied Wagner all musical acumen, calling him a bombastic noise-maker.

"He is a showman," she declared with bitterness, "not a musician!"

Showmanship was of course the very quality that Robert lacked. Nor did he have a sense of theater. His *Paradise and the Peri* would never enter opera repertoire. Critics dubbed it a chorale or, at best, a pagan oratorio. His *Manfred* failed to attain even this classification, since only the overture was destined for survival. Among Schuman's dramatic works only *Genoveva* would gain a hold on the lyric stage, but it was a precarious hold that did not outlast the century. In sum, what Clara never grasped was that her beloved Robert's talents lay outside the field of opera.

With Wagner the opposite was true. The stage was his element, whereas the subtleties of abstract music escaped him. Such piano solo compositions as came from his pen are puerile beyond belief. His true worth lay in creating for operatic ensemble.

Clara could not concede that two divergent artists like her husband and Wagner were not to be compared. With uxorious pettiness she carped against the mighty Richard and belittled him on all occasions. Almost, though not quite, she blamed him for Robert's poor showing as an opera craftsman. But her rancor encompassed also Dresden and its doctrinaire citizens who were incapable of appreciating the genius in their midst.

Naturally the Düsseldorf offer appeared to her a godsend. It promised a change of scene and of spiritual climate, plus a fixed salary that was by no means to be disdained. With Clara the salary weighed heavily. Where five growing children must be cared for, the family budget took some deft manipulating. Robert's lofty indifference toward mammon repeatedly gave rise to anxiety. The prospect of a regular monthly income was definitely cheering to a harassed mother.

While this situation was still in flux the Schumanns were shocked and distressed to hear of Chopin's death in Paris on October 17, 1849. The friends had not met in recent years due to the Pole's much publicized involvement with George Sand. When Madame Sand left him subsequently for Pierre Leroux, the socialist writer and apostle of Saint-Simonism, Chopin had rapidly gone downhill. In need of money, he toured England and Scotland without profit, since he was much too ill to fulfill his commitments. He returned to Paris, coughing blood. His sister Louise and a circle of friends gathered in the sick man's attic room at 12 Place Vendôme. Among the devotees were the Polish poet Adam Mickiewicz, the painter Eugène Delacroix, the cellists Auguste Franchomme and Moritz Karasowski, and a Polish priest. Liszt also came, as well as several ladies who at different times had shared Chopin's heart and couch—these were the Princess Marceline Czartoriska, the Countess Delphine Potocka, and an obscure but well-to-do Miss Jane Sterling. Madame George Sand, engrossed in a new lover, was absent.

Delphine Potocka had a lovely voice. In the words of the critic Francesco Giacobbe it was "chaste and sensitive, as is so often the case with women who are neither." Her lyric repertoire included Bellini and Mozart. She sang for Chopin in his final hours and also at his obsequies in Père Lachaise Cemetery.

In the same month of Chopin's death, and also at the age of forty, the grandson of a general in the American Revolution drew his last breath in the alcoholic ward of a Baltimore hospital; he was Edgar Allan Poe, master of the modern short story (he wrote more than sixty fabulously constructed tales) and a versifier of facile rhythm though slight poetic depth.

As so often, at the hour of an endowed spirit's departure, Nature provided compensation in some related sphere. The year of Chopin's and Poe's passing was marked by the birth, in Stockholm, of Sweden's leading dramatist-to-be, August Strindberg, destined to follow the tormented school of realism currently ruled by another Scandinavian, Norway's twenty-year-old Henrik Ibsen. Their gentler and more amenable disciple, the Viennese Arthur Schnitzler, was not to be born for another dozen years.

Robert and Clara Schumann were spiritually far removed from these agitated parallel currents. Had they glimpsed the mundane setting wherein much of Chopin's life took its course, their grief at his premature end would have been tempered by moral indignation. They ranked, themselves, among the most decorous Victorians of the Victorian Age. In weeping for Chopin they mourned a pristine ideal that never existed.

Some months after these happenings the question of the Düsseldorf position had to be decided. With misgivings Robert bowed to Clara's counsel. During the summer of 1850 his acceptance was at last forwarded to the city on the Rhine.

CHAPTER 14 More often than not, change is accompanied by vexations. Though greeted in Düsseldorf by a reception committee and a speech and an escort to the Hotel Breidenbacher Hof, the Schumann family noted with disappointment that the town was smaller and less picturesque than Dresden. Looking about for a house to rent, Clara in particular found fault with local architecture. Walls were too unadorned and flat, there were no eighteenth-century rococo cornices with dimpled cherubs smiling down, and the preponderance of wide modern windows seemed to her an obstacle to privacy. She did not reflect that if one liked Dresden and wished other places to resemble Dresden one had best never leave Dresden.

Another Düsseldorf peculiarity, annoying to newcomers, was the prevalence of amateur acrobats dedicated to turning cartwheels on street corners and other public places. These *Düsseldorfer Radschläger* or "wheel-turners" were both the pride of the city and the bane of uninterested and peaceful travelers. Since small children no less than hulking clods of every age and description indulged in the sport, unsuspecting strangers found it at times difficult to cross a sidewalk without getting tangled in a whirl of upside-down human beings. But that was not all. The voluntary performers expected a reward for their feats. Between cartwheels they paused to beg for coins. If these were not forthcoming the recalcitrant onlooker might end up against a wall, hemmed in by a whole horde of *Radschläger*, whose heavy-cleated shoes whizzed past in uncomfortable proximity to his nose.

While Robert and Clara would carefully dodge such street exhibitions, the Schumann children delighted in them. Before long they were

111

to be seen practicing cartwheels on their way to and from school, and the jingle in their pockets left no doubt that they played the game with all its rules.

Before the end of the first week a house was found on Grabenstrasse, which did not altogether satisfy the family's needs. The street was noisy, with the daily passage of an organ grinder adding to the din. As Robert could neither work nor rest under such circumstances he chose a back room for his study. But here the abominable "wide windows" of Düsseldorf looked out upon the rear courtyards of other dwellings, with cackling chickens, flapping clotheslines, and the chatter of laundresses and housemaids supplanting the commotion on the street. It was Clara who at this point gave way to an access of nerves. On October 1, she made an ill-tempered notation in her diary:

> . . . I absolutely can't get used to the lower classes here, people for the most part coarse, cocky, and pretentious; they consider themselves our equals, not even saying good-day. . . .

Nevertheless, no fault could be found with Düsseldorf's cultural elements. Beginning with Hiller, who had postponed his own departure in order to help Schumann get established, an eager and friendly circle gathered about the newcomers and gave them welcome. Among them were local officials, musicians, and university professors as well as prominent members of society. Their names would appear at random in the diary which of late was carried forward mostly by Clara, as Robert's former punctiliousness had given way to apathy toward most matters outside music.

An appalling incident occurred on the evening of Schumann's debut as conductor of the Düsseldorf Orchestra. An ovation with three trumpet flourishes had greeted him. The program contained Beethoven's *Overture, Opus 124*, Mendelssohn's *Concerto in G-Minor* (with Clara as soloist), Schumann's own *Adventlied*, and the cantata *Comala* by Gade. All went magnificently; Clara's performance especially aroused admiration as, for the first time in years, she played again by heart—a feat to which German audiences were still not accustomed. The evening ended with a reception at which the toastmaster, Hiller, committed a *faux pas*. Instead of raising his glass in homage to the guests of honor, man and wife, he forgot Robert and drank a pledge to Clara alone. Even then there would have been time to follow through, in guise of climax, with a more resounding toast to Düsseldorf's new conductor. But, on realizing his lapse, the unhappy speaker flushed and grew tongue-tied. By the time a spontaneous voice rose to repair the damage it was too late. A shadow had fallen on Robert Schumann's face; the Russian experience was repeating itself. The famous Clara Wieck, even with the handicap of dropping her own established name and adopting his, managed to blot him out. It was a bitter pill to swallow.

No one could have been more distressed at this awkward mishap than Clara herself. Her love for Robert counted in her life above all else. If she appeared as soloist at one of his concerts it was at his request and because she felt that by so doing she helped consolidate his position. She found it less easy to perform nowadays. At thirty-one, with six pregnancies behind her—and no chance to resume the rigorous practice regimen of her girlhood—she harbored doubts regarding her pianistic future. With fear and trembling, and only for Robert's sake, she had got through the Mendelssohn *Concerto* from memory, certain that at any moment she might break down. Her diary, following the event, contained the following:

> After many years this was the first time that I again played an orchestral number without score. Could this mean a return of youth's freshness and power? I don't think so, despite this evening's good result. The audacity required for memory playing is, after all, a concomitant of youth. . . .

There was no denying that in spite of the hazards and tensions she had enjoyed stepping once more into the limelight. Like a race horse on a long-missed track she had felt herself swept forward in an excitement that imparted itself ineluctably to the watching crowd. But it was Robert's debut. It was to have been his first great moment in Düsseldorf. The limelight won unwittingly by Clara was Robert's due. A surge of anger and remorse came over her as she alternately berated the well-meaning Hiller and gave way to outbursts of self-blame for having furnished him the occasion to put her in the wrong. Decidedly she must draw from this a lesson for the future. In the interest of her marriage and out of veneration for her husband's genius even more, she must efface herself to a far greater degree. She vowed to herself that the Hiller *gaffe* would never be repeated.

8

Withdrawal from the public eye proved easy during most of the following year, as Clara found herself again expectant. Her seventh child, Eugénie, was born on December 1, 1851. By this time it had become apparent that Schumann, apart from having got off to a wrong start at Düsseldorf, was not going to thrive in his new job. For one thing, he lacked two qualities essential in an orchestra conductor: the gift of handling people and winning their unlimited co-operation, and the ability to exchange the composer's untrammeled freedom for a job-holder's harness. The taciturnity that had subsided under the stimulus of the Rhineland atmosphere was to return before long, straining communications between the body of musicians and their distinguished leader. Resentments and repeated splutters of insubordination confronted Robert, and he found no way to bridge the widening chasm. Furthermore, the long hours of rehearsal tired him excessively so that he found no time to pursue what he considered his true vocation, composing. Sleeplessness, nervous morbidity and mental blackouts reappeared, fitfully at first, then with increasing frequency. Before long the directing board of the Düsseldorf Symphony questioned the wisdom of having engaged the eccentric Herr Schumann at all.

Despite his threatened health, Robert worked through long nights and early morning hours on his own music scripts. He finished his *Rhine* (or *Cologne*) *Symphony in E-Flat, Opus 97, Number 3,* and several overtures to operas that would never be written. Under the spell of a recent performance of Handel's *Messiah* he was impelled to try his hand at an oratorio, choosing for his subject the life of Martin Luther. This project fell through, however, when Robert and his librettist Karl Ferdinand Pohl failed to agree on length and poetic meter of the text.

A further drain on Schumann's strength, and one for which he had not been prepared in Dresden, was the directing of a mixed chorus made up of ladies and gentlemen from Düsseldorf high society. No serious love of music prompted these idle songsters. Rehearsal nights proved occasions for flirtatious *causeries* and general horseplay, and little attention was paid to antiphons or madrigals. "They don't come to learn," Robert complained to Clara, "but to amuse themselves." It is an arraignment easily seconded by choral directors everywhere.

Again Clara sided with her husband, denouncing Düsseldorf green-horns for their lack of respect and appreciation in the presence of genius. In Schumann's current fever of activity she saw no danger signal but only the wondrous phenomenon of divine afflatus. How proud she was of him! How deeply gratified to be soulmate to such a one, and mother to his children!

There were others who observed Schumann at this time and thought differently. During 1852 unfavorable comments began appearing in the press after each subscription concert. Professional journalists and amateur critics alike hinted that something must be done to salvage the remainder of the season. When, in the summer months, Robert suffered a fainting seizure on the podium, and a local musician named Julius Tausch took over the baton, there were murmurings in favor of making the change permanent.[*]

The following winter a visiting soloist, the Danzig violinist Joseph Wilhelm von Wasielewski, called on the Schumanns and found Robert engaged in a table-rapping spiritistic séance.

"Listen!" the composer whispered, without giving any sign of recognition to his guest. "The table is playing Beethoven's *Symphony in C-Minor. . . .*"

Wasielewski heard nothing. Schumann however was swaying back and forth, beating time with his upheld hand and issuing orders: "Much too slow, dear table! Wait, I'll give you the right tempo——"

In grave alarm Wasielewski spoke to Clara. "Your husband, Frau Schumann, is very ill." He hesitated. "I think you should consult a special kind of physician, an—er—alienist."

She was outraged. Very likely Wasielewski had been sent by Tausch, the substitute conductor, who wanted Robert's job. As for table-rapping or planchette experiments, these were in vogue just now as an amusing pastime. In America something called a ouija board counted among modish parlor games. Surely Robert could alternate his working schedule with a bit of innocent diversion? No, there was no need for summoning any kind of doctor.

Rebuffed, Wasielewski withdrew. A few days later Clara admitted to herself that there was something odd about her husband's behavior. He had opened a newspaper, then suddenly crumpled the pages, exclaiming, "I can't read! I hear A-major all the time. . . ."

From the orchestra came complaints. Schumann had again taken command, but during rehearsals he went motionless at times, his eyes staring vacantly into space. When spoken to he gave no answer. Eventually emerging from some kind of fog, he took up his baton and resumed work, unaware that he had suffered a mental blackout.

Periods of betterment followed upon these as yet trivial incidents. Repeatedly that year Schumann was invited to appear in Holland and Switzerland as guest conductor. Clara accompanied him, and all went well, obviously due to the distractions of travel and the enforced break in Robert's frenzied composing schedule. Passing through France, they found a new atmosphere, or rather, an old and retrogressive one: the Second Republic was dead since, on November 21, 1852, following some skillful political maneuvers, the erstwhile republican champion Louis Bonaparte had himself proclaimed, by plebiscite, Emperor Napoleon III. A festive era opened now in Paris, full of promise for architects, painters, musicians. It would not be long before Schumann won plaudits in the capital on the Seine.

At Düsseldorf, however, things went from bad to worse. Returning home, Robert again succumbed to the destructive routine of daytime work and night-time composition, with corresponding loss of sleep.

Yet even now Clara was able to exclaim, enthralled, "Ideas and melodic inventions simply pour from him. How joyful it must be, to find oneself so blessed!"

Others disagreed, especially the board of directors of Düsseldorf's Symphony Orchestra. In the fall of 1853, with the new concert season under way, a deputation made up of two gentlemen named Illing and Herz approached Clara with a tactful suggestion. Keeping in mind its contract obligations no less than Herr Schumann's obviously imperilled health, the board proposed to relieve its official conductor of all routine concerts (subscription evenings) and request him to direct only his own compositions. The assistant conductor, Herr Tausch, was already in agreement with such a course of action. It required, said Illing and Herz, merely a persuasive conversation between Clara and her husband to clinch the matter.

Clara irately refused to become a party to so degrading a machination. A contract was a contract. Furthermore she deemed it a gross insult that the quite subordinate Herr Tausch should have been consulted before Robert's consent was assured. No, she would not lend herself to this kind of malevolent intrigue.

The gentlemen shrugged, then warned: "A signed agreement works two ways. Unfortunately your husband is not living up to his obligations toward *us*."

There was a pause, followed by a clearing of throats. "If a friendly compromise is not accepted by Herr Schumann, we shall have to take other steps."

Clara bristled, but she saw the point. With trembling hand she reached for the proffered protocol which contained an outline of the board's decision. She did not know when or how she was going to make Robert read it. But there was no further dodging the issue.

To her departing callers she said: "You will have an answer, gentlemen, later this week."

CHAPTER 15 Schumann's reaction to the Illing and Herz mission was not unlike that of Clara. With severity he gave reply by letter on November 9, 1853. What angered him—as it had angered his wife—was that the substitute conductor Tausch had been approached before he, the incumbent director of the orchestra, was consulted. Did the convenience of Herr Tausch, then, have paramount importance? For the rest, Robert made clear that unless *all* concerts were conducted by him, as stipulated in his contract, he would take up the baton for *none*. He also gave notice that on termination of the present season he planned to depart from Düsseldorf. The committee might begin, as of now, to look for a permanent replacement.

Actually Robert's first impulse was to pack up and leave at once. In Switzerland and Holland he had met with acclaim, and there remained always Leipzig or Vienna. But an evening's applause, however enthusiastic and prolonged, did not guarantee a full-time salaried job. Clara too shared Robert's chagrin; she was all for walking out on the unworthy Düsseldorfers, but there was the economic angle to remember. She confessed this to her diary: ". . . With six children one can't just lift anchor and steer into the unknown!"

In addition to this sober thought she had something else to consider. By Christmas of that year she knew that she was three months along in her eighth pregnancy. Decidedly this was no time to pull up stakes. They must make the best of a disagreeable situation.

Since he had no other choice, Robert bowed humbly to the inevitable. He conquered moroseness and obeyed each summons (there were not many) to the podium when Tausch was not in action. Thus the year 1854 began under a cloud. Despite the natural animation and

118

cheer furnished by the young brood, there hung over the household a growing tension. The contract difficulties had been discussed throughout the town. Düsseldorf citizens, generous and hospitable at heart, grew piqued. The Schumanns continued to be treated politely but without the warmth once lavished upon them. In the attitude of friends and professional associates there was already a feeling of estrangement and farewell.

Withal Robert's passion for overwork continued. He seemed beset by a fear that time might be running out before the treasure within him was fully brought to light. And that treasure pressed and urged and forced itself to fruition. During the Düsseldorf years Schumann published his *Sonata in A-Minor for Piano and Violin, Opus 105*, three *Fantasies, Opus 111*, the *Trio in G-Minor for Piano, Violin, and Cello, Opus 110*, the second great *Sonata in D-Minor for Piano and Violin, Opus 121*. He was also giving melodic structure to several opera projects based on Shakespeare's *Julius Caesar*, Schiller's *Maria Stuart*, and Uhland's epic poem *Des Sängers Fluch (The Minstrel's Curse)*.

Again Clara stood by, thrilled and confident. "What glory there is," she wrote, "in so tireless and potent a creative spirit; how fortunate I hold myself, that Heaven should have given me comprehension and heart to grasp fully the worth of such genius. Often I am overcome with acute fear when I regard my happy lot above that of millions of other women, and then I ask Heaven if it is not too much. . . . What are all the shadows of material existence compared to the joy and bliss which I possess in the love and the art of my own Robert! . . ."

That her judgment was blinded by devotion is evidenced in the writings of contemporary critics as well as later biographers. There was Philipp Spitta, who at twenty-three heard Schumann's two violin sonatas. It was Spitta's subsequent and well-weighed opinion that the master's inspiration had already flagged when these works came into being. "One can hardly listen to them," declared Spitta, "without a feeling of embarrassment."

Others shared this reaction. They squirmed on hearing a song cycle *(Opus 135)* composed to some lyrics supposedly penned by Mary Queen of Scots. In this case Robert had a legitimate excuse. When the house in which the Schumanns lived was abruptly sold, the family was forced to take lodgings at the opposite end of town, on Herzog Street, with a construction gang working in a vacant lot nearby and an assortment of obstreperous neighbors overhead. A second move had followed upon this one to more agreeable quarters on Bilkerstrasse. With all this unrest, Clara conceded, the verses of the unhappy royal Mary had not been dealt with fairly.

In the year 1854 outside factors also caused tremors of anxiety. Russia, England, and France had got entangled in a tussle known as the Crimean War, brought on by Muscovite yearnings for a warm water port on the Mediterranean. To this end Tsar Nicholas I sent an attacking force to Constantinople with the intent of driving the Sultan Abd-ul-Hamid II from the Dardanelles. If anyone took umbrage at this Romanov move it should have been the nearby powers of Austria-Hungary and Germany. But, in the words of H. G. Wells, the "passion of the foreign offices of France and England for burning their fingers in Russian affairs has always been very difficult to control." With no good pretext, since the Turk had always been regarded as an enemy of Christendom, the chancelleries of London and Paris took up the defense of the Crescent. Actually the French had colonial designs on Syria while the British saw their route to India threatened by Russian shipping in the Mediterranean; these factors alone impelled their fealty toward the Ottoman Empire, for which they felt normally only contempt.

The war put a damper on musical activities in most European capitals as public interest focused on a thirty-four-year-old Italian-born Englishwoman, Florence Nightingale (her Christian name was that of her birthplace), whose ministrations to the wounded of both fighting contingents would lay the basis for .the humanitarian organization known as the Red Cross. Women, heretofore excluded from civic and military concerns, began taking an interest in welfare work. The care of the sick, a servant task up to now, assumed the character of a profession. The modern career of nursing was being foreshadowed.

Reading the newspapers, Robert Schumann now heard sounds other than music. The names of remote places like Balaklava, Sebastopol, Inkerman, Traktir, Mamelon-Vert, and the Tower of Molakhov evoked in his ears the din of battle mingled with the stridencies of creatures in pain.

Into this period of malaise which slowly wore down Clara's optimism—for she admitted to herself at last that all could not be well with Robert—there came an element of reviving buoyancy and joy.

Recommended by the violinist Joseph Joachim, a Hamburg music student—aged twenty and named Johannes Brahms—arrived at Düsseldorf for an audition with Schumann. The youth was fragile of build but handsome and enormously talented. He brought with him an extraordinary assortment of his own compositions, all of them remarkable for their originality and imaginative flair. Nowhere in his efforts was there a trace of the trite banality so characteristic of the beginner. Both Robert and Clara were dumfounded.

"There's nothing more to teach this boy," they told each other. "He was born a finished musician!"

Without hesitation Schumann urged his own publishers, Breitkopf and Härtel, to bring out whatever this singular young man submitted. Immediate popularity might not be assured, as the Brahms style was uncommon and demanding. But there remained no doubt that such gifts were headed for immortality.

Johannes himself had little knowledge of his worth. He was of an ingratiating simplicity, cheerful and brimming with energy. His admiration for the Schumanns knew no bounds. Thus, though they could not in conscience accept him for a pupil, he refused to be sent home. He stayed on well into the spring of 1854, calling daily on his new friends and spending long evenings at their piano. His playing was bold and spirited, though undisciplined. Clara saw at once that he would never submit to the strictures required of a true virtuoso. Like Schumann, Brahms possessed the creative spark in the highest degree.

"Like John the Baptist," declared Robert fervently, "Johannes is one that cometh in the name of the Lord!"

Clara's initial impression was perpetuated in the following diary lines:

> It is truly moving to observe this person at the piano, with his interesting young face transfixed while playing; his beautiful hands, surmounting with the greatest ease the greatest difficulties (his things are very hard to play); and then those remarkable compositions. He studied with Marxsen in Hamburg, but what he plays for us is so masterful that one would think the dear Lord has sent him into the world a finished artist. A splendid future awaits him, for once he starts writing for orchestra his imagination will find its real scope! Robert says one can ask for nothing else but that Heaven may preserve his health. . . .

Again here was emphasized the most extraordinary fact about Johannes Brahms: in him the world would see that rare phenomenon, the absolute musician, born, not made. He was the answer to the casuistic question, "Were there no musicians before there were teachers of music?" The issue touched upon all the arts. Could painters paint without having been taught to paint? Was the poet incapable of writing poetry unless he read another's poem?

In Brahms, assuredly, natural genius was vindicated. His music-master Eduard Marxsen (of Nienstetten near suburban Altona) had acquainted him with keyboard fundamentals. But had Marxsen never existed, the voices in Johannes would not have remained silent. Even without a knowledge of scales, clefs, notes or crotchets, there was no holding back the harmonies that poured from him. Lacking all training in conventional forms of expression, he would have devised a magic of his own to capture the attention of his fellow men.

From their first meeting, Schumann became warmly attached to Johannes. He wrote an enthusiastic letter to the youth's parents assuring them of the bright future awaiting their son. The elder Brahms, Johann Jacob, had been for years a double-bass player with diverse Hamburg orchestras. The family came originally from Heide, a small town in Holstein, where the name had been spelled Brahmst. The boy Johannes was born on May 7, 1833. He had an older sister, Elisabeth, and a younger brother, Friedrich.

The Brahms household occupied rented quarters all over Hamburg, living at different times in the Ulrikus Strasse, the Bäckerbreitergang, the Anselar Platz (birthplace of Johannes), the Dammthorwall, and lastly at Number 74, Fuhlentwiete. Money was scarce, although Frau Brahms (born Henrika Nissen, and seventeen years older than her husband) possessed some savings from a gift shop and rooming house operated before her marriage.

At the age of four, Johannes delighted listeners with his angelic soprano voice. He sang at street corners and collected a bounty in coins, which supplemented the meager family budget. At ten, still chanting in alleys and public squares, he was run over by a delivery wagon. This put him in a hospital for six weeks with a crushed chest. He recovered miraculously and, having studied piano with his father almost since nursery days, Johannes now played at fairs and in beer gardens for pay. He improvised with astounding ease, composing new tunes faster than he could write them down. The center of his existence seemed to be music.

Because of the late hours they kept, and the frugal meals served by Henrika, the Brahms children grew neither big nor strong. Johannes in particular was slight of build, fine-boned, and subject to migraine. But he had good features, luminous blue eyes, and the happiest of dispositions.

At fourteen he fell in love with a young girl named Lieschen Giesemann, for whom he wrote two songs. When these were not appreciated he took them back. The following year he composed the first of his published works, the *Sonata in C-Major, Opus 1,* and turned his back on romance. His pen remained busy. The *F-Sharp-Minor Sonata* became his *Opus 2,* with an *E-Minor Scherzo* and the *Fantasy on a Favorite Waltz* soon to be added.

Playing these numbers in concert, Johannes was heard by a visiting Hungarian violinist, Edouard Reményi, who engaged the youth as accompanist for a farflung tour. At Göttingen in Hanover Province, a phenomenal happening occurred that underscored the Brahms acumen. Beethoven's *Kreutzer Sonata* was on the program. On reaching the concert hall Reményi discovered that the only available piano was tuned half a key lower than his violin. It would seem that the solution lay in re-tuning the four strings of the fiddle. But to this, Reményi, who was the feature attraction, would not consent. His sensitive ear, he claimed, could tolerate no change in pitch.

At this point Johannes spoke up brightly. With the audience already in its seats, there was no time for argument. He would simply read off the score as written, while playing it in the required higher key. What was more, after a few measures he pushed the music aside and carried on from memory, still transposing as he went.

Word of the feat reached the ears of Liszt, who came to hear Brahms at Weimar. Later, at Liszt's home in Altenberg, impressions were exchanged and the host volunteered to perform one of his own favorite compositions, the *B-Minor Sonata.* At a particularly moving passage Liszt turned toward Johannes for some gesture of response, only to find the latter fast asleep. Still an adolescent, the boy had just not been able to catch up on his rest.

In Weimar the tour ended as, due to a case of mistaken identity, Remenyi was threatened with arrest. A brother of his had, with Richard Wagner, taken part in the socialist demonstrations at Dresden in 1848. The authorities were still tracking down ringleaders of that uprising, as well as relatives of ringleaders. The nonpolitical violinist Reményi was persuaded to leave Germany for a while. Before departing he left with Johannes an assortment of Magyar folk tunes and gypsy airs which would one day inspire the Brahms *Hungarian Dances, Opus 65,* and two subsequent *Rhapsodies, Opus 79, I & II.* The so-called *Rhenish Rhapsody, Opus 119, IV,* would be derived from Rhineland rhythms.

On parting with Reményi, Johannes decided to spend his earnings in further study. The idol of Germany's younger musicians was Robert Schumann. Armed with a letter of recommendation from Joseph Joachim, and another by the always gracious Franz Liszt (who held no grudge over the Altenberg "nap"), Johannes presented himself in Düsseldorf.

The surge of sympathy between himself and the Schumanns was instantaneous. Robert in particular, on learning of the humble (and musically undistinguished) Brahms background, marveled at the emergence of the phoenix Johannes. Was there an answer to this enigma? Schumann, who had looked in vain for manifestations of genius among his own offspring, reached the disillusioning conclusion that heredity was not to be relied upon.

Johannes responded unreservedly to Robert's friendship. But his candid veneration would soon belong only to Clara.

Now in her thirty-fourth year, musically inactive, and grown big with child, she appeared to him the noblest of women. Her serene face and the cadence of her voice cast a spell over him from which he could not and would not escape. As if this were not enough, her musicianship won his fullest admiration. When she consented to play, in the intimacy of a family gathering, he felt himself transported into regions of highest bliss.

But there was something more that drew him toward Clara, not romantically, though with a chivalrous and protective impulse. Fourteen years her junior, and certainly unschooled by life, he saw nevertheless what the loving wife and mother was blind to: the progressive disintegration of Schumann's mind. To be sure, there was little chance to speak to Clara alone, nor would Johannes have found the courage to confide to her his observations. Might he not be in error, dramatizing what was only a temporary ailment?

He addressed himself to Dr. Hasenclever, Schumann's physician: "The master's ear affliction grows worse. He can't sleep, and he suffers severe headaches. . . ."

Hasenclever shrugged helplessly. For some time he had urged his patient to enter a clinic for treatment, but to no avail. The sounds heard by Robert were "heavenly choirs with voices of angels," which furnished him with untold inspiration. Clara supported her husband in his claim that such "celestial symphonies" must not be checked.

Under these circumstances Brahms had little hope of studying under Schumann or learning from him anything of value. In 1853 he departed again, to concertize alone at Cologne, Berlin, Leipzig, and other German cities. The parting was almost painful. Robert and Clara had come to look upon Johannes as another son (their eldest child Marie was nearing thirteen) and they were loath to see him go.

Soon after, Schumann's condition became aggravated. The melodious carols in his head turned into diabolical screeches and obscene sounds. He began seeing visions of demon faces that leered and gesticulated from the corners of his room. At night he refused to retire, begging Clara to lock her own and the children's doors, for fear he might do them unwitting harm.

Now at last she faced the truth. She allowed Hasenclever to call a nerve specialist, the Rhineland military zone's psychiatric authority, Dr. Böger.

As the latter examined him, Schumann spoke up suddenly: "I belong in a lunatic asylum, is that it?"

The doctor's answer was evasive. "We shall see. First we shall try a new routine at home—" In an aside to Clara, Böger indicated that a manservant must be engaged to guard the patient.

Robert meanwhile was seized by an *idée fixe*. He packed his night clothes, shaving utensils, cigars, a stack of music scripts. He put on his coat.

To the others he said, "Good-by. I am going to the asylum."

They had some difficulty dissuading him and putting him to bed. Clara wanted to watch at his side, but the attendant led her from the room.

As the Christmas season came and went, Robert was kept under sedatives and meekly did as he was told. Then, on February 26, 1854, he rose in the early morning hours and, barefoot, slipped from the house in a pouring rain (the manservant had momentarily dozed off). By the time Robert's absence was discovered no trace of him could be found.

Police and firemen were alarmed, and a searching party combed the town.

The downpour continued when, an hour later, Robert Schumann was brought home on a stretcher. Some dockworkers on the riverbank had seen him leap from a bridge into the turgid waters of the Rhine. They had followed after and saved him from drowning.

Clara was not in the house. Soaked to the skin, she was trailing the searchers through streets and alleys. When at last she returned to her doorstep, the doctors barred her entry.

"Herr Schumann is alive, but in a state of terrible excitement. It will be best for you and the children to stay with friends."

She was too tired to protest.

Robert alive! Thank God, thank God . . .

Sobbing with joy, she let herself be led to a neighbor's house where the wide-eyed and bewildered children were being quieted with an impromptu supper.

CHAPTER 16　　　　　　She never saw him again, save under supervision. For several days, Robert was confined to his room watched by two keepers now. He alternately spent some hours in bed, then paced the floor or sat at his desk and engaged in tireless scribbling. On March 1 Clara sent him a violet plant and some fruit—oranges, a luxury in middle Europe, since they were imported from Italy and Spain.

He wrote a note of thanks, assuring her that he was feeling better. But even as he wrote, a burst of violence came over him. He tore up papers, threw furniture about, and fought off anyone who came near. Summoned by Bertha, the housemaid, Hasenclever and Böger arrived in haste. A decision was taken at once: Schumann must be institutionalized. In particular it was essential to remove him from all things and persons familiar, or any activity reminiscent of his former life.

Clara's permission was needed for commitment. She recorded the poignant hour:

> . . . And so Böger and Hasenclever came to me with the most awful news, namely, that they wanted to take him to a private clinic at Endenich, half an hour from Bonn. . . . Him, the marvelous Robert, to an institution!—how was it possible that I bore it? And they refused to let me see him and to press him to my heart just once more! this greatest of all sacrifices I had to bring, myself, to my Robert. . . . They wrote to Dr. Richarz at Endenich, whom Hasenclever knew personally as an excellent person and distinguished physician. . . .

An affirmative reply from Endenich came two days later, and Hasenclever made preparations to transfer Schumann on March 4 to the clinic. From Berlin arrived Clara's mother, Frau Bargiel, who had been informed by letter of the tragic developments. Brahms, seeing a report in the newspapers, broke off his concert tour at Hanover and likewise rushed to Düsseldorf. Again Clara's pen described the hours that followed:

> . . . Saturday, the 4th, arrived! Oh, God, now the carriage stood at the door to our home. Robert dressed in great haste, climbed into the vehicle with Hasenclever and the two keepers, without asking for me or his children—and I sat at Fräulein Leser's, in dull numbness and thinking I must now collapse! The weather was glorious, so that at least the sunshine reached him! I had given Dr. Hasenclever a bunch of flowers for him, which he gave to him along the way; he held it for a long time unconsciously, but all at once he breathed the scent while gripping Hasenclever's hand with a smile! Later he passed a bloom to each one in the carriage. Hasenclever brought me his—with bleeding heart I have kept it! That evening at 6 o'clock I returned to our home with Mother— the moment of entering his room! I cannot write about it. . . .

Fräulein Rosalie Leser, at whose house Clara and the children had found refuge during the days and nights since Schumann's breakdown, was a blind spinster, of wealth and cultural background, who had befriended the musician and his family since their arrival in Düsseldorf. Now, on the arm of her companion-secretary Elise Junge, she came to the Schumann home to keep Clara company on that first difficult night-fall. Brahms also came, and on the following day Joseph Joachim canceled a violin recital to join the faithful circle at Clara's side.

Monday, March 6, brought a resumption of practical duties. The older children must attend school once more, while Clara took steps to enlarge her class of piano pupils. Not only would work absorb her thoughts and banish despair, but she needed the money. The large household, Robert's asylum bills, and her own confinement (only three months away) called for substantial reserves.

Dr. Hasenclever returned from Endenich with a description of Robert's quarters. The patient's room and small visitor's vestibule looked across the Rhine to the Siebengebirge or Seven Mountains, made famous by the Brothers Grimm because of the Seven Dwarfs found there by Snow White. Richarz had received Schumann with warmth and tact, assigning him a male attendant toward whom Robert showed immediate trust. In short, Clara had reason to feel reassured that all would go well and her separation from her beloved husband was to be only temporary.

She got through her days by keeping busy, but the nights were terrible. In thirteen years of marriage they had known no parting. This made his absence doubly felt. But there was another worry to keep her awake; would she lose too many pupils, and consequent earnings, during the time taken off for the birth of her new baby? Could she afford another servant, so as to gain practice hours with a view to resuming her former concert career?

Meanwhile news of Schumann's illness continued to occupy journalists at home and abroad. A profusion of mail arrived daily, much of it from strangers whose words of sympathy were both crude and ill-advised, as they spoke of Robert as one already dead. Such missives constantly undermined what Clara tried so desperately to cling to: courage and hope. Among the writers there were also, however, devoted friends who betokened their loyalty in concrete ways. Paul Mendelssohn, brother of the late Felix, sent a sizable bank draft for Clara's use. She declined this courteously, as she did a sum of cash brought in person by another Schumann admirer, Avé Lallement, who made a special trip from Hamburg to bestow his offering. Similarly the music-publishing firm of Breitkopf and Härtel intended sponsoring a benefit concert in Leipzig, with an all-Schumann program, provided Clara gave her consent.

She refused. "Give me work!" was her plea. Let them employ her as teacher, music copyist, or in the role of performer, which had once been hers. Robert's wife and children must not be thought destitute; when he returned to his fireside, restored to health, he was to face no humiliating obligations. "No, thank you," was her answer to all gestures that carried a hint of charity, "we shall manage." One offer alone did she accept in pride and without loss of face. This was the continuance of Robert's salary as conductor of the Düsseldorf Orchestra, through the remaining term of his contract. Here she did not flinch. It was a question of her husband's reputation and honor.

April came, and another report from Endenich. Schumann appeared less disturbed, the spells of violence and panic were subsiding. He spoke little, and never of his family. But he spent long hours at an open but barred window, listening to the nightingales. At such times there was a smile on his face.

Clara read into this more promise than was warranted. Her Robert

9

was soothed, and growing calm. And in the woodland surroundings of the asylum there was the sound of nightingales! That noblest of songbirds did not come within a mile of industrial Düsseldorf. . . . Ah, perhaps in May, when the rains stopped and nature was in fullest bloom, she would have him home again. The nightmare would be forgotten.

By end of the month a note of disillusion crept into her diary pages. On April 25 she wrote:

> . . . A letter [from Dr. Richarz] states that it is not yet possible to predict a favorable outcome of the illness, such as I want to believe in. . . . I am crushed, all courage leaves me, since I never for a moment harbored serious doubt regarding complete recovery, though I feared it might take a long time; never did I believe in the sickness leading to a bad end. . . . I feel paralyzed, deprived of all will power; how shall I continue working under the blight of such hopelessness! . . .

In May her physical condition grew burdensome. She was in the last month of gestation, her girth was great, a swelling of feet and ankles gave her constant pain. On the twentieth she wrote:

> My body causes me much suffering right now. My nervous fatigue is such that I want to lie down all the time. . . . I can do very little, and am only glad still to manage my teaching commitments. . . .

All this time Brahms was in Düsseldorf, where he had taken lodgings near the family of the admired master. Having with Robert's help entered the ranks of published composers, he had sufficient income to stand by in the capacity of "protector." Clara smiled at this. A pink-cheeked stripling, as irresistible and high-spirited as her own brood, hardly brought her surcease from sorrow. What was more, in an effort to supplement his possibly quite temporary mammon Johannes quickly acquired a few pupils himself, mostly fluttering females with less talent for the piano than interest in the young and personable pianist. Thus, while trying to help, Brahms was actually giving Clara competition.

Even so, she took comfort in his company. On May 27 her pen revealed the following:

. . . I prefer to speak of Robert to Brahms above all others, primarily because Robert loved him so, and then on account of that sensitivity which—despite his youth—does me so much good! His entire personality is impressive, with a culture far beyond his years, yet on the other hand his emotions are those of a naive child. . . .

June 8, Robert Schumann's forty-fourth birthday, dawned without better news from Endenich. Clara walked into his abandoned study with an armful of roses which she distributed in vases long empty. No visitors were received until, toward noon, Burgomaster Hammers refused to be sent away. Relenting, she learned from this good man that the city of Düsseldorf had voted in favor of continuing Schumann's salary not only for as long as his contract specified, but indefinitely, until the composer himself returned and handed in his resignation. A splendid gift, admitted Clara, weeping. A noble community, this town of Rhinelanders.

Later that day Johannes arrived, not his usual cocksure self. What he secretly dreaded had come to pass. His royalties were petering out and, with the start of summer, there was a paucity of piano students. He could not afford the posies with which Clara's heart might have been gladdened. Instead, he had sat up most of the night penning the score of some Hungarian folk tunes, remembered from his tour with Reményi. These he left at the Schumann door, without entering, on that melancholy date.

In another three days, on June 11, 1854, Clara took to her bed and gave birth for the eighth time. The child, a boy, was to receive the name of Felix, after the great Mendelssohn, from whose family had come the first spontaneous offer of help.

From the moment of this delivery (it was her slowest and most difficult) Clara experienced a psychic change. As her body was eased of its burden she felt a surge of new courage. All at once she realized that the poorly paid teaching career on which she had embarked would not insure her future. The education of the children, apart from Robert's institutional bills, called for bigger earnings. In short, she must return to the concert stage.

Within a week after her confinement she was at the piano, practicing with a fervor she had not known since early youth. It was appalling to discover how much she had fallen behind. How grueling was the effort to regain lost disciplines of hand and mind! But no challenge frightened her. The compulsion under which she worked was dynamic, unflagging. She felt herself again her father's daughter, Clara Wieck, who once had scaled the heights of fame.

And now she faced her hour of truth. She had known well-being on those heights, a well-being she needed and must have again. Wifehood, motherhood, economic need, all these were secondary factors. Mere pretexts, even. In her heart she knew that there could be for her only one destiny: her path was the virtuoso path.

Into this delirious realization there now obtruded the problem of the children. Who was to care for them while she went off on tour? Her mother, Frau Bargiel, offered a partial solution; she would take the third daughter, nine-year-old Julie, to Berlin. The older girls, Marie and Elise, could aid the housemaid Bertha with the school-age boys. The toddler Eugénie and the bottle-fed Felix most likely would need a nurse.

At this point Brahms came to the rescue. Since he had no intention of ever leaving Düsseldorf again, he promised to look after the Schumann brood in Clara's absence.

She agreed. He had a way with children, and all children liked him. It seemed a perfect plan. Perfect, that is, for all but Julie, who, in Berlin, cried herself to sleep each night with homesickness. If the Bargiels had no idea of this, Clara was even less aware. In coming years she would "farm out" her remaining offspring, never grasping that the break-up of brother-and-sister relationships was to bring her children untold harm.

For the moment she was ruled by a force she had believed long dead: the artist creed of Friedrich Wieck. She was again, as her father would have her be, wedded to music.

CHAPTER 17   Thirty-five was an uncommon age for starting a concert career. But that was what Clara intended to do.

It was not a question of making a comeback; too long a time had elapsed since Friedrich Wieck had exhibited his child prodigy across Central Europe. As for her rare appearances after marrying Robert Schumann, these did not count. Clara knew she must begin anew, minus the advantages she had formerly enjoyed. That is, she could not afford training with a professional coach but must rely on memory for recapturing what her father had taught her.

There would be other hurdles. The modern impresario system had not yet evolved. Singers traveled with some former teacher who pocketed a part of their fees, in payment for lessons given on faith. Instrumentalists, however, had to build up their own public by performing in test recitals with non-paying orchestras, and depending on word-of-mouth advertising for bookings.

Clara faced all this without a qualm. She worked tirelessly, practicing day and night so as to regain her former brilliance of technique. Astonishingly, her fingers had never stiffened. She was fortunate in possessing a natural limberness of hands and wrists.

Her mental state during this period of preparation is evidenced in the diary pages. In July of 1854 she wrote:

> . . . I am haunted by music as never before; at night I cannot find sleep, and by day I am so absorbed by music that I lose track of all else, which is not like me. . . .

Two months later, in a note to the violinist Joseph Joachim, her emotions found even fuller expression:

. . . Oh, dear Joachim, what a glorious thing it is to be an artist! I always thought I knew this, yet complete realization comes to me only now, since in God-given music there is release from sorrow and joy, and I am made whole again. . . .

Her birthday month, September, brought two surprises. The first was a little concert by her daughters Marie and Elise, whom Brahms had coached in secret. The girls showed no exceptional talent but their earnestness and application delighted Clara. As yet (and this is characteristic of virtuoso self-absorption) she had never thought of even one among her children as potential artist material. It had been Robert who, off and on, had called them to the piano for a brief *solfeggio* lesson.

The second September event was a letter from Endenich, written by Schumann himself. In it he recalled not only every member of his family but spoke rationally of things once important to him. He asked about his manuscripts, opera libretti, the autograph album with signatures of Goethe, Weber, Richter, Mozart, Beethoven (the latter two having been heirlooms, not personally obtained), as well as the correspondence exchanged between himself and Clara during their courtship years. All this was accurate and clear, yet the words carried a fading, hollow quality, as of an echo rather than a living voice. The writer spoke of past matters, without acknowledgment of present or future. In the words of the great Schumann biographer Berthold Litzmann: "Like a voice from the grave is this letter, not of someone resurrected but of one buried who does not know that he is dead. Touching, of childlike delicacy, there is no breath of life, the only thing occupying a tired imagination is the past. The future has died."

Clara did not share this reaction. To her, Robert's first message since their parting brought jubilant assurance that the cure progressed and his final recovery was in sight. She failed to observe the pathological deterioration in the sick man's script. "Robert always wrote illegibly," she explained to Brahms. Nor did certain strange phrasings alarm her, such as:

Oh, if I could only see you and talk to you, but the road is too far. I would like to know so much about you, what your life is really like, where you are staying, and whether you still play as marvelously as you did once. . . . Oh, how I would love to hear your wonderful playing. Is it a dream that we went to Holland last winter?

The trip to Holland was something which Schumann in his right mind could never have forgotten nor would he voluntarily have brought it up again. For at The Hague he had suffered one of those unfortunate humiliations that cut so deeply into his soul. After conducting a concert before the royal family, with Clara as soloist, Robert had been addressed subsequently by a Dutch prince who did not recognize him:

"Are you also a musician?"

Amused, Schumann had nodded.

His Highness, Friedrich of Nassau, wished to parade a certain familiarity with matters cultural. "What instrument?" he persisted.

This brief dialogue plus the fact that no carriage had been made available to take the artists back to their hotel (Clara had ruined her satin slippers while sloshing through the snow), turned the Netherlands visit into an indelible memory. No, Schumann—while master of his senses—would not choose Holland for reminiscence.

Even so, a degree of betterment in his condition seemed to make itself evident throughout the close of 1854. Under supervision and in the company of other nonviolent patients Robert was allowed to stroll around the asylum grounds. Once he was taken on an excursion to Bonn, and again to visit the cathedral at Cologne. But contact with his family remained forbidden; neither Clara nor the children were permitted to make the short journey to Endenich. A complete cure, maintained Dr. Richarz and his psychiatric colleagues, depended on the constant absorption of new and altogether innocuous impressions.

Robert continued writing. In a second letter he recalled the joint diary started with Clara on their honeymoon. It ran into fifteen volumes by now. He begged her to send him one or two. Then he wanted a list of the children's birthdays—"They are in the little blue notebook." It had been a secret joke between them that the four sons and four daughters of their marriage had been born each in a different month, with only May, August, October, and November "unused."

In this too Clara saw a reawakening of impish merriment, nay, wit. Similarly, Robert's mention of having beheld the great Beethoven statue on his recent jaunt to Bonn gave her renewed hope that his musical roots would burgeon anew. But all this was, again, according to Litzmann: ". . . only a nostalgic response of the senses, like the sigh of an Aeolian harp."

Christmas approached and Clara trimmed a tree, not for the children alone but because she counted on Robert's coming home. Till the last moment, as the candles were being lit on December 24, she expected the door to open and the beloved figure to appear on the threshold. However, when the brass knocker was lifted and she rushed forward to answer, her eyes did not behold him whom she awaited nor any messenger with news from the asylum. Instead, the smiling Brahms walked in, carrying a small sack of bakery goods. She could not hide her disappointment, though in the end it was Johannes who saved the evening. As Clara gave way to melancholy, and soon sought the quiet of her room, the children clung to the young man whose gay resourcefulness (he knew an assortment of piano tricks and was a crack storyteller) turned the occasion into a happy party.

With the new year the spurt of correspondence from Endenich began to flag. On May 5, 1855, Schumann wrote one last letter which dealt again with memories of things long past but in no manner gave answer to Clara's own constant probing into plans for present and future. She had hoped for some emotional reaction to the birth, nearly a year ago, of the baby Felix. But beyond approving the baptismal name (it evoked recollections of the loved Mendelssohn!) Robert made no mention of the child. His thoughts moved in a vacuum, detached from earth's realities. The writer of that final letter breathed, but he no longer lived.

In this period of desolation Clara found refuge nowhere but in music. Feverishly she threw herself into the task of building up a new repertoire. The excitement of the Crimean War was dying down, Russia's defeat was clearly in view. By 1856, when peace terms were dictated in Paris, Europe would swing back from humanitarian enterprises to pursuits of pleasure and the arts. By 1856 Clara Schumann would be ready.

The list of works she mastered at the outset of her second emergence as a concert artist was impressive. It included numbers studied long ago and only partially forgotten. A few refresher sessions put her again in full command. But there were new offerings added, in keeping with the purpose she had set herself, namely to win homage from the world for Robert's genius. The composer Schumann would figure prominently on her programs. At the same time a sense of gratitude toward Johannes, who in such selfless devotion lived at her beck and call (he helped the older children with their schoolwork, played nursemaid to the little ones on the servants' day off, and did most of the

family shopping), caused Clara to present a cycle of Brahms compositions, some of them still in manuscript. Her repertoire ran now as
follows:

Beethoven: *Sonatas for Pianoforte and Violin, Opus 47, A-Major;
Opus 96, G-Major; Opus 30, C-Minor*
 *Sonatas for Pianoforte, Opus 7, E-Flat Major; Opus 27, E-Flat
Major; Opus 31, E-Flat Major; Opus 106, B-Flat Major; Opus
28, D-Major*
 Variations and Fugue, E-Flat Major, Opus 35
 Variations in C-Minor

Bach: *Chromatic Fantasy*
 Prelude and Fugue, G-Major (Wohltemperiertes Klavier)
 Prelude and Fugue, A-Minor, for Organ (piano arrangement by
Clara Schumann)
 Sonatas for Piano and Violin, *E-Major* and *A-Major*
 Concerto for Two Pianos, *C-Major,* with Quartet
 Sarabande and Bourrée, English Suite, A-Minor
 Sarabande and Passepied, English Suite, E-Minor
 Gavotte, English Suite, D-Minor

Brahms: *Sonatas: Opus 1, C-Major; Opus 5, F-Minor*
 Scherzi, Opus 4 and *Opus 20*
 Gavotte (in manuscript)
 Sarabande (in manuscript)
 Hungarian Dances (in manuscript)

Bargiel (Woldemar, half-brother of Clara Schumann): *Phantasies-
tück, Opus 8*

Chopin: *Nocturnes, C-Minor, Opus 48; F-Minor, Opus 55*
 Scherzo, A-Minor, Opus 20
 Impromptu, A-Sharp Major, Opus 29
 Phantasie-Impromptu, C-Sharp Minor, Opus 66
 *Waltzes, D-Sharp Major, Opus 64; C-Sharp Minor, Opus 64; A-
Sharp Major, Opus 34; A-Minor, Opus 34; A-Sharp Major, Opus
42*
 *Etudes, Opus 25: A-Sharp Major; F-Major; C-Sharp Minor; G-
Flat Major; C-Minor*
 Ballade, G-Minor
 Mazurkas, Opus 7, A-Minor; Opus 40, C-Sharp Minor

Mozart: *Sonatas* for Piano and Violin, *Opus 24: F-Major; A-Major; G-Minor; C-Minor*
  Concerto, D-Minor
  Rondo, A-Minor
  Sonata for Two Pianos, *D-Major*
  Andante
Mendelssohn: *Concerto, D-Minor*
  Sonata for Piano and Cello, *Opus 45, B-Major*
  Rondo Capriccioso, Opus 14, E-Major
  Caprice, Opus 33, E-Major
  Scherzo à Capriccio, F-Sharp Minor
Scarlatti: *Tempo di Ballo, D-Major*
  Andante, C-Minor
  Allegro Vivace, F-Minor
  Allegro, C-Major
  Allegretto, A-Minor
  Allegrissimo, G-Minor
  Presto, G-Major, A-Major
Haydn: *Sonata, G-Major*
Handel: *Suite No. 7, G-Minor*
Schumann: *Jugendalbum, Opus 68*
  Sonatas for Piano and Violin; *Opus 105, A-Minor; Opus 121, D-Minor*
  Symphonic Etudes, Opus 13
  Nachtstück, Opus 23
  Trios; Opus 110, G-Minor; Opus 80, F-Major
  Introduction and Allegro Appassionato (with Orchestra), *Opus 92*
  Phantasiestücke for Piano and Violin, *Opus 73*
  Märchenbilder for Piano and Viola, *Opus 113*
  Schlummerlied, Opus 124
  In der Nacht, Opus 12
  Jagdlied, Opus 82
  Stücke im Volkston, Piano and Cello, *Opus 102*
  Romanze, Opus 28, F-Sharp Minor
  Kreisleriana, Opus 16
  Carnaval, Opus 9
  Canons, Opus 56, A-Flat Major and A-Minor

Concerto, Opus 54, A-Minor
Davidsbündler Dances, Opus 6
Vienna Faschings-Schwank, Opus 26

In addition there was need for some encore numbers requiring superficial skill rather than serious musicianship. For this Clara chose Liszt, whom she admired but did not esteem. That is, his keyboard gymnastics staggered her as would the feats of an acrobat; her inclusion of such feats in her own repertoire was purely a concession to showmanship. Clara did not want audiences to murmur that the flashy Hungarian's technique was beyond her. It wasn't. Even so she selected none of Liszt's original compositions (she thought them abominable!) but only his transcriptions—brilliant indeed—of other people's work. In this case: Schubert's *Serenade* and the same composer's *Gretchen at the Spinning Wheel*.

Lastly, though she no longer thought well of her own compositions, she added a Clara Schumann number. It was only partly her own since the melody had been left unfinished by her husband at the time of his collapse.

Her version of this work was called *Variations, Opus 20, on a Theme by Robert Schumann*.

CHAPTER 18 In 1856 the Crimean Peace Treaty was signed in Paris. Its terms were hard on the Tsar. A permanent watch was placed by England on the Dardanelles, with international control of Danube navigation to follow. Russia's hope to sit in Europe's front parlor had thus again been dashed; she was assigned her usual place at the back door.

While the parleys were under way a brief interruption livened up the solemn conclave. On Sunday, March 16, the boom of guns from the Hôtel des Invalides (twenty-one shots, silence, and then eighty more) announced to France the birth of the Prince Imperial. After repeated miscarriages the Empress Eugénie was at last, in her third year of wedlock, delivered of a son. Congratulations arrived from many lands. Théophile Gautier wrote a poem for the occasion; Alfred de Musset, ill of heart disease, could not manage so much (he died the following year). The American novelist Henry James, vacationing in Paris with his brother William, chanced to be among the first to see the royal infant wheeled in his pram through the gardens of the Tuileries.

War clouds having been banished, the cause of art revived across the Continent. Dramatists, painters, sculptors, composers, all faced a newly avid public. In Germany music festivals dotted the calendar, especially at Düsseldorf where Jenny Lind, Joseph Joachim, Franz Liszt, and Clara Schumann formed the main attractions. The program also featured Robert Schumann's *Paradise and the Peri,* a gesture by which loyal Düsseldorfers showed their compassion for the sick composer.

Though delighted at seeing her husband so honored, Clara could not rejoice in the presence of Liszt. Her antipathy toward the wizard of the keyboard had grown to the point of intolerance. The extremely high musical standards to which she adhered made her scornful of individualistic departures from the consummate best, and Liszt was guilty of many such departures. He permitted himself pianistic somersaults that bewitched audiences and left artists of unquestionably greater worth sadly in the shade. This, Clara could not forgive. On seeing the popular Magyar perform (it was a question of *seeing*, not of *hearing*) she anathematized in her diary:

> I could weep over his abominable playing. . . . How Liszt banged the instrument, and what tempi he takes!

Another matter she took exception to was the forty-seven-year-old artist's much publicized love life. Since 1835 Liszt had paid court to a married woman, the Comtesse d'Agoult (née Marie de Flavigny), who wrote historical novels under the name of Daniel Stern and still had time to bear her lover four illegitimate children. One of her daughters, Cosima, was to marry the pianist-conductor Hans von Bülow, to leave him later for Richard Wagner.

Clara Schumann, uncompromising in issues of morality, had simply no words for such conduct. On the subject of Liszt's amours (the d'Agoult liaison had been preceded and would be followed by many others) the sacred diary was without comment.

Oddly, a cooling occurred likewise between Clara and the beloved Jenny Lind, though not on moral grounds. During her American tour in 1852 the Swedish Nightingale had married her accompanist, Otto Goldschmidt, in Boston. Clara could only rejoice over such news. But at the Düsseldorf Festival a difference arose between the Goldschmidts and herself over the music of Brahms. Clara attempted to interest Jenny in a set of *Lieder* by her protegé, only to meet with hesitant demur. Unfamiliar with Johannes, the Goldschmidts did not take readily to his difficult style. Jenny thought it sufficient risk to be singing Schumann's *Peri*, a departure from her standard and sure-fire successes. She did not want to take an additional gamble.

Brahms smiled indulgently on hearing of this. Unencumbered as yet by fame, he had humility and patience. What troubled him far more than Jenny's snub was Clara's maternal attitude, for his admiring devotion toward her had grown to a passion. Now twenty-three, he was consumed with yearnings that thrilled and shamed him. Despite his deep filial love for Robert Schumann and knowledge that his feelings for the latter's wife were inexcusable, he could not help himself.

As for Clara, her rectitude was such that she could not (or would not) take cognizance of what went on in the young man's heart. By nineteenth-century standards she belonged, at thirty-seven, among the matronly and staid. Had she for a moment considered herself alluring or seductive, the spare room in the Schumann home would certainly not have been made available to the paying lodger, Brahms. No, she never beheld in him the lovesick swain. His presence under her roof was a calculated measure, dictated by her touring plans. She needed him to look after her children and servants during the time she meant to spend abroad. Having a way with youth, he was ideally suited to the job. Also he appreciated good food and had already become a favorite with Bertha the cook.

In reply to Clara's quest for bookings, after the Düsseldorf Festival was over, answers were coming in from major cities in Germany, Austria-Hungary, Holland, Belgium, France, and England. The response astonished her. Not only had the daughter of Friedrich Wieck not been forgotten but there was sympathetic concern for the wife of Robert Schumann. People were interested in knowing how she fared since her husband's breakdown—she and all those children. Agents and entrepreneurs saw the publicity value of her situation. There would be no empty houses with her name on the billing. England in particular, where she had never played, urged that she come as soon as possible.

With some timidity she started her tour in Vienna, city of fond memories. Here she again saw the poet Grillparzer, now sixty-five and still her loyal admirer. She also met the much younger Friedrich Hebbel, working currently on a new version of the *Nibelungen* epic. Other intellectuals in her audiences (she gave five recitals in the Danube capital) imbued critics with respect and awe, though Clara had no need of their sanction. Her musicianship was on so high and compelling a plane that press and public were overwhelmed.

She was billed as the interpreter of Robert Schumann, though she would also acquaint the Viennese with the modern idiom of that musician's musician, Johannes Brahms. A courageous undertaking in the land of operettas and Strauss waltzes!

To Clara's chagrin she found her Vienna stay coinciding with a sojourn of Franz Liszt in the Danube city. The elegant Franz, it appeared, was visiting one of his newest lady friends, the Countess Nicholas Bánffy. At his instigation, indeed, Clara was entreated to give a recital at the Bánffy residence. She agreed with the understanding that this was to be a serious professional engagement. On arriving at the salon of her hostess, however, she saw herself surrounded by a horde of chattering men and women, none of whom showed the slightest inclination to quiet down. Reproachfully she turned to Liszt, who was responsible for her being there:

"I could cry over the beautiful numbers I came prepared to play— each one of them is too good for such a gathering as this!"

He smiled his handsomest before answering with irony: "Why don't you play some bad stuff of Liszt's, which would fit perfectly?"

She paid him back in kind. "You are so right, but I can't bring myself to that."

While in Vienna she paid a visit to the graves of Schubert and Beethoven, grieving at the thought of Mozart lying unknown in a pauper's ditch. On February 13, finally, she left for Budapest. Here three concerts were scheduled, at which she entranced the emotional Hungarians with her husband's *Carnaval* and Beethoven's always powerful *Appassionata*. For herself, Clara was impressed by her first contact with the gypsy orchestras she heard nightly on the Danube bank, under her balcony at the Hôtel de l'Europe. She rejoiced in the talent of these unschooled children of nature whose capacity for improvisation seemed to her miraculous. Above all, in this homeland of the violin, she thought with tender reverence of Robert's and her own good friend, Joseph Joachim, the greatest string artist since Paganini. After coming to Hungary, one understood Joachim better.

March found her playing in Prague, then Leipzig, and Dresden, where a family reunion took place under her father's roof. Friedrich Wieck had aged noticeably in the years since their last meeting. He wore a fretful look, perhaps of disappointment at having been unable to turn one of his younger children into another Clara. Yet he tactfully refrained from recalling his prediction regarding Robert's ill health and the obvious hereditary taint in the Schumann family. The tragedy borne by his daughter gave him sufficient pain. There was no need to aggravate it.

What Papa Wieck could not refrain from showing was curiosity about Clara's offspring. Did even one of them show traces of musical endowment? If so, why not give him a chance to make some tests? Why not send the older girls to Dresden for their schooling?

Clara could not but see the wisdom of such an idea. So long as she was embarking on the vagabond life of a touring artist it would be helpful indeed to know that Marie and Elise, on the threshold of adolescence, were safe in their grandfather's care. That would leave only Ludwig (now eight), Ferdinand (seven), Eugénie (five), and the baby Felix for Brahms and the servants to look after. Wieck's plan was accepted and the two older Schumann daughters were transferred to Dresden forthwith. They underwent rigorous training at the hands of their well-meaning grandparent, but no marvels resulted. Nature did not squander her gifts epidemically; she doled them out with grudging thrift.

In April of 1856 the Channel crossing to England was at hand. Clara set out with fear and trembling, for she knew neither language nor people of that island world. What correspondence had taken place between her and the Yorkshireman John Ella, manager of London's concert organization "The Musical Union," was accomplished with the aid of translators. But how was she to get on with Henry Wylde, leader of the "New Philharmonic Society," with whose orchestra she must go into rehearsal immediately on arrival? Fortunately a conductor with this group was Sir William Sterndale Bennett (another Northerner, from Sheffield) who almost two decades ago had spent a year in Leipzig and there befriended Robert Schumann. She counted on Bennett's help, since he spoke German with some fluency. She hoped likewise to make contact with Pauline García (Madame Viardot), who was singing in the English capital.

The journey from Ostend to Dover, in fog and drizzle, was appallingly dreary. Had there been a port stop midway in the Channel, Clara would have stepped off the ship and turned back. As it was, she found herself welcomed on English soil by an Ella representative who escorted her to the London train and then delivered her into the solicitous care of the Misses Busby, a pair of spinsters who ran an economical rooming house while giving piano lessons on the side.

Clara would soon learn that all Britain was in the grip of a musical frenzy. Whether this stemmed from the cultural soirées sponsored at Buckingham Palace by Albert the Prince Consort, or was an emotional reaction to the tensions of the recent Crimean War, would be difficult to ascertain. But that nerve-wracking nineteenth-century phenomenon, the drumming of piano scales in every parlor of the land, was at its peak among the allegedly lethargic islanders.

To Clara's surprise, England was well ahead of the Continent in recognizing Robert Schumann's worth as a composer. The fact that he not only created but re-created fresh new music from worn-out classic patterns, was readily accepted in the land where Dante Gabriel Rossetti and his Pre-Raphaelites were doing the same for painting, and the Algernon Charles Swinburne school of writers hoped to create a new form of English verse.

The London visit had its hazards nonetheless. The first number rehearsed by Clara with the Philharmonic was Schumann's *A-Minor Concerto, Opus 54,* under Wylde's baton. Things did not go altogether well due to differences in interpretation. An outstanding quality of Clara Wieck, as of Clara Schumann, had always been her sense of rhythm. Here she and the somewhat rigid Mr. Wylde came into conflict. Thus, during a sold-out concert on May 12, piano and orchestra lost rapport and went off suddenly in opposite directions. Clara reported to Brahms:

> . . . Incredibly, we got together again thanks to quick action by a twenty-five-year-old cellist, Antonio Piatti, who ignored the conductor's dragging beat and swept the ensemble back into line.

The evening ended in triumph, as did Clara's entire stay. During her three-month sojourn she met many hospitable Britons, and drank an unconscionable amount of tea.

Her appearances were not confined to London. At Manchester, where a German-born conductor, Karl Halle of Hagen, Westphalia, was introducing so-called "pop" concerts, Clara gladly supported the new music-for-the-masses movement. She chose her husband's lighter works, the *Childhood Scenes, Papillons, Youth Album,* and the happy *Carnaval.* All were received with unreserved enthusiasm. What satisfaction, she reflected sadly, these plaudits would have brought to the sick man at Endenich!

Back in London during early June, Clara received an invitation to Buckingham Palace. While the pianistic portion of the visit absorbed the Prince Consort, Her Majesty Victoria could not wait for the program to end so that she might engage Madame Schumann in private conversation. The Queen, herself the mother of eight, liked nothing better than to exchange data on nursery matters. Her son Bertie, the future Edward VII, had been born the same year as Clara's eldest, Marie. The Princess Royal, later Empress Frederick of Germany, was one year older. On the other hand her baby, Prince Leopold (Duke of Albany), and the last-born Schumann child, Felix, were also of equal age. With such womanly points of contact it was inevitable that "Dear Vicky" and Clara should end in happiest accord. However slight its artistic significance, the evening at Buckingham Palace wound up with the coziest of confabulations between two German hausfraus.

A few days later Victoria, who seldom appeared in public, wished to honor Clara by attending a theater presentation of Schumann's *Paradise and the Peri.* Jenny Lind was to sing, with Robert's admiring champion, Bennett, on the podium.

Clara was thrilled. But her joy turned to wretchedness within minutes as, on the night in question, the Queen's amiable gesture backfired into a near calamity. On seeing the sovereign materialize unexpectedly in the royal box, the audience succumbed to a wave of hysteria. Forgotten were the Swedish Nightingale and Schumann as, throughout the performance, binoculars and *lorgnons* were fixed ecstatically on the squablike, dimpled, jewel-bedecked Queen. Nor did the trancelike seizure soon subside. On the contrary. As the evening wore on, Clara observed countless spectators (they had ceased being listeners!) wedged sideways in their seats, so as to keep their sights focused the better on Her Majesty's box.

Beyond question, the English loved music. But they loved royalty more.

After the ordeal (to her it could be nothing else) Clara tried to slip unnoticed from the theater. But Prince Albert trapped her on the grand staircase. He had some questions of harmony and counterpoint to discuss with her. In his idle moments, the Prince Consort fancied himself a composer. He had written a chorale as well as an operetta, and was now in the throes of perpetrating an opera on the subject of the legendary Jean le Fol (John the Mad). Would Madame Schumann have the goodness to drive back to Buckingham with Albert and Vicky for a look at the embryonic masterpiece?

Clara would not. She packed her bags forthwith and departed, leaving the royal dreamer to his whim and the Queen awed by such lack of reverence. It would take the Prince Consort exactly ten years to finish *Jean le Fol*—and store it away in camphor balls.

The "opera" was never commercially produced, and few readers or listeners would identify its central character with an obscure historic personage named Bagnières de Bigorre. A certain amount of public notice did however accrue to the royal composer. "*Jean le Fol*, folderol!" chanted brash elements in the Commons when there was need of embarrassing the Queen's Lords. Also, the Scottish critic Andrew MacKenzie, who attended a private showing, was quoted soon after: "It's the triple distilled quintessence of balderdash! I fearrr for the human rrrace—"

Such commentary did not, of course, reach the ears of Albert. But the silence greeting his artistic efforts was more deadly than the sharpest ridicule.

CHAPTER 19 In looking back over her English season, which covered twenty-six concerts, Clara could be well satisfied. Aside from the *Peri* misadventure she had experienced only one other vexation, which she was able to pass off as humorous. Invited to a dinner at Lady Overstone's, Clara had been asked to favor the company with a small piano number. Politely, if reluctantly, she had acceded. The hostess thereupon had clapped her hands for silence, so as to make the corresponding announcement.

Vacant stares greeted whatever Her Ladyship had said, since this was Mayfair where voices were adenoidal and hard to make out, even by the initiated. A pause ensued as Madame Schumann stepped onto a daïs. But no sooner had she touched the keyboard than the magpie chatter, characteristic of most blueblood soirées, exploded in her ear. She played a few measures, hoping to fight noise with noise, until the indignity of such an effort shamed her. Abruptly she stopped and let her fingers rest in her lap.

The silence struck like a thunderclap. Instantly the squeals of aristocratic small talk died away as startled eyes fixed on the pianist. The audacity of it! The foreigner was sitting there, doing nothing!

Quite calm, Clara stared back. Then, carefully choosing her words in a tongue she was only beginning to master, she declared:

"Either you talk, or I play. It cannot be both."

The effect was paralyzing. Whether for love of music or because they were too flabbergasted to find speech, the assembled lords and ladies fell silent. In the beautiful peace that followed, Clara got through the *Carnaval* in brilliant fashion. The applause was earsplitting, and the next morning Madame Schumann received a letter of profuse apologies from Lady Overstone plus a basket of roses.

"If more musicians took the stand I did," wrote Clara in her diary, "our profession would earn greater respect." In summing up the experiences gained across the Channel she added: "I like the English character very much. At first there is coolness and reserve, but once these people warm to you it is forever. They have a tremendous gift for friendship."

While in London, Clara had received several reports from Endenich, most of them forwarded by Brahms. They brought distressing news. Robert was losing ground and, in the opinion of Dr. Richarz, must remain permanently institutionalized. Johannes had made several trips to the asylum but the sick man no longer recognized him. Whether or not speech-control centers of the brain were becoming affected, Schumann's silences had returned. When he became vocal at all the words were muffled and unclear, sometimes fading into mere animal whimpers. Also, though the patient showed a steady loss of weight, his feet were swollen and it was feared that he would soon become bedridden.

On July 4 Clara returned from Britain to the mainland, disembarking at Antwerp. Here Brahms awaited her, intent upon easing the shock of the Endenich news and making her homeward journey less desolate. At Düsseldorf she found her boys and the little Eugénie full of vitality and cheer. All but the toddler Felix had learned by now to do handstands; all were bound to become Düsseldorfer cartwheelers. In part, Johannes was at fault. He admitted having spent many an idle Sunday with the children in an open field, practicing gymnastic tricks.

At home again Clara had no peace. After repeated letters to Dr. Richarz begging permission to visit her husband, she tired of medical secretiveness and evasion. On July 14, without warning, she left for Bonn and thence by local coach to Endenich. At the asylum she was led straightway into the administration wing, far from the cottages harboring the sick. And now the doctor in charge spoke a hard truth:

"Your husband has not a year to live. The time will be even shorter if you insist on seeing him, as such an experience causes the patient extreme shock."

Meekly she let herself be sent away. A year. How short was a year, and without hope of meeting! Back in Düsseldorf she tried to resume teaching, for now there was no thought of traveling again. The doctors could be wrong; an improvement might occur even yet, in which case she must be on hand.

It was not to be a year. Less than a fortnight after Clara's Endenich trip a message came from Dr. Richarz. If she still wished to see her husband alive she had better come at once. If?! For two and a half years she had pleaded for a moment, an hour, a day at Robert's side. . . . And now, when they at last relented, it was done with the cynical warning that she might be too late!

Frantic with worry she rushed again to the train, this time accompanied by Johannes. It was Sunday, July 27, and they arrived in Endenich at dusk. This time there were no frustrating obstructions. Clara described the scene:

> . . . I saw him, it was in the evening between six and seven o'clock. He smiled and with greatest effort, for he could no longer command his limbs, put his arm around me—never am I going to forget this. Not for all the treasures would I trade that embrace. My Robert, it had to be thus that we should meet again, how desperately I tried to make out your beloved features; what a painful sight! Two and a half years ago you were torn from me, without farewell, and leaving such sorrow in my heart! . . . I crouched silently at his feet, hardly daring to breathe, and only now and then drawing from him a glance, befogged, yet indescribably tender. Everything around him seemed holy to me, even the air breathed by his noble self. He seemed engaged in a long dialogue with ghosts, couldn't stand people for more than short intervals, became restless and almost completely unintelligible. Once I understood 'my,' probably to be followed by 'Clara,' since he looked at me affectionately; then again, 'I know'—'you,' most likely.
>
> . . . On Monday, the 28th, Johannes and I spent the whole day there, partly with him, but often just keeping watch through the peephole in the wall. He suffered terribly, though the doctor denies this. There was a constant jerking of arms and legs, also violent talking efforts. Oh, out of love for him I begged God for release. For weeks he has taken nothing but wine and fruit jelly. Today I served him and he ate happily, with greatest haste, licking some wine from my finger—ah, he knew me. . . .

Tuesday, July 29, death came quietly at four in the afternoon. Clara and Brahms had gone to the telegraph office to send a wire to Joseph Joachim. Patients and asylum personnel were enjoying their after-lunch rest period. Thus no one witnessed the actual end.

At four-thirty Clara entered the room and beheld the still face on the pillow, the peaceful eyelids, the high, almost childlike bulge of brow. He looked handsome in death, strangely youthful, and remote. "I have no love left," wrote Clara that night. "He has taken all with him."

The burial took place two days later, at Bonn. Not many people were present since obsequies held at Endenich Chapel received little publicity. By the time Germany and the rest of the world took notice, it was all over. Clara had gathered her husband's few personal belongings, his final music notations, books, photographs of herself and the children (how puzzling, that they were not to see him, yet he had been allowed to keep their pictures!), and she had trudged homeward.

"So is all happiness gone from me with his going," she concluded the pages of their joint existence. "Another life has now begun for me."

The wrench she felt would cut even deeper into the lives of Robert Schumann's children. Already the three older daughters had known the loosening of home ties after their father's breakdown, more than two years ago. In seeking to rebuild her professional career Clara had unhesitatingly accepted the help of relatives in caring for the girls, not balking at the fact that such offers came from different cities and that the children faced an additional separation from one another. She would soon take similar steps with her three boys and the younger daughter Eugénie, again failing to see the peril of robbing them all—and much too soon—of the enfolding warmth of her own heart and hearth.

Clara herself was only a few weeks away from her thirty-seventh birthday when widowhood became her lot, and she did not possess a normal woman's fitness for the task that now lay ahead of her. For one thing, she was not by nature domestically inclined. Her extraordinary musical endowments plus the specialized education she had been subjected to in tenderest youth were hardly conducive to housewifely prowess. Nor had the early divorce of her parents, and the purely pedagogical relationship between Clara and her father, left her with any ken of mother-love or its immense importance.

What she remembered of her own childhood was achievement, fame, financial success—all attained at far too immature an age, and without any contributive emotional factor. Thus her attitude toward her brood was conscientious rather than caressing; she put intellectual development above the spiritual or purely sentimental. One must become a useful member of society. To this end she did not hesitate to shorten the fledgling years by sending her children out on their own, each into a private loneliness that—had she but known!—was to bear bitter fruit.

The first to leave the Düsseldorf family circle after Schumann's death had, of course, been Brahms. While there was still hope of a cure for Robert, the presence of a boarder under Clara's roof aroused no commentary in the town. The widowed Frau Schumann could not, however, continue indefinitely with a personable bachelor in the house. Brahms offered to grow a beard, but that would scarcely have helped. The only solution lay in his going back to his former home in Hamburg.

Clara accompanied him to the railroad station. The parting saddened her. She described her mood on walking back: "It was like returning from another funeral. . . ."

The following weeks were crammed with activity. This was good, for she dreaded nothing so much as sitting idle. There was a mountain of correspondence waiting to be answered, mostly letters of condolence from friends and well-meaning strangers.

But Clara also intended renewing professional contacts, and she began negotiating as soon as possible for the resumption of her concert tours. During early September an offer had come from Niels Gade, now conductor of the Copenhagen Music Society, for three recitals in the Danish capital. She accepted gladly. Calls came from England, too, where she was wanted for another extensive season, though not before April of the new year. Meanwhile she fretted over the handling of her two older boys. "Where to put them?" she questioned her diary. "This worries me very much, as they need masculine supervision." By mid-October she had solved the problem; Ludwig and Ferdinand were placed as boarders at the home of a private tutor named Herchenbach. Clara made mention of this in a note to her girlhood friend, Emilie List:

> . . . How much weighs on my heart, of which I want to tell you, but it must wait until we meet. Right now I am so terribly busy that my head whirls—what I must bear is often really too much. Just think, having five children boarded out in three different places, and getting their wardrobe in order for the changing seasons. . . . Such work, with the enormous correspondence, giving lessons, and pursuing my own repertoire studies. What sorrow, what desolation in my heart!

All this was unquestionably true, yet the words that gave so telling a picture of the writer's distress revealed nothing of what might be the emotional state of the five children. Emilie List gained a clear grasp of her friend's discomforts: she could visualize Clara in the act of tying clothes parcels for the offspring who were now no longer underfoot, and Clara answering letters, drilling students, practicing the concert numbers with which she would step again before the world. The "sorrow and desolation" were manifest, both in the bereaved widow and the newly burgeoning artist. It was the portrait of the mother which grew blurred.

A stream of homesick missives came from Brahms during this period. His adoration of Clara was intensified by distance. "My love for you is indescribable," he wrote on October 28, 1856. "Send me news of you, as it is my greatest joy. Farewell, my dearest beloved. Your Johannes." For years to come the tenor of his letters would be the same: loving, passionate, nostalgic. Her replies carried a dash of caution. She let her pen pour out enough sentiment to keep the altar fires burning, for she drew comfort from the worship with which he enveloped her. But there would never be a moment when Brahms was allowed to forget the indissoluble union between Clara and Robert. Johannes might adore her, but he could never have her.

To retain additional bonds of contact he interested himself continually in the children. When she complained about Ludwig and Ferdinand not taking warmly to the Herchenbachs he spouted owlish wisdom:

> What you say about today's youth makes me think of the boys of my friend Otten. He laments violently that none of them wants to study. I blame this on the fact that children are too spoiled nowadays and have nothing left to wish for. They possess every kind of toy, every kind of book. They have seen all the great paintings, in reproduction at home; the other day I absolutely could not think of a Christmas present for the youngest Otten boy. I ascribe even his pale complexion to this surfeit of good things —though he does take a lot of exercise. . . .

This plaint of a "too-muchness" in privilege and earthly possessions is the more remarkable at a time when the modern uses of electricity and mechanization were still many decades away. While Brahms wrote this harangue the automobile, telephone, phonograph, cinema, radio, airplane, television, and space rockets were nonexistent save in the imagination of a twenty-eight-year-old Frenchman from Nantes, Jules Verne.

If small schoolboys were considered blasé at Yuletide of 1856, what was to be said of them a century later?

CHAPTER 20 The year 1857 began for Clara with a concert engagement at the Leipzig Gewandhaus.

En route there she stopped in Berlin to visit the Bargiels, in whose care she had left her daughter Julie. This child, nearing her twelfth birthday, was the most similar to her mother in physical appearance. She had the same immense eyes and serene gaze, as well as the daintiness and grace, that had once characterized the young Clara Wieck. There, however, the analogy ended. Julie was a shy, withdrawn child, difficult to fathom. Toward her mother she displayed an uneasy attitude in which wistfulness and resentment played equal parts. It was plain that the girl did not comprehend or accept as valid any reasons put forth in explanation for her removal from home. "Wouldn't it be nice to stay with Grandmother?" she had been asked when first taken to Berlin. But that had been more than two years ago, and "staying with *Grossmama*" had lost its novelty.

Julie suspected by now that what had been formulated to her as a happy treat was in reality a convenience for the grownups, specifically her mother and Brahms. Her pre-adolescent mind dwelled on this subject with unwholesome insistence, until she looked upon Johannes as the plotter who had turned her into a homeless waif. The news of her father's death, coming to Julie (as it did to her older sisters in Leipzig) only as an echo from afar, increased her sense of forlornness. She had not seen Papa since he fell ill. They had not fetched her or Marie and Elise to attend his funeral.

"We're not wanted in Düsseldorf," the child told herself fiercely. "There's no place where we belong."

Julie's melodramatic exaggeration contained an element of truth, especially regarding the life her mother was embarking upon. Only now did the career of Clara Schumann begin its rush to glory. She would thenceforth be gypsy, vagabond, bright bird of passage without nesting place. The full-time role of wife, widow, mother, had ended. A new personage emerged: the priestess dedicated to but one holy office—music.

This did not mean that Clara would neglect the material welfare of her family. Her obligations in this respect had been the initial spur that drove her back to concertizing. The education of Robert Schumann's children would remain her foremost, though hardly innermost, concern.

Testimony to the latter fact can be gleaned from the mass of letters and diary pages she would one day leave behind. A musicologist's storehouse, these writings provide a record of more than seventy years of cultural development in nineteenth-century Europe as witnessed by an extraordinarily privileged individual. Clara herself is highlighted in her capacity of brilliant interpreter, formidable trouper, sublime artist.

But of the children there is little.

Only when destiny dealt harshly with them, and the individually tragic lot of each of them impinged on Clara's peace of mind, do they enter the long narrative. The diaries are rich in musical shop talk and travel minutiae but fail to mention whether a birthday celebration for one of her boys, or a coming-out party for a sister of theirs, ever took place. One fact alone stands out incontrovertibly. The memoirs of Clara Schumann admirably illustrate the artist life that is enmeshed in peripheral earthy problems but is itself essentially aloof. The dominance of such a life over its environment is often devastating; genius sometimes resembles the queen bee that must drain substance from her vassals in order to survive. It will be seen that of Clara's seven living children only one would attain belated fulfillment. Lumped together, their paltry destinies could nowhere match the plenitude of vigor and exaltation known by the titan who was their mother.

While concertizing in Leipzig, Clara had her two older girls brought over from Dresden for a reunion. She found them gangling, ill at ease, and devoid of visible talents. Both Marie and Elise had long ago grasped the aura enveloping their father's name, an aura they saw concentrated now upon the great Clara. Abashed by their own insignificance, they gloried in being linked to this awe-inspiring and applauded woman. Genetic ties being accidental at best, the young sisters saw in Clara less of the maternal being than of the goddess. Their timid love, having little to feed on, transmuted itself into the related ecstasy of worship.

The same note of worship is evident in a letter from Brahms, which reached Clara on tour. He wrote from Hamburg on New Year's Day of 1857:

> I have stopped making resolutions toward betterment, on specified days, as this is useless for me. May God merely consent to work some improvement within me, toward which I shall do my part. As to you, one can only wish for outward blessings since inwardly you have no need—you are beautiful. May I always be able to give you joy, and may I become worthy of your friendship. . . .

After a succession of engagements in Hanover, Göttingen, Elberfeld, Barmen, Cologne, Berlin, Dresden, and again Leipzig during March and April, Clara left for England. It was early in the season and things were slow. She wrote a discouraged line to her stepbrother Woldemar Bargiel:

> . . . Up to now the season is very bad. If it doesn't improve by June, I am leaving. For May I have only two dates; if I am lucky and get two more, the earnings will just cover my expenses. . . .

Nevertheless, matters picked up. June proved a profitable month for her, besides bringing a number of diverting experiences. On the eighteenth she heard Anton Rubinstein, of whom her diary says:

> He played several of his own compositions, which interested me partially as they do reveal talent, but I missed in them the charm that is also lacking in his playing. From the moment he struck the piano I was horrified at his hard touch, and I don't like his preliminary keyboard runs; it seems to me unartistic to sweep up and down the piano in galloping thirds and sixths. His technique, incidentally, is notable. We spoke of Joachim and Johannes, whom he called *Tugendpriester* [deans of virtue, because of their musical purity]—I can well believe that he has nothing in common with them. . . .

Another lasting impression would be her first visit (for a Handel festival) to London's Crystal Palace, with its seating capacity of some 25,000. Finally she attended a performance of Ernest Wilfrid Legouvé's *Médée,* with the thirty-six-year-old Italian tragedienne Adelaïda Ristori in the lead. "A marvelous artist," Clara went on record concerning Ristori, "a genius through and through. I don't understand Italian, but since Schroeder-Devrient I have not been so uplifted by an actress. . . ."

The English tour over, Clara returned to Düsseldorf where she gathered up the younger children and, with servant and governess (Joachim and Brahms would join the group later), spent the summer, till September 5, at Oberwesel and St. Goarshausen on the Rhine. Here, between hikes and picnics or boat rides, she plunged into preparation of her winter concerts.

The "middle-period" and "late" Beethoven were her present delight. She worked on four great sonatas: *Opus 28, D-Major* (Pastorale); *Opus 101, A-Major; Opus 109, E-Major;* and *Opus* 110, A-Flat Major. With the last of these she made the discovery so gratifying to most earnest musicians: the passage of years gave increasing scope and enlightenment; the genuine performing artist is never so good in youth as in his mature or, often, final years. Clara herself admitted: *"The A-Flat Major Sonata* used to appear chaotic to me, yet all at once it is wonderfully clear."

Shortly after her thirty-eighth birthday Clara pulled up stakes and moved to Berlin. If this step was dictated by a desire to live near her older daughters she thereby removed herself the more from the two boys, Ludwig and Ferdinand, who, being younger, had surely greater need of her. Her reason was actually professional. Berlin offered metropolitan advantages over the provincial town on the Rhine. With a first-rate conservatory, the Hochschule für Tonkunst, there beckoned an active musical field not only for the concertizing artist but for teachers as well. The latter fact could not be overlooked by Clara. Unless she planned to be on the road twelve months of the year—a grueling prospect!—she must consider her pedagogic possibilities. She could of course not buckle to a rigid schedule. No famous virtuoso could. But music schools and private pupils adjusted to this, aware that the celebrity of a teacher outweighed any break in curriculum. It lent prestige to say, "My voice instructor is in Milan this week, singing at La Scala." A teacher on whom the world made such demands was worth waiting for.

An apartment was readily found at Schöneberger Ufer 22. But the transfer of chattel from one town to another, this time without the help of Robert, proved more burdensome than Clara had expected. Also, arriving in Berlin as a private person rather than a publicized performer made a difference. There were the Bargiels, to be sure, and Julie, who would now live with her mother. But apart from these no one else had been informed and hence no official cognizance was taken of Clara's presence. Although she had lived in Düsseldorf only three years, and had experienced there her deepest sorrow, she now regretted having left. Berlin seemed to her cold and unutterably drab, especially as one of her best friends there, Joseph Joachim (only two years older than Brahms), was away on tour. During October a desolate letter from Clara reached Joachim in Bonn:

> God knows how miserable I feel here! I am still in the worst mess, although I've been unpacking and settling for two weeks. I feel as if I were no longer myself, not a sound [of music] lives in me. Oh, this joylessness inside me is dreadful. Berlin seems terrible to me, I think of myself as of someone in banishment. . . .

When she wrote in the same vein to Brahms he answered sternly, urging her to apply self-discipline:

> . . . You must seriously try to take care that your dismal mood does not grow excessive and interminable. Life is precious; such mental depression works powerful destruction in the body. Don't persuade yourself that life means little to you. This is not true; it is true with very few people. If you surrender completely to such moods you will also fail to enjoy whatever good things come your way. The more you strive and get the habit of taking sad times with equanimity and calm, the more you can appreciate the better days that always follow. To what end has the heavenly gift of hope been bestowed upon mankind? You don't have to be afraid of hope, since you know that happy months will follow upon the present as upon every other unpleasant period. Don't take this lightly, it is quite important. Body and soul deteriorate under prolonged dolefulness; this must absolutely be conquered or not allowed to prevail in the first place. . . . Such an unwholesome

spiritual diet as your enduring melancholia will harm body and soul, like the worst plague. You must seriously change yourself, my dearest Clara.

Do decide every morning quite earnestly and simply to be more equable and cheerful, that day as well as at all times. Passions are not natural to the human race. They are the exception and the excess. He in whom they go beyond moderation must consider himself sick, and in need of cure. . . . Composed in happiness or pain or grief is the truly beautiful person. . . .

Undoubtedly this friendly philippic contained valuable advice, but within a fortnight Clara had found a more congenial solution. An offer came for a series of concerts in several southern cities, with Munich as the final goal. She accepted forthwith. Rugs could remain rolled into a pile, curtains and curtain poles stacked in corners; Julie slept once more at Grandmother Bargiel's, while wanderlust dispelled Clara's doldrums. She enjoyed the trip to the hilt, including another of her verbal tilts with Franz Liszt, whom she ran across in Dresden. The subject was Bach, a classic perfectionist not loved by the unruly Magyar.

"All bone, no flesh," said Liszt deprecatingly.

Clara and Joachim (the latter's tour touched Dresden at the time) snapped back in unison: "Better than jelly, anyhow!"

At Munich, both triumph and calamity awaited her. The Bavarian capital had up to now given only reluctant acceptance to compositions by Schumann and Brahms which formed the bulk of Clara's programs, but this time she found warm applause, especially from fellow musicians (she played predominantly with orchestras nowadays) after a thrilling rehearsal of Robert's *A-Minor Concerto*. However, her own fire and verve in rendering this number led to a strained tendon in her left arm, and an ensuing nerve inflammation that extended from fingertips to shoulder. The accompanying pain lasted all night and grew so excruciating the following day that her second concert had to be called off. Two engagements in nearby Augsburg were also canceled.

The financial loss for Clara, involving not only the lack of box office receipts but also additional hotel bills and medical expenses, was considerable. The ailment, known in modern parlance as neuritis, seemed to be of ambiguous origin; doctors ascribed it to occupational fatigue combined with an incipient arthritic condition loosely referred to in those days as rheumatism. Ample cause existed for both deductions: pianists were prone to overwork their hand and arm muscles, while drafty and unheated nineteenth-century concert halls caused an overwhelming number of musical luminaries to complain of pain in their joints. This "ague" affected audiences as well, to such an extent that during cold weather the prudent theatergoer never doffed coat or earmuffs. Often as not he also carried a fur-lined foot bag or, in extremity, a hot water bottle.

The artist on stage had no recourse to such aids. If his wrists ached or his fingertips turned blue he could blow on them. The breath employed for this purpose would vary only slightly in temperature from the surrounding chill.

For Clara the Munich seizure proved a cruel ordeal. After a week of suffering she returned to Berlin, her pain-wracked arm in a sling.

A winter of discouragement lay ahead.

Clara's arm required absolute rest, and, for a performing artist, this was the ultimate in punishment. She chafed under the enforced idleness, as her mind was set on a concert tour through France.

By mid-January of 1858 she would thank her stars for the ailment that had kept her at home. On the fourteenth of the month, while driving with his wife to the Paris Opera for a performance of Rossini's *William Tell*, Napoleon III became the target of a bomb attack. Their majesties escaped unharmed, entering the theater minutes later with forced smiles on their lips and fluctuating heartbeats beneath their gala trappings. The city was placed under martial law.

The reason for the attack sprang from Italy's long-seething resentment of Austrian rule over the provinces of Lombardy and Venice, a matter in which French intervention was being sought. Since Napoleon was reluctant to pick a quarrel with the Habsburgs, a conspirator called Felix Orsini (disclaimed by the famous Roman family of that name) concluded that a charge of dynamite might spur France to action.

Orsini's effort won him a death sentence, but it also led to a conference between Napoleon and Count Camillo Benso di Cavour, during which a Franco-Italian alliance was formed and an acceptable pretext for war against Austria headed the agenda. Shortly thereafter a colorful freedom fighter, Giuseppe Garibaldi (he had seen service in

11

Latin America), roamed the Apennines and made fiery speeches, while armies were recruited on both sides of the Alps. Contemporarily there was born at Naples an infant later to be known as Ruggiero Leoncavallo, and at Lucca one Giacomo Puccini. But this was neither here nor there.

At Vienna the bellicose bustle could not go unnoticed. Austria's inexperienced young Emperor Franz Joseph, twenty-seven at the time, engaged in angry saber-rattling, but no one took much notice; his beautifully costumed troops, the handsomest in Europe, were considered more efficient in ballrooms than on battlefields.

The year went by with war clouds gathering darkly. At last, during April of 1859, Franz Joseph went too far. He sent an ultimatum to Cavour, giving Italy seventy-two hours to demobilize. This was a glove hurled at an enemy who had been all too eager for just such a challenge. Cavour now had his *casus belli:* the sovereign dignity of his country had been insulted. Napoleon was informed, and he decided promptly that France must take umbrage too. It was Easter Sunday when Parisians, attending Mass, heard from chancel and pulpit the shocking news that *la patrie* was now at war.

The conflict lasted only a few months. In the words of Philip Guedalla: "It has been for two centuries the misfortune of Austrian generalship to provide with victories the armies of other nations, and in 1859 its traditions were well maintained." With only moderate fighting preparation and no particular strategy the Franco-Italian allies trudged over the peninsula's dusty roads to face Habsburg might at Magenta and Solferino, where—almost by accidental collision—two battles were fought. In both cases the Austrians could be relied upon: they lost. On July 11, at dusk, Franz Joseph put his signature to the peace terms which cost him two of his fairest provinces, Lombardy and Venice, while Italy in turn would have to pay off her French helpers by handing them a neat portion of her Riviera, including the city of Nice.

Politically these events did not touch Clara Schumann deeply. She had only the vaguest notion of the issues involved, and certainly no bias toward one or the other warring party. But she and all other musicians, except those who played wind instruments and could sign up with military bands, found little demand for their talents. As in the Crimean War, public attention focused on the fray in northern

Italy, which—who could tell?—might at any moment have drawn other powers (Germany, England, Russia) into action. With such a possibility in mind few people were in the mood for entertainment. The theater, the ballet, the concert artist, all suffered losses at the box office. In France, where a Clara Schumann cycle had been under consideration, booking plans were abruptly dropped; Paris society was busy with humanitarian pursuits, foremost among which was the plucking of old linens into charpie for the binding of wounds (absorbent cotton had not yet been discovered).

In May of 1859 Clara nevertheless undertook a trip to England. John Ella, the London agent, presented her in a few recitals which were poorly visited. On June 5, the day after the battle of Magenta, she wrote to Brahms:

> All music festivals [in England] are canceled. How do things look to you? Martial? This hapless war has spoiled everything here, shopkeepers are wringing their hands. A while ago fifty firms went bankrupt in one week—

Returning home with only a slim profit which would scarcely see her through the summer, Clara faced other exasperations. One was the publication by Wasielewski of a Robert Schumann biography for which she had not given her consent. That is, the author had, soon after Robert's funeral, sought Clara's permission to inspect diaries, correspondence, and manuscripts for a study of the composer's life. She had answered evasively, stating that the burdens of widowhood were too great to afford her the proper leisure for sorting the documents involved. Since this was not an outright objection to Wasielewski's purpose, he went ahead with such material as he could lay hands on, namely, quotations of his own (he had known Schumann for many years), letters from colleagues and music publishers, some vital statistics obtained in Robert's birthplace of Zwickau, and a fairly accurate report of the last days at the Endenich asylum.

The resulting book was sadly incomplete. Also, its tone disappointed Clara. Her adoring heart demanded that the departed be spoken of worshipfully. Wasielewski was a sincere Schumann admirer, but he wielded nevertheless an objective and by no means uncritical pen. In indignation Clara considered bringing suit for libel, besides seeking an injunction to stop further printings. But Brahms pointed out the folly of such action. To prove Wasielewski wrong would have necessitated disclosing many private matters, particularly concerning Robert's illness, which the general public did not know. Also, the long feud with Papa Wieck during Schumann's courting days would become glaringly exposed. Clara would regret this since she was now at peace with her father. In short, Johannes urged that the whole matter be forgotten. *Schwamm drüber!* ("Wipe it off the slate with a wet sponge!")

A different problem, not to be put aside lightly, confronted Clara with her daughter Julie. The girl showed an early desire for independence. Now fourteen, she aspired to become a singer (she scorned any thought of competing with her mother in the pianistic field, even if she had possessed the talent). But after a term at the Berlin Conservatory it became evident that something was wrong with Julie's lungs. Doctors diagnosed incipient tuberculosis, and recommended a southern climate.

What to do? Clara had just begun to take root in Berlin, where Joseph Joachim had recently accepted a permanent job as orchestra conductor. Through this most loyal of friends her own prospects for the coming season would be greatly enhanced. Apart from local engagements she might obtain a well-paid teaching post at the Hochschule. With such negotiations already under way, she had summoned her daughters Marie and Elise to join her Berlin household. Julie, now no longer at the Bargiels, was to become reacquainted with her older sisters.

The medical report threw these plans overboard. A place must be found where Julie might absorb sunshine and, above all, have proper therapeutic care. This would take money. Clara must go on tour again. Even as she corresponded with concert organizations in German cities (Leipzig, Dresden, Hamburg, Düsseldorf, Vienna, Amsterdam) where she was always certain of a welcome, news came from Jena that her two boys—Ludwig and Ferdinand—were unruly problems for the boarding school in which they had been placed. The principal of the institution requested their removal at the earliest convenient date.

What was wrong with the boys? For some time Clara had known that her son Ludwig differed from other children both in temperament and mental reactions. He was affectionate and had great charm, but could not adjust to life away from home. In consequence he learned poorly and lagged behind the younger and more easy-going Ferdinand. Educators of that day, however, did not concern themselves with differences in personalities. They judged their charges along a uniform pattern, fixed for all. By this standard Ludwig was found backward, a case of mental retardation. Clara was advised to put him under special tutelage.

This she could not bring herself to do. The boys, only eleven and ten respectively, ought not to be separated as yet. She had seen, to her rue, that Julie and the older girls would have fared better if they had been left united. Julie's tart sullenness, even her lung ailment, might perhaps not have developed in the comforting presence of her sisters. In any case, so long as the boys could not remain in Jena, Clara sent them to a private school in Bonn, run by a Dr. Breusing. At the same time she wrote some friends in Switzerland, the Schlumberger family, regarding a place where Julie might receive treatment. To her relief the Schlumbergers answered at once, offering to take the girl into their home; perhaps all Julie needed was mountain air, in the ozone-laden Alpine woodlands. Should medical attention still be required, this too would be furnished. The Swiss were specialists in the treatment of tuberculosis.

With these problems temporarily solved, Clara spent the balance of 1859 and most of 1860 on increasingly extensive concert tours. Her frame of mind was not optimistic, however. On February 5, 1860, she learned of the death (in Coburg, at the age of fifty-six) of the fervently admired soprano Schroeder-Devrient. The latter had abandoned three husbands and four children, and had spent the past decade in a vain struggle to retain her eminence despite a fading voice. Finally, incurably ill, she had retired to Saxony where her third husband—the Latvian Dr. von Bock—nursed her with tenderness and utmost abnegation. Clara mentioned the sad finish in her diary:

> . . . The news of the death of Schroeder-Devrient has deeply shaken me. Still, I must deem her fortunate in passing away, for she outlived herself and that was something she could not stand. May heaven spare me such misery, for I should be unspeakably wretched if I could not continue an artist's life in fullest vigor. Therefore, just not to grow old! There was only one for whom I would have wished to face decline; for him, who was dearest, I could have renounced outward success, finding my heart amply

rewarded in its dedication to *his* art and *his* whole being. But he lives no more. . . . People often say I have, after all, my children! True enough, and surely I feel as strongly as any mother the bonds that still tie me to earth—but only until they are educated and can stand on their own feet, when each will go a separate way and my later years will see me alone. . . . This I shall not be able to endure. My need for love is too great, since it makes daily living bearable; without love all vitality would drain from me!

It was extraordinary that she should be so aware of her own emotional hunger without recognizing the far greater need, in this respect, of her own children. Again, by her own testimony, their "education" was all that mattered. She had to work and earn sufficient money to set them up "on their own feet." But there is no trace of deeper concern with such imponderables as the spiritual development of her brood. When a mother is in the public eye it is particularly important to protect her children from developing acute inhibitions: Clara's daughters should not have been made to feel overshadowed, nor her sons rendered shy and inept, by the effulgence of the parental genius. Yet this is exactly what was happening. Great artists live, and cannot but live, unto themselves. It was Clara's personally believed fiction that had Robert Schumann survived she would have dedicated herself to him to the point of self-effacement. Nothing could be more preposterous. Had she not, in the early years of her marriage, been tethered by almost uninterrupted pregnancies, it is certain that the potency of her talent would have driven her from hearth and home to seek fulfillment in the world outside. The gifts of excellence are bestowed on those with fortitude to bear them, since the weak would cast them thoughtlessly aside. If Clara Wieck was never weak, the wife of Robert Schumann would be even less so.

She had sporadic periods of maternal solicitude. July of 1860 was one of these. During the slack musical season Clara had chosen the small Rhineland spa of Kreuznach for a rest, and she gathered all her children—save the two elder boys—about her. With commendable industry she gave them daily piano lessons, noting with pleasure that Marie and Elise had gained notable proficiency under the guidance of their grandfather. Even Julie, much improved in health (she had enjoyed a holiday with the Schlumbergers on the French Riviera), showed pianistic aptitude. But Clara was not misled. She knew the limits beyond which the trio would not go. In her correspondence with the faithful Emilie List she declared:

> The three girls play very nicely, having great talent for teaching; I would like to help them a lot more if only we could always be together. At present, here [in Kreuznach], I teach them quite regularly, but there's always the question of finding the time. . . .

Late that month Brahms and Joachim made a Rhine journey. They stopped to see Clara for a few days. How long since Johannes had played nursemaid to the younger Schumanns! Marie and Elise were grown young ladies, and Julie, at fifteen, unquestionably had become the beauty of the family.

Shyness overcame all three girls on meeting their former companion who, now twenty-seven, had achieved world renown. This was the Brahms of the ineffably beautiful *Sextet in B-Flat Major, Opus 18,* (two violins, two violas, two cellos), due to have its première that year before the blind King Georg of Hanover. The second movement of this work, developed from the composer's earlier *Variations in D-Minor,* was purest melodic sorcery. It would be used as tonal background, a century later, in a prize-winning French motion picture called *Les Amants.* It would be difficult to find a cadence more spellbinding or so finely attuned to love.

Although the *Sextet* is without dedication it was clearly written for her whom Brahms venerated above all others: Robert Schumann's widow. Months earlier he had sent her a piano version of its principal themes, which she delighted in. Nor was she stinting with praise. But her reaction was aesthetic, impersonal, rather than passionate. She continued to regard the loving and beloved Johannes not as an ardent suitor but as her always cherished older son.

Brahms had suffered long and poignantly under this. Now for the first time, at Kreuznach, his torment was eased. For here his eyes beheld a vision that overwhelmed him: the semblance, in the flower of youth, of her who over endless years had denied herself to him.

For the first time Clara's image emerged in unfavorable perspective, with the true outlines of a forty-year-old matron.

His eyes fixed on Julie.

CHAPTER 21   Johannes Brahms belonged to the generation of masterful males who liked their women weak. His passion for Clara had been inspired by pity over the suffering she faced through her husband's illness. With Robert Schumann's death the ardent youth saw himself as the widow's shield against a harsh world. Little did he suspect her strength and self-sufficiency, or that she, the matriarch, could look upon him only as upon another son. Years of sterile longing had gone by, a longing sustained with fervent letters that poured from him in an endless flood, yet never—like Swinburne's "weariest river"—wound "somewhere safe to sea."

He was not himself aware of the moment when his devotion to Clara was transmuted into love for Julie. The second-elder sister Elise, herself deeply fond of Johannes, was the first to notice. She kept the discovery a secret, pining in silence until the opportunity of taking a job away from the family gave her release; a certain Frau Böcking of Kreuznach accepted Elise as companion-housekeeper in her home. At the same time an offer came from Clara's friend, Frau von Pacher (a sister of Emilie List), to take Julie under her wing. As the Pacher villa near Munich assured the girl of amenities not otherwise attainable, Clara agreed. Her one concern was to see all her children safely housed and cared for by end of summer, as the concert season would soon begin and she must bestir herself to replenish the family purse. It never occurred to her that the move would bring sorrow to Brahms.

The education of the littlest ones, Eugénie and Felix, began to demand more attention. For the first time Clara thought she had reason to believe one of her children exceptionally endowed; the six-year-old Felix showed an early love and aptitude for music. She expressed herself to the governess, Elisabeth Werner:

"Will this decide his future? Will music bring him happiness? How wonderful it would be to have one of the children follow the trail of their father."

However, she had no time to dwell further on that joyful prospect. Ludwig and Ferdinand had to be separated at last since all the educators consulted thus far agreed that they needed different handling. Ferdinand was therefore placed in a regular boarding school while Ludwig came under the tutelage of a Lutheran pastor named Altgelt.

Private harassments left Clara unaware of major events stirring the world outside. In America an important election campaign had ended with Abraham Lincoln gaining the presidency; he would be inaugurated early the following year, and the United States soon after would face the outbreak of the Civil War. Smaller storms occurred also in smaller teapots. In March of 1861 a story was carried by German newspapers concerning the fiasco, in Paris, of Wagner's opera *Tannhäuser*. Hoots and catcalls had interrupted the performance (witnessed by Napoleon and Eugénie from the royal box), and the affair had ended in a missile-throwing tilt between audience and singers on stage.

The news drew no lament from Clara Schumann. She continued to regard Wagner and the Wagner cult as an abomination. "Bravo for those French," she cheered, "they want no part of that noisy charlatan!" In opera she held with Gluck, Mozart, Beethoven; the latter's *Fidelio* with its theme of marital fidelity was to her, both musically and ethically, the art work supreme. She had less use for the Italian school of Rossini, Donizetti, Verdi. "Such screaming!" was her verdict here.

Along with the *Tannhäuser* report a hushed-up horror tale escaped from Paris by grapevine. Henri Murger, author of *Scenes of Bohemian Life* (on which, a generation later, Puccini's *La Bohème* would be based), had died in January of a mystifying disease. Over a period of time his nose and cheeks had strangely disintegrated until one morning, as he brushed his mustache, part of his upper lip came off. People had as yet no knowledge of cancer; its study was just beginning. Rumor spread that Murger had contracted leprosy while on the Marseilles waterfront seeking local color for a story. In any case, his misfortune caused tourists and artists (Clara Schumann among them) to avoid Paris for the better part of that season.

In avoiding France, Clara also did not cross the Channel during

1861. But in April of 1862 (the year of Jacques Halévy's death and Claude Debussy's birth) her faithful English public again rejoiced in welcoming her. She returned by way of Paris, still somewhat uneasily, and fulfilled a number of postponed commitments. For the summer holidays she would choose Baden-Baden.

It was here, in July, that Clara arrived at an important decision. Since lodgings were always hard to find (hotels and tourists were not yet big business), she had long toyed with the idea of investing in some property. Now, as she strolled one afternoon along the verdant outskirts of the town, a roomy cottage surrounded by trees and a rose garden caught her eye. It was for sale, and the price appeared reasonable. She made a bid for it, which was accepted. On August 1 her diary contained the following entry:

> Inasmuch as I travel all winter it would certainly be sensible to have a fixed home for the summers, where I could periodically gather the children around me. The life I currently lead is awful, never feeling at home anywhere nor finding time or concentration for my studies. Here in Baden I would have beautiful surroundings as well as artistic contacts, since everybody comes here— maybe even in too great numbers.

When the transaction had been concluded (the cost was 14,000 *Gulden,* or approximately 3,000 American dollars) she wrote to Joseph Joachim on October 8, 1862:

> Since I don't want you to hear this through the gossipers, who snap up everything fast, you are herewith informed that I have just left Baden after buying, in the Avenue Lichtenthal (Number 14), a modest but nice little house, into which I shall move in April of '63 with my whole family, to spend most of the summer with the children, and then continue traveling as always or perhaps choosing Vienna or Paris for winter headquarters. For three months I have been harboring this plan, which needed careful reflection, hence I did not want to speak of it until all was resolved. Thus you and Fräulein Leser [in Düsseldorf] hear the news first—I am writing Johannes in the next few days. I concluded the purchase myself, yesterday in Baden, and hope this decision will bring me many advantages and satisfactions. I can give lessons there in the summertime, with good earnings, while enjoying such a wonderful natural setting! I am so excited, I can hardly write, there is so much pressing upon my soul! A new home, what will it bring me?

While Clara was thus rejoicing in her freshly planted roots there came from Brahms a bitter lament. For the second time he had suffered disdain in his native city of Hamburg. After having been refused the post of philharmonic conductor some years ago, he had recently been under consideration for a subordinate job (assistant conductor) at the Sing Akademie. The matter appeared practically settled when, at the last moment, a slightly older man named Ludwig Deppe was chosen. There was in this not nearly so great an affront as Brahms insisted. The alternate candidate presented himself very late in the proceedings and had been rejected when someone reviewed his qualifications as a mere formality; it was then discovered that Deppe had notable teaching experience whereas Brahms was regarded primarily a composer. The selection therefore was dictated by prudence, not malice.

Johannes received the news by mail while on tour in Austria. It put a definite end to his dreams of returning to Hamburg to live. He complained to Clara in a letter from Vienna, dated November 18:

> This is a much sadder blow to me than you think or can perhaps understand. Just as I am a somewhat old-fashioned person I also don't belong among cosmopolites, for I love my native city as one does a mother. Now you must know that since autumn the Sing Akademie seriously looked for a second conductor. Before I left on tour (Deppe and I had been under consideration) the proposition was privately put up to me. . . . How seldom do we in our profession find a permanent post, and how gladly I should have accepted it in my birthplace.
>
> At present, here in Vienna—where there is so much beauty in which to rejoice—I feel and shall always feel myself a stranger, without peace. You probably have already heard about the Hamburg affair and have thought of me without realizing how deeply I have been hurt. But it isn't difficult to see how much is lost to me. If Vienna does not satisfy my longing, what place can? You saw with your husband what it is to be left adrift, alone and far away, when one wants to be tied down, achieving the things that make life worth living—for one is afraid of loneliness. To work companionably and surrounded by a happy family—who is so inhuman as not to crave this? . . .

Clara comforted him by pointing out that the Hamburg disillusion must be looked upon as a mark of recognition. Johannes ranked too high as concert artist and composer to lose himself in the anonymous herd of conservatory teachers. The true creator made a poor jobholder.

On the personal (and sentimental) side she thought it time to deal out some advice: Brahms was twenty-nine and ought long ago to have married. He had good looks, sufficient savings to support a bride, and the kind of talent that vouchsafed a brilliant future. What was more, Clara knew of a girl named Agatha von Siebold, who had heard Brahms play in Osnabrück and since then was bombarding him with ardent letters. Why did he not take Agatha to wife? And if not Agatha, why not the daughter of his Vienna landlord? Brahms had commented on the latter girl's prettiness in a recent postscript. To clinch her words of counsel, Clara added a quotation from Robert Schumann's notebooks:

> *. . . Nimmt ein liebes Weib man sich,*
> *in jeder Stadt*
> *den Himmel man hat!*°

Johannes agreed. But he did not want Agatha, nor his amiable landlord's equally amiable daughter. His heart was torn between two impossible goals: the love of Clara, who was fourteen years older than himself, and that of Julie, twelve years his junior. While his emotional life remained thus throttled there came a surprise announcement from Joseph Joachim. At thirty-one the latter had become engaged, in February of 1863, to the young operatic soprano Amalie Weiss (her real name was Schneeweiss, i.e., "Snow White").

"There you are," Clara wrote Johannes, "Joachim has set you a proper example!"

But she triumphed too soon. The marriage turned out unhappily due to career rivalries, and was destined to end in divorce. As an example it served only to confirm Brahms in his bachelorhood. Besides, he was very busy nowadays on a new work for strings, of which a rumor reached Clara. She sent him an impatient note:

> What is this I hear about a *C-Minor Sextet!?* Will you not, dear friend, send it to me? Or am I to be left in ignorance of it?

° . . . If you take a loving wife,
in every town
you've a heavenly life!

The composition was his second sextet, *Opus 36,* one of the finest things ever to come from the pen of Johannes Brahms. He wrote it at a time of heartache and spiritual confusion. Had his musical output stopped with this masterpiece and its counterpart, *Opus 18,* his place among the immortals would already have remained assured.

But there was more, much more, to come. Forming the high point of the creative triangle Robert Schumann-Clara Schumann-Johannes Brahms (Clara was not a simple interpreter but, in the best sense, a creative one), Brahms alone raised the work of his partners-in-art to fullest flowering. That is, he had the scope not reached by either but grasped and initiated by both. Brahms completed the step foreshadowed by Beethoven, going from the strict purity and mathematical perfection of Bach, Mozart, and Haydn to the liberation of rhythm. This liberation gave emphasis to spiritual content, hitherto fettered by metrical limits.

The change was dictated by an inner need of the age, and it bespoke organic growth no less than psychic. In painting the phenomenon was being called Impressionism. Its disciples scandalized the current art world with their daring projection of life, light, action, mood. Contemporary masters of the new brush magic imparted to canvas not only the shimmer of sunshine but a sensation of heat, a feat Rembrandt himself never achieved. No classic artist heretofore had ventured beyond rule-bound limits of portraiture. The sensory effects commanded by the present crop of young painters (they were all in their thirties or under) would forever consecrate their names: Camille Pissarro, Edouard Manet, Edgar Degas, Paul Cézanne, Claude Monet, Pierre-Auguste Renoir. The best of them, Paul Gauguin (aged fifteen at this time) and Vincent van Gogh (ten), were still toying with school crayons, unconscious of their rendezvous with destiny.

In literature the Goncourt brothers, Edmond and Jules (the former was to institute the Prix Goncourt) embodied the same movement, variously qualified as naturalism or modernism, but for which they furnished title and definition:

> *Impressionnisme—forme d'art, de littérature, et de musique qui consiste à rendre purement l'impression telle qu'elle a été matériellement ressentie.**

---

* Impressionism—a form of art, literature, and music in which an impression is rendered with the truthfulness one has actually experienced.

This was far removed from the pretty-prettiness into which Classicism had drifted. It conceded that the great works of the past would live on, losing none of their eloquence and dignity. But mere formalism and imitation were doomed.

No one knew this better than Johannes Brahms. To him the essence of music lay not in its literal effects, such as the simulated patter of rain, the chirping of crickets, or what passed for whispering forest sounds. These sensations should be experienced in nature at first hand. Why bother with feeble approximations? In short, Impressionism was to Brahms an abstract concept, and therefore Brahms must be listened to with the soul as well as the physical ear. He is the supreme master of abstract music.

Herein lies no implication of esoteric dissonance. Quite the contrary: Brahms had a royal gift for melody, felicitous, highly original, never trite. To him the words of one of the subtlest American humorists (Kin Hubbard, who disguised himself as a rustic character named Abe Martin) could not be applied: "I don't like music we keep hoping will turn into a tune." All of Brahms is just that: tune that does not deteriorate into ditty.

A musician's musician, he seldom wrote anything "easy." Nor did respect for tradition prevent his taking bold liberties with structure and timing. To structure and timing he gave new facets that startle and challenge the performer, especially the pianist. Here was revealed a credo: his would never be stock, pastime music, grown quickly hackneyed through the thumping of dull amateurs. Few amateurs indeed will tackle Brahms, for he is of the élite.

There may be even those who protest: "Correction. He *is* the élite!"

The house in Baden-Baden gave Clara
CHAPTER 22   many years of serene contentment. It
served as a retreat for intense study
between her long and exhausting concert tours, and also as a haven
where she could periodically gather the children about her for a sample
(it was never much more than that) of family life.

Little is known of Clara's taste in furnishings, but her correspondence
mentions that the cottage could not accommodate two grand pianos;
hence, for a second instrument, she chose a pianino or upright. Incidentally, recognized artists of her time enjoyed great advantages in this
respect. Important firms put pianos at their disposal, either at nominal
cost or entirely free, because of the publicity returns. Even for her
daughters, untouched by fame, Clara would repeatedly be able to
make use of this privilege.

The eldest and least attractive of the girls, Marie, had gradually
taken over the role of secretary-housekeeper, when she did not serve
as her mother's travel companion at home and abroad. In March of
1864 Clara undertook another trip to Russia which, with the self-
effacing Marie at her side, proved far more satisfactory than the visit,
years ago, with Robert. The Channel crossings to England were likewise eased by the devoted handmaiden who, apart from industry and
competence, overflowed with daughterly solicitude; quite naturally
Marie seemed to find in these ministrations her fore-ordained purpose.
At twenty-three it could be easily guessed that she was destined to
remain a spinster.

Clara was being increasingly approached by people of fashion for
private lessons in piano and composition. Among her summer pupils
at Baden-Baden was the young Princess Elisabeth von Wied, later
Queen of Rumania (through her marriage to Carol I, a Catholic Hohen-

zollern-Sigmaringen invited to the throne at Bucharest in 1881). Elisabeth had lived with her widowed mother at Neu-Wied on the Rhine, dreaming of a musical career. Her real talent did not, however, lie in this direction. The time would come when, after having given an heir to the newly-founded Rumanian dynasty, Elisabeth would turn to literary endeavors. Under the pen name of Carmen Silva she was to publish some quite acceptable poetry as well as a collection of exotic fairy tales.

Clara had other royal pupils, among them a Princess of Prussia, a second of Hesse, and one of Lippe-Detmold. These three were less gifted than they were determined, and their keyboard banging gave listeners many an hour of torment. But the pay was excellent and Clara could not afford to hold aloof. Similarly she was often asked to the court of the aging blind King Georg of Brunswick-Hanover, for private recitals in which Brahms and Joachim likewise took part.

In her private life Clara faced graver tests. Following a consultation with a Swiss doctor named Lazarus she learned that her son Ludwig showed definite psychotic aberrations and must be confined in a mental institution. Soon after, it was found that her youngest son Felix, the only outstandingly talented among her children, had the same pulmonary affliction as Julie. The boy needed immediate attention since he was only ten when the disease first showed itself, and the lung damage seemed already considerable. Added to this worry was the fact that Felix lagged behind in school, since he lived in the grip of only one overwhelming obsession, the study of music; it was the violin, not the piano, that absorbed him.

During 1867, while Felix was at his grandmother's in Berlin, Clara wrote cautiously on this subject:

> : . . There is something burdening my heart, about which I must talk to you in particular. Grandmother and Ferdinand write me that you think constantly about becoming a violinist; that would be a big step, far more difficult than you may believe. No matter how good a violinist you might become, if you did not achieve *eminence* you will remain insignificant because you are the son of Robert Schumann. You can live up to that name only if, in music, you give evidence of extraordinary genius—and with it an enormous capacity for work. Now, although I am convinced that your talent suffices for amateur purposes and to give pleasure to others (even to this end one must be industrious) I do not believe you have in you what is required for highest artistry.

Therefore do consider carefully, my dear Felix. You have other fine gifts which will open up many paths, allowing you to become outstanding in any field you choose, though none will be possible without serious study. It is certain in any case that greater honor will accrue to you in the world with any career save that of artist. People like Herr de Ahna (an idealistic teacher) can easily say "become a musician!" I know from almost forty years of experience what it takes; for this reason I have always suppressed the desire to make one of you follow in my footsteps. . . . Even so, for your peace of mind and my own, I shall have Herr Joachim test you. . . . He will be the best and most impartial judge. What do you think of this? Write me your opinion.

At the time Felix received this maternal admonition he was thirteen and undergoing medical treatment. Clara thought it unwise to focus on his illness as the main obstacle to a musical career. From personal knowledge she realized that the performing virtuoso, even more than the composer in his retreat, must possess indestructible health. For this reason she regretfully minimized the musical heritage which was by no means negligible in her youngest son. She knew quite simply that a life patterned after her own would mean an early death for Felix. To tell him so was cruel and demoralizing. Far better to discourage his artistic leanings and steer him toward a safer profession. To do this she must hurt him. But not to hurt him would almost surely be fatal.

While worrying about Felix, Clara was by no means at ease regarding the welfare of her daughter Julie. In August of that same year the girl had come to Baden-Baden with symptoms of a new relapse. A line in Clara's diary states: "Julie excites pity to behold, so wretched does she look."

Again the kindly Frau Schlumberger came to the rescue. She offered to take the girl to Divonne-les-Bains, a French spa dedicated to cold-water therapy, the craze of the age. Years ago this kind of "cure," Clara might have remembered, had done her own husband no good. But mankind is ruled by fashions, and the current fashion was elegantly called *l'hydrothérapique*.

Julie stayed at Divonne most of that year. By Christmas of 1867 her condition had become so aggravated that she was bedfast and Clara was summoned to her side. The trip through the center of France proved strenuous and overshadowed by anxiety, yet it had its light moments; en route Clara managed to stop in Karlsruhe (nothing ever really defeats a genuine musician!) to attend a performance of Robert

Schumann's so-so opera *Genoveva*. The date was January 3, 1868. By the sixth, returning from Divonne, Clara reported to her friend Rosalie Leser:

> The performance of *Genoveva* was magnificent, and one of the greatest treats I have had in years. What all went through my mind—since, after all, a large part of my life is enmeshed with this work! It was extraordinarily beautiful, leaving me to puzzle all evening and even now about some nice thing I might do for Levi [the conductor].

That same day, in reply to a worried letter from Brahms regarding matters at Divonne, Clara stressed the impossibility of bringing Julie home; the girl was too ill to be moved. The very next morning the indomitable Madame Schumann traveled to Belgium; at Brussels and Antwerp she gave two of the most notable concerts of her career, then set out, on January 24, on another triumphant tour of England.

Johannes meanwhile underwent spiritual torment. His unclear attachment to mother and daughter had crystallized, fixing with ardor upon Julie. He made no secret of this. Aware for a long time that Clara's feeling for him remained irrevocably maternal, he confided in her now with filial candor. On February 2, 1868, he begged her for more urgent action in behalf of Julie, "that poor girl, of whom I can't think without rapture, now so far away and ill. . . ."

Brahms had been at work for some time on a religious choral composition to be titled *German Requiem*. Its text, contrary to custom, was not in Latin but taken from the vernacular of Martin Luther's Bible. While occupied with such sacred matters he received a preposterous report from home: his aging parents were getting divorced. Papa Brahms, so went the sad tidings, had strayed into the snares of another woman.

Johannes blamed his mother for the not uncomical situation. After a long and harmonious marriage during which the elder Brahms had been a model husband there happened upon the scene, introduced by Mama Brahms herself, a gracious and highly cultured widow. To please his wife, Herr Brahms treated the lady with deference, nay, affability. What followed was characteristic of wifely reaction everywhere: the very friendship she had instigated became now for Frau Brahms a goad to fiercest jealousy. Teasingly at first, then with a waspish sting, she cast a distorted light upon her Jakob's quite artless urbanity. More than that, the widow she had herself embraced as bosom friend, appeared to her now a dangerous Circe.

On visits home during his concert tours Johannes had observed a changed atmosphere under the paternal roof. His mother had turned into a snapping termagant, while Papa Brahms, stimulated by the so far unfounded accusations against him, began believing that there survived in his seedy person some trace of tempestuous youth. In short, he thought himself irresistible, a view in which the naughty widow more than supported him.

The lamentable result was now at hand. Johannes could not but admit that his mother's pigheadedness had driven matters to the extreme, namely a divorce in which she had the most to lose. He also blamed his sister Elisabeth who, well past thirty and unmarried, had taken a faded virgin's hostile attitude toward her father. Now mother and daughter alone, submerged in despair. The emancipated Jakob on the other hand was anything but forsaken; the widow had opened her house and arms to him.

The drama did not end there. A short time after these events Mama Brahms took to her bed and died, aged seventy-six, perhaps of remorse and heartbreak. Johannes rushed to Hamburg for the burial. On this occasion he met his father's lady friend of whom, admittedly, he gained an excellent impression. When, some months later, Papa Brahms and the widow were married, Johannes approved. The late Frau Brahms might turn in her grave, but her son had to concede that his father was showing rare good judgment.

A cheery epilogue followed soon after in that Elisabeth Brahms, liberated from her mother's strangling devotion, found herself at loose ends in a dangerously exciting world. For the first time in her life she was forced to stand alone, and since no one now required her daughterly ministrations she had nothing but time on her hands. Briefly, Elisabeth went out to look for work.

In so doing she rediscovered her unlived youth. She stumbled across a timid bachelor whom she conquered forthwith despite her vestal inexperience. The next thing Johannes heard, his sister was married and —not long thereafter—properly with child.

By having had the grace to die, Mama Brahms managed to do a considerable amount of good.

CHAPTER 23 In the manner of lecturers, theater companies on tour, traveling salesmen, and other professional gypsy folk, Clara Schumann complained throughout her life about the hardships of "the road." Yet fundamentally she could not endure being long at rest. The pretty cottage at Baden-Baden delighted her so long as it was a novelty, but she soon admitted to Johannes that its idyllic quiet put her nerves on edge. She had bought the place with a view to spending her summers there, devoted to study and the re-acquaintance with her scattered children. Actually, however, the family was reunited only for a few weeks at a time, with the old schedule of hopping to Switzerland, Italy, Austria or the Bavarian Alps dominating the idle season. As the sailor who has longed for port can't wait to put to sea again, or the grounded aviator frets for his lost wings, so Clara—having attained serenity—did not know what to do with it. It was this fact which proved so disastrous for her children: lacking a true and lasting refuge, an anchor, they successively broke down.

During 1869 the mental state of Ludwig Schumann (he was now twenty-one) had become greatly aggravated. Clara had not heeded the dictum of Professor Lazarus regarding permanent commitment to an asylum. Instead, the youth had been apprenticed with the publishing firm of Breitkopf and Härtel, at Leipzig, where he was handled with special indulgence and consideration. This proved only a temporary solution, as Raimund Härtel soon informed Clara that her son would remain forever unemployable. Like Lazarus, he urged internment.

To Clara such a thought was horrifying. It revived memories of Robert's last illness besides underscoring the rumor heard in the days of Clara's courtship regarding insanity in the Schumann family. Ludwig in a madhouse? No, this must be put off as long as possible.

Defiantly she hit upon an eccentric plan. She would send the boy to his grandfather—yes, to Friedrich Wieck at Dresden. There, in the lion's den, Ludwig would be aroused—out of sheer fright—to show himself at his best. The famous Wieck discipline would make a man of him. Why hadn't she thought of this before? Surely here was all that would be needed.

Alas, she couldn't have been more wrong. Ludwig was, and had been for some time, a man. A very sick man. Nothing Papa Wieck could do would change the pathological picture. In unvarnished terms Clara heard the truth for the third time. And now she could procrastinate no longer. With heavy heart she allowed her father to escort Ludwig to a psychiatric hospital at Colditz. It was high time. A feeble-minded adult in the full vigor of physical manhood was a danger to others no less than to himself.

From Julie at Divonne there came, happily, much better news. In the picturesque spa she had made the acquaintance of an aristocratic Italian widower with two small daughters, Count Vittorio Radicati di Marmorito, who within seven weeks of daily association declared his love for her. In a letter to her mother the erstwhile declining Julie appeared joyous and brimful of health. The young people begged for Clara's approval of their engagement, though—at twenty-four—the girl was legally entitled to make her own decisions.

Clara's reaction was one of alarm. Having baptized her children in the Lutheran faith, she could not look with favor on a mixed marriage, especially to a Roman Catholic. Furthermore, a poor linguist herself, she knew that she would never be able to converse at ease with an Italian son-in-law. Then there was the discrepancy in social station, even if Clara could not admit a cultural or an intellectual one. What sort of "countess" would Julie make? How were they all, in the family and within Clara's circle of musical colleagues, to get along with a fellow hampered by a title?

In her diary the troubled mother gave expression to her doubts:

> . . . I have told her [Julie] all my misgivings, though more to ease my own conscience, since love will not be thwarted; this I know from my personal experience! Seldom has anyone had more obstacles to surmount than did my dear Robert and I!

Her surmise was correct. Even over objections from the Marmorito clan in Torino the lovers became engaged on June 11, 1869. At Baden-Baden, where he stopped for a visit after a performance of his *Requiem* at Karlsruhe, Johannes Brahms received the news. Clara described his bafflement:

> ... He seemed to have expected nothing of the sort, and was completely shocked.

Julie had rejoined her family during these days, which led to almost unbearable tensions. Brahms had taken rooms at the nearby lodging house of a Frau Becker, and he now froze into miserable silence at sight of the happy young betrothed. On July 16 (why did he not jump on a train and leave?) Clara's diary complained:

> Johannes is a changed man. He seldom drops by, and then shows himself taciturn even toward Julie whom he formerly treated with such affection. Could it be that he truly loved her? Yet he was never marriage-minded, nor did Julie harbor deeper feelings for him. ...

A month later Clara wrote to her friend Rosalie Leser at Düsseldorf:

> From the moment I told Johannes about Julie's engagement he became transformed, falling into a dismal mood which it took him a fortnight to conquer. He is improving, but hardly speaks to Julie whom he used to pursue with words and glances. ... [Hermann] Levi said to me a few days ago that Johannes loves Julie with an absolute frenzy!

His heartache notwithstanding, Brahms composed a chorale, *Opus 53,* for orchestra, male voices, and a contralto solo, as a wedding chant for the bridal pair. He drew the text from Goethe's "Journey Through the Harz Mountains," a happy choice for its lyric scope. Future generations would speak of this work as the *Alto Rhapsody.*

Julie's wedding took place in the Lichtenthal Catholic Church at Baden-Baden on September 22, 1869. It was followed by a breakfast in the Schumann cottage before Marmorito carried off his new countess to Italy. Brahms hung on, visibly in need of solace. He clung to Clara as a storm-tossed mariner seeks shelter in his home port.

In the months to come, perhaps impelled by a sense of guilt, Clara again attempted to steer him into wedlock with various willing ladies of her acquaintance. She was not blind to the fact that over the years her own demands on his loyalty had done Johannes infinite harm. To-day his devotion to all that bore the name of Schumann was beyond uprooting. It had reached the irreparable phase: habit. Thus no mat-ter how many marriageable damsels Clara recruited to work their blan-dishments upon the determined bachelor, all was in vain. At thirty-six he was a skittish fish, wary of bait.

A recent encounter with a young woman in Vienna intensified his aversion to marriage. Angela Peralta, the Mexican soprano, now twen-ty-four, had displayed an extraordinary vocal capacity at the age of eight. In 1862 she made her international debut at La Scala, winning plaudits for her mastery of the *Cavatina* in Donizetti's seldom-heard *Belisario*. As a woman, La Peralta did not interest Brahms. She was pockmarked (her countrymen spoke of her as *"picadita de viruela"*), and so nearsighted that she fell over the furniture on stage. But her greatest handicap was a beastly little husband at whose hands she en-dured a thousand offenses, not excluding public drubbings. True, the bantam bully had his civil moments when he indulged in a hobby, the stitching of petit point and crewelwork. If she was not shaking with fright at his always impending tantrums, La Peralta liked to display a chair (it traveled with her from hotel to hotel) for which the tapestry had been embroidered by her spouse.

Brahms had been treated to a view of this piece of furniture, so bright with color, just as his eyes had taken in the rainbow hues left on the singer's cheek by her needle artist's fist. No, if marriage could turn into such grim buffoonery, Johannes wanted no part of it.

Oddly La Peralta, who by rights ought to have loathed the entire male sex, evinced no bitterness. Patiently she let her obnoxious mate snarl and storm into an early grave, whereupon, sweetly confident, she entered a new union. Her second marriage proved quite happy, lasting until Angela's death in 1883 at Mazatlán. Through it all her voice was to grow steadily more glorious. A true artist, she always knew how to rise above earthly miseries, in song.

Brahms did not profit from La Peralta's example. After that single Vienna meeting with the lady of the pitted face and unbreakable heart, his path and hers were never again to cross. Her country, Mexico, was for most Europeans but the bloody stage on which in 1867 (only two years before) the drama of Maximilian of Habsburg had played itself out.

As for Clara Schumann, she soon gave up all matchmaking efforts in behalf of her friend. She knew he would not listen, and she had other cares to exact her attention. She must begin a new course of treatments for her ailing arm—the rheumatic and neuritic pains were on the increase—in preparation for the winter concert tours. Despite unmistakable signs of physical infirmity, she was at the age of fifty playing better than ever in her life. A glorious realization manifested itself to her, daily anew: he who abides with music will grow in capacity and enjoyment. Only the passing of many years could bring what she now possessed in tone color, sureness of touch, technical ease, and a rich depth of expression. Her audiences too were well aware of this. From London to St. Petersburg their cheers turned into ovations such as the youthful Clara Wieck had nowhere elicited.

To Clara Schumann the Franco-Prussian War of 1870 brought a worry over one of her children who had never before caused her a day's distress. Her son Ferdinand had managed to come of age just two days before the outbreak of hostilities. With admirable Prussian efficiency his name was inserted in the first lists of draftees, and soon thereafter he marched to the front. At the same time Clara's youngest, the sixteen-year-old consumptive Felix, was going from bad to worse. After being subjected to expensive treatments in renowned Swiss sanatoria at St. Moritz and Davos, he had recently transferred to Pirna on the Elbe, in Saxony. It was from here that the resident physician now sent Clara a tragic dispatch: Felix was no longer a simple pulmonary case, for he had meanwhile contracted tuberculosis of the spinal marrow. There was, said Dr. Lehmann, no hope.

Oddly, she did not rush to the sick boy's side though this news reached her before autumn when she was still at leisure and the war would cancel out concerts in any case. Her diary contains a woeful if somewhat self-pitying passage:

> Not since the tragedy of Robert have I suffered such grief as this. . . . But I decided to master my sorrow out of duty toward my other children. Immediately I started playing [the piano] industriously, wrote a great deal, and, in short, absorbed myself as much as I could. The nights were often the worst, for then I saw the poor boy before me, with his kind and loving eyes which I never could resist. . . .

This attitude appears callous and heartless. Yet in Clara there manifested itself simply a trait peculiar to German and Slavic races, the voluptuously subjective view: "Ah, how *I* suffer!" In the voluminous writings of this diary-keeping mother the fate smiting her children is not delineated with half the eloquence employed in telling posterity how those children's broken lives impinged distressingly upon her own. In a lament to the Düsseldorf friend Rosalie Leser occur the words:

> . . . If only I could go [to Felix] at once! We talked about it a good deal yesterday, whether to bring him to Doctor Roller at Illinau, where we would have him closer; yet how to transport him? I would so like to write him, but how and what? My heart bleeds as it has not since I went through all that with my poor Robert! I thought I had grown insensible through the years; still, here I am, utterly overwhelmed!

She unburdened herself to Rosalie, to Brahms, to Joachim. News of her son's fatal illness was transmitted by her busy pen to friends in England, Switzerland, the Baltic provinces. But the primary need of dispatching a word of comfort to Felix drew from her the impotent wail of "how and what?"

Here again lay the enormous and dehumanizing detachment of the dedicated artist, the artist dedicated unto himself, not unto others. In this detachment rested strength, absolute and uncompromising, but a strength that answered only its own need.

Day by day, meanwhile, the war was piling up civilian problems. On July 17 Clara wrote again to Rosalie:

> . . . If we didn't have the house [in Baden] I would flee, but we must remain and protect it as far as possible. Only if Algerians come shall we drop everything, for these are said to be like wild beasts. Just think, my poor boy [Ferdinand] has already been drafted and beginning tomorrow he must undergo training for four to five weeks after which, if the emergency continues, he will be sent to the front. But one cannot stop to think of one's child at such a time as this, when all Germany is anxious for her sons. . . .

The bathos of the closing words, if the stupidity of the war was kept in mind, did not diminish their sincerity. Through several millennia mankind had made of discord a noble passion, and of war a worthy trade. In every country and under all flags humanity cherished the tradition of dying for "the fatherland" when, quite conceivably, it might be more useful and certainly jollier to *live* for it. This dedication to slaughter always left behind a crop of widows, orphans, and desolate mothers whose tears were genuine even if brought on by skillfully perverted patriotism. In the present instance, when the question of who occupied the Spanish throne was really Spain's business and no one else's, both Bismarck and Napoleon might have engaged in reasonable discussion and (perhaps even with a dash of humor) have come to terms. But reasonableness and wit are commodities notoriously lacking among saber-rattlers. The Emperor of France and the master-Junker of Germany (Bismarck handled all decisions for his sovereign, the seventy-three-year-old King Wilhelm of Prussia) were itching for combat and only too elated to have found their pretext at Madrid.

It was a long way to go for a pretext. But the possible plum of a possible victory might possibly be worth it. Impassioned bludgeoners never tote up the damage. Their fanatic stare is fixed only on triumph.

The Franco-Prussian War lasted less than two months, but this was long enough for France to suffer humiliation and for Victor Hugo to publish a collection of poems entitled *L'Année Terrible* (*The Terrible Year*). The final battle at Sedan on September 1 brought Napoleon's surrender, and news for Clara Schumann from Torino that—one day earlier—she had become a grandmother. At nightfall of August 31 Julie had been delivered of a son.

Politically Europe faced some changes in the aftermath of the storm. France had stripped herself of all monarchic claptrap and proclaimed the Third Republic. The victorious Germans moved in the opposite direction. Under Bismarck's guidance the loose federation of ducal provinces, principalities, and midget kingdoms was welded into a *Deutsches Reich* over which the Prussian king would rule as emperor. At the Versailles peace conference the patriarchal Hohenzollern (he had a British daughter-in-law, eldest of Queen Victoria's children) was addressed as Kaiser Wilhelm I, while Bismarck became his Iron Chancellor.

Well ahead of such developments Clara Schumann had returned to the concert stage. She gave many benefit recitals for hospitals, war widows, and orphans. Patriotic duties behind her, she returned in February of 1871 to London, on her own. She discovered here a certain amount of anti-German feeling, explained by her more intimate British friends as "a national characteristic to side always with a loser,

in this case France." Clara's own popularity remained nevertheless un-
diminished, not only because true music lovers rose above politics but
because—miraculously—her playing seemed ever to improve. This was
the more remarkable as her muscular pains had become chronic and
she suffered lately of a disturbance in both ears. She ascribed the latter
to a head cold, though it soon disclosed itself as of a more serious order.
In a note to Johannes the following explanation occurs for Clara's
neglectful correspondence:

> I should not have remained silent for so long a time, but an acute
> ailment has plagued me these three weeks. A chill affected my
> ears to such a degree that all voices were audible to me only at
> closest range, while any word of my own echoed horribly inside
> my head. Musical notes rose to highest descant for me when they
> did not sink to bass where I lost them altogether. . . .

Most of Clara's letters nowadays were dictated to her daughter
Marie, to save the ailing artist's fingers for the podium. The auricular
trouble proved now a new handicap. With the reverberations set up
in her skull at every utterance of her own, speech itself had become
torture.

Repeated medical opinions finally agreed that both complaints, the
muscular and the auditive, must be ascribed to the inroads of age.
Clara was fifty-two, a venerable mark in those days. According to her
doctors she must accept the decrepitudes considered axiomatic at her
time of life.

All the same, her response to medication and rest proved that hers
was not a rheumatic case. What afflicted Clara was a strictly occupational cachexy. That is, the inflammation and gradual atrophy of
organs (in this instance tendons of arms and hands as well as mem-
branes of the ear) sprang from their overuse.

Robert Schumann had suffered the same ear trouble before the onset
of his mental collapse, though the two were not necessarily related. In
short, Clara faced the professional hazard against which every practicing musician must be on guard.

Surprisingly Franz Liszt, whose assaults on the piano ought long ago
to have produced muscle damage, suffered no ills. Having had his fill
of glory he was now living in Rome, content at sixty with a life devoted
to Christian charities. In 1866 Pope Pius IX had conferred upon him
the title of *Abbé*, permissible to "unbeneficed secular ecclesiasts" who

could wear clerical robes and enter the monastic condition, though without authorization to say Mass.

Clara was not impressed by Liszt's benign and pious sunset. The handsome *bon vivant* had turned to God only after living his best years to the hilt.

"*Er hat nichts anbrennen lassen,*" she said contemptuously. "He let nothing burn before enjoying it first!"

Virtue on those terms was too easy.

For the rest, Clara was growing daily more conscious of life's speedy flight. The words of a future American writer, Gertrude Stein, had not yet been said: "We are always the same age inside. . . ." Nor would Clara have taken comfort from them, for she lacked imaginative perception in any field save music. St. Augustine, more than 1,500 years earlier, had written:

> All of our years are with us, nothing is lost, not even childhood. For how would childhood leave us? Where could it go?

Here was much of Christian dogma, expressed in the Sermon on the Mount. Blessed the simple of heart who are as little children!

But Clara read no religious books. Her creed, as that of most aesthetes, centered on beauty. Yet while all art surely is Heaven-inspired, too much must not be asked of it. Though mystically related to the pulsations that held in place the universe with its planets and stars, music could not of itself sustain the prayerless heart.

Yes, Clara was short of faith. And she was tired. All of life seemed to her nowadays one long process of getting tired.

This attitude was rooted in a fundamental cause, the rectitude of which she would have fiercely defended. From the day of Robert Schumann's death she had passed sentence upon herself, ceasing physically to be a woman. At thirty-seven an egregious sense of virtue closed her heart to all passion save that which was to find release in art. She allowed music to turn her into a priestess, as religion would surely have made of her a nun.

Viewed from a hedonist and worldly angle, such chastity was tinged with priggishness, if not vainglory. There is a post-mortem fidelity not far removed from pride. And there is a pride as cold as marble.

CHAPTER 24   Nowadays Clara was obliged to re-edit her programs, eliminating certain numbers which made such technical demands that she was incapacitated sometimes for as long as a week afterward. Among these compositions was the piano portion of the *A-Major Quartet* by Brahms, and also his brilliant *Variations on a Theme of Handel*. Of the latter she confessed to Brahms, in a note of April 8, 1871, from England:

> I had wrecked myself with your *Variations* which I absolutely wanted to play in my recital [a London matinee] but had to give it up because I simply hadn't the strength. I can't tell you how sad I am that these *Variations*, which so enthrall me, are now beyond my capacity. . . .

Some time earlier she had written:

> God knows how I shall master the fear that so often grips me! At the same time my playing is mostly as fortunate as ever, yet from one number to the next I fall into a panic which I can't describe. . . . On the other hand I can't make up my mind to play from score [instead of memory playing] since this always seems like clipping my wings, which still possess some *élan*, if not for life with its never-ending blows, then for art. With my hearing, things are alternately better and worse! Thank God that our worries over Ferdinand are at an end, and he is no longer in danger.

Her son was in Paris with a German occupation force which would remain until the peace terms had been fully carried out. In June of that same summer Ferdinand would return with his regiment to Berlin, to be discharged soon after.

While still in London, Clara attended a performance at Covent Garden of Vincenzo Bellini's *La Sonnambula*. The composer had finished the opera at twenty-nine (he died four years later), basing his plot on a flimsy tale by Eugène Scribe. Adelina Patti, looking lovely and much younger than her thirty-one years, sang the role of the sleepwalking Amina who is found in the wrong chamber of a rustic Swiss inn. Clara Schumann reviewed the experience in her diary:

> Complete disappointment. I found [in Patti] a purely superficial personality; no trace of depth, such as I have seen in Jenny Lind, Schroeder-Devrient, and some others! La Patti has a stringy voice [*Zwirnsfaden*—thin as a thread] but she is clever, flirtatious, her eyes are always directed at the boxes. She has vocal agility, though not my idea of technical perfection as I remember it from Lind and Persiani [Fanny Tacchinardi, married to the composer Giuseppe Persiani]. . . . Also, she is pretty!

The last comment seems to have been added almost as a reproach. Clara was intensely and hopelessly feminine: she found it difficult not to resent good looks in other women. For the rest, her moderate enthusiasm for *La Sonnambula* was shared by other listeners, due to an unfortunate circumstance: a parody of the opera had been presented many years earlier in New York's rowdy Olympic Theater, under the irreverent title of *The Room Scrambler*. With such a handicap even the Swedish Nightingale might have had trouble in bringing dignity to the occasion.

To cap her English visit, Clara became the victim of a burglary two days after the Covent Garden night. Money and jewels were stolen from her room, including a diamond brooch and her prized *léontine*, a waist-length gold watch chain.

Since the newspapers reported the incident, a quick letter came from Mrs. Goldschmidt (Jenny Lind) who resided currently in London. Highly indignant, the diva wrote in Stockholm-flavored accents:

> Dear Madame Schumann! It is too cruel, too shocking, for you to have been robbed! It can cut one's heart, so! There must be a Hell for the bad, bad people. At least they are distant from God—and that is Hell enough. . . .

With this autographed outburst there arrived a jeweled pin that had been presented to the singer by the Queen of Sweden. "Please let me give you this," begged Jenny, "since both you and your husband have given so much to the world. . . . This pin I have worn much. Oh! How sad it makes us that you were be-stolen!"

Returning to the continent at last, Clara played a special concert at Baden-Baden for the new German Emperor. Whether the exalted graybeard knew much about music or not, the event marked a personal triumph in her career. She had appeared as a child prodigy before this monarch's brother, Friedrich Wilhelm IV, on her long-ago stage-coach tours with Papa Wieck. Now she was Europe's foremost pianist, and the former Kings of Prussia had advanced to Emperors. Yes, honor was indeed coming her way.

Possibly as a result of this command performance Clara received an invitation to join the faculty of the Berlin Music Academy as artist-teacher, under terms to be set by herself. She pondered the matter long and soberly before submitting her conditions: a substantial salary of 4,000 *Thaler* per year and lifelong pension, five months' vacation time, freedom to admit or dismiss pupils and also to give private lessons to students not enrolled in the school, and freedom to accept concert dates (in which case the teaching schedule would be rearranged).

These almost preposterous terms are an indication of Clara Schumann's immense prestige. In point of fact she did not really want the job since it meant putting up with the vile Berlin climate, stifling in summer and bone-chilling during winter with little modulation in between. She expected a categorical and prompt refusal.

Incredibly, her demands were accepted. With Joseph Joachim at the head of the Hochschule, this could perhaps not have been otherwise. He knew that Clara Schumann was the pianistic wonder of the century. Undisputed. Supreme. To win her, Berlin was prepared to make any sacrifice.

The contract did not become effective till October 1 of 1872. This would permit Clara to accept her favorite annual tour of England where she had her most ardent (and financially generous) public. Offers were also coming from America, one of these promising $10,000 for a series of concerts across the United States; but no mention was made of hotel and living expenses which, experience had taught her, came high away from home. Six months overseas might easily swallow up half the stipulated fee. What remained could, in her case, be earned more comfortably in Europe and with less expenditure of energy and time.

Britain on the other hand proved particularly profitable to visiting artists, due to the extraordinary hospitality of that land. Despite the proverbial aloofness and frigidity of the English character, Clara found herself nowhere more warmly·received. After her first London season, when she stayed in a rented room, she never again saw a bill for lodging, meals, or local transportation. Town and country houses opened their doors to her for months at a time, with landau, gig, or even pony trap at her disposal for getting about. Throughout her professional career Clara Schumann's annual British profits topped whatever the balance of each year totaled in fees.

A further source of astonishment was the acceptance, on the part of almost painfully conservative English, Scottish, and Irish listeners, of the modernism so evident in Clara's programs. She treated them to overwhelming servings of Robert Schumann and Johannes Brahms, against both of whom one still encountered resistance on the Continent. To be sure, these *avant-garde* composers had never shown hostility toward the classics. Whenever audiences seemed in need of appeasement, Clara readily chose Robert's *Kinderszenen* or the Brahms transcription of Gluck's *A-Major Gavotte* (from *Iphigenia in Aulis*, a model of eighteenth-century grace and symmetry). With such concessions she was always able to lure diehards toward an occasional departure from too-rigid convention.

This had been particularly important at Buckingham Palace in the days of Prince Albert. Since the Royal Consort's death no court musicals had been held, but in April of 1872—just as she made ready to leave London for home—Clara received a call from the Queen. Her immediate impulse was to give a negative reply since Frau Bargiel, her own mother, had died on March 10 in Berlin, and Clara's commitments had prevented her attending the funeral; her schedule concluded, she had now no excuse to delay longer.

There is, nevertheless, a compulsion about a royal summons to which even the most self-possessed artist is not immune. Clara was more self-possessed than most, yet she succumbed. Her subsequent regret is immortalized in a diary description of High Tea with Queen Victoria:

Her Majesty invited me to play at Buckingham Palace. It was an unbelievable concert. . . . Madame [Amalie] Neruda, Miss [Anna] Regan, some gentlemen and I took part. The room was fine for music, though not very big. Seven hundred people had been invited (from five p.m. to seven)—about one hundred were in the salon, most of them standing behind their empty chairs. With the Queen sat the Duchess of Cambridge and Princess Louise. The Queen did not greet us at all, she sat half turned toward our room, talked incessantly, heard only the closing measure of each program number and then applauded faintly. How— but how—she looked! With white muslin cap and the most ordinary black silk dress. . . . Above the music one could also hear the mumbling of the other six hundred persons scattered through adjoining salons.

The most incredible thing happened during the intermission: the Queen rose to have her tea, and in the meantime the royal band blared a folk medley, followed by two bagpipers (in kilts!) who cut loose in the next room. I was speechless, unaware at first of what this could be, until Madame Neruda explained that this was the Queen's favorite music! . . . Beside myself, I was ready to leave right then. But the second part now began and the Queen was half seated when it must have occurred to her that we ought to be spoken to. So she came forward and, look- ing at us in a lump, said "very nice playing," after which she returned to her chair. . . . When it was all over she did not utter a word of thanks. Never in my life has such a thing happened to me. This Queen is not going to see me under her roof again; of that I am sure! . . . A dinner had been prepared for us in the anteroom where we left our coats! But I declined . . .

Following this onerous episode Clara came to the conclusion that the most un-English and unmusical phenomenon in the United Kingdom was its Germanic sovereign.

She was back at Düsseldorf for a concert early in May, having also played in Brussels en route. A summer reunion had been planned at Baden-Baden with the two youngest children, Eugénie (now twenty and working toward a music teacher's certificate), and the ailing Felix, who in an interval of deceptive improvement had enrolled at Heidel- berg University. Later in the season Julie with her husband and two babies would arrive for a short visit.

Meanwhile an Easter greeting from Brahms waited in Clara's piled-up mail. It gave a clue to the loneliness of the soul that has strayed onto a road apart. He wrote:

Holidays are always spent by me in great isolation, all alone with a few dear ones in my quiet room—these dear ones being either dead or far away. What joy I then feel, to find that love can fill the breast! Yet I am after all dependent on the outer world, its clatter and confusion; I don't join in its laughter or hypocrisies but move through it as half a person, the other part of me escaping in a dream. . . . How happy you are (by contrast, with a family to cherish)—how beautiful, how good, how right.

This would, of course, have been true, had Clara ever in her high-pressured life found pause for counting blessings. But the greatest of these, the joys of motherhood, had invariably been stifled by the overpowering and all-dominating demands of her artist-self. In time it would be seen that none of her children's lives would come to full flowering, and thus bring the enrichment of a golden sunset to her own declining years; each would know grief and early withering. The bliss envied by Brahms was simply not there.

For the moment, at home once more in Germany, Clara was confronted by a loud and (to her) distasteful hullabaloo in Bavaria. On May 22, 1872, Richard Wagner—now in his sixtieth year—was laying the cornerstone for his Bayreuth Festival Theater. Her diary took caustic note of the fact:

That Wagner has again been much on my mind, since he appears currently in all the papers and occupies everyone's thoughts. The cornerstone for his Bayreuth Theater has been laid, with all the great celebrities of the art world present except Johannes and Joachim. . . . This Wagner craze seems to me like a disease that spreads from land to land and sweeps away the best.

She, the interpreter of music in its purest abstract sense, would never become reconciled to the composite uses for which Wagner enlisted the world of sound. She, the absolute musician, could neither comprehend nor tolerate the musical showman. Only recently, after meeting Liszt once again (at a private reception in London—she had long given up attending his concerts) Clara observed that the Hungarian's bravura was as swaggering as ever. "He gallops over the keys with superb skill," she admitted grudgingly that day, "but is it music?"

There was in her attitude more than a shade of pedantry. Yet for the cause of art at its unimpeachable best such martinets as Clara

Schumann, Robert Schumann, and Johannes Brahms were needed. Without their veracity and scorn for musical prestidigitation the heritage of Bach, Mozart, Beethoven, Weber, Gluck, and countless others would reach the modern listener only in adulterated form. Without such Draconian sticklers as these three the performing musician might as well move from the concert hall to the pantomime or circus tent.

CHAPTER 25   For Clara the year 1872 was to end on a tragic note. When the Marmoritos arrived in mid-August, Clara was shocked at the sight of her married daughter. Julie looked wasted and ill following two births in quick succession, and a third pregnancy was now under way. The tuberculous condition, ignored in the first flush of wedded bliss, reasserted itself with grim force. Doctors counseled the young mother against spending another winter in the damp cold of northern Italy, and Julie herself longed for another visit with the kindly Frau Schlumberger in the south of France. The latter project was carried out, with the Count taking the children back to his drafty Piedmontese palazzo.

On November 9 Clara left for Heidelberg to fill a concert engagement. Two days later she received a telegram reporting Julie's sudden death. It was too late to cancel the recital. Clara went on stage that same evening and, in the opinion of local critics, played "wonderfully as never before."

Nothing is known from diary, correspondence, or other biographical sources about Julie's obsequies, disposition of her body, or its final resting place. Clara's itinerary seems to have gone on unbroken, showing her departure from Heidelberg on November 13 for Munich, and thence on the sixteenth for further professional activities in Vienna.

During this period she became the object of a generous tribute on the part of a group of music lovers in Cologne who, through a spokesman named Wendelstadt, sent Clara the following message:

> For some time there has arisen among your most devoted friends the wish to furnish you, the widow of the immortal Schumann—

196

yourself an incomparable and universally admired artist, noblest of women, excellent mother—a means of easing the strains of your career, and of contributing to your future security. . . .

Continuing in a more specific vein, the writer announced that Clara would receive a donation of 30,000 *Thaler* in Rhineland Railroad Securities (she was, of course, one of that railroad's steadiest customers) bearing a five per cent interest rate. In addition the circle of music lovers pledged itself to contribute annually another 1,000 *Thaler* to the already handsome basic pot.

Clara accepted after a week of careful consideration. Her cogent reply contained, in part, the following text:

> I am deeply touched at thought of having friends who in remembrance of him, the sublime artist who was my life's companion, are now concerned over my welfare. I feel humbled since the work I carry out is only my duty, in which the gift bestowed on me by God, my enthusiasm for music, and my good health have sustained me. . . .

Yes, the pleasing windfall thus coming her way would indeed banish financial worries from Clara's mind, though it in no wise affected the intense pace that ruled her life. Travel, concerts, audiences, applause, these were the elements making up her permanent need. Barring short breathing spells at Karlsbad, Gastein, the Bavarian or Swiss Alps, the Italian or the French Riviera, she grew restive when long chained to one spot. Like all incurable wayfarers, she complained about the hardships of the road, yet nothing in the world could have persuaded her to trade those "hardships" for domestic repose. Anything smacking of fixity, torpor, inertia was, to her, synonymous with death. Under no circumstances would she slacken her nomad's pace.

During this time (she was fifty-four, and plagued with increasing neuritic pains) Brahms urged her to slow down. He pointed out that Clara herself had, in past years, criticized other artists (in particular the singer Wilhelmine Schroeder-Devrient) for not retiring in time and with good grace. In proffering advice, Johannes employed an unfortunate phrase. "At your age," he wrote without guile, "you ought to take it easy!"

At your age.

This was a phrase no woman would forgive—least of all Clara, who admitted no comparison between herself and others. Her reply to the above counsel was swift and acrimonious. Schroeder-Devrient had lost her voice, she reminded Johannes, and needed to be shooed off the platform. Clara Schumann, on the other hand, remained in fullest possession of her faculties, a more compelling artist than ever in youth. Ah no, there was no driving *her* into the shadows.

She was right. There was manifested in her a vital truth, priceless to instrumentalists. Time, to the performer, need be no enemy. Perfection lay not behind, but always ahead. One had but to realize this. Clara did.

She had currently a young pupil from Poland named Nathalie Janotha, who would soon be ready for a Leipzig debut (at the same Gewandhaus where the small daughter of Friedrich Wieck had started). Clara was vitally interested in this girl, the first spectacular talent to emerge from her tutelage. Retirement now, when her name shone at its brightest, even in the teaching field? Johannes certainly was not in his right mind.

Johannes, as a matter of fact, was passing through a difficult period spiritually. Very successful as a composer (the third of his great symphonies was just being acclaimed by an at last awakened public), he had achieved economic security which permitted long annual vacations in Italy, Switzerland, or wherever his fancy might dictate. But there was desolation in his heart. If the marriage of Julie Schumann struck him a cruel wound, her death—so soon after—drove the stab even deeper. There was now no hope of occasional encounters with the beloved, no bittersweet observance of her happiness at the side of another man. At the same time the relationship between Brahms and Julie's mother had undergone a change. While not estranged, the devoted friends of yore met seldom nowadays, their correspondence lagged, and they exchanged fewer confidences. In addition there was Clara's pout over the unforgivable, the unpremeditated "at your age." It would take some time and many conciliatory gestures on his part before the *gaffe* was forgiven.

Actually Clara herself no less than the fashion of the era was at fault if she had, prematurely, acquired the aspect of a venerable dowager. The Biedermeier style prevailing in her youth had already turned freshly baked brides into matrons before the age of thirty.

This trend was not altered with the advancing century. Before her fortieth year Clara wore the appurtenances of a great-grandmother: a voluminous gown of black brocade, white ruching and a square brooch at the neck, besides a lace cap perched above the severest of middle-part coiffures. This, plus the fact that time had coarsened her formerly fine features (the nose had enlarged, the chin was more prominent, the mouth firmly set and severe), gave to her person a forbidding air. No, here was not the pliant, feminine creature to whom Johannes could return in search of Julie's image, as once he had sought in Julie the image of Clara. Both were lost to him, as youth itself was lost.

From now on the world would know a different Brahms. At thirty-nine the slight, handsome charmer who loved and was loved by life turned semi-hermit. His artistic output increased, but he grew taciturn and indifferent to praise. Also, with a lessening of his wanderlust and of the physical verve that had once characterized him, he took on weight.

Being more famous now, he was photographed and portraitized with frequency. In consequence, posterity is well supplied with like-nesses of the portly, bearded Brahms of the middle and late years. But the slim and fair-haired lad whom Robert Schumann loved is al-most nowhere depicted. The saving of family albums and sentimental keepsakes is a woman's, not a man's, hobby. Though the world's best biographies are unquestionably of male authorship, their illustrations for the most part derive from female sources. The bachelor Brahms, at all events, hoarded nothing; hence, and more's the pity, our physical image of him remains incomplete.

With the autumn of 1872 Clara's Berlin teaching job took up a fixed part of her time. She had transferred to the Prussian capital with heavy heart, depressed by the thought of having to sell the property in Baden-Baden. For a while she procrastinated by renting the house to strangers. Her secret hope was that the Berlin move would turn out to be temporary and that the sinecure she had not the courage to relin-quish (this would be rank ingratitude) might yet be taken from her. Even losing a life pension seemed acceptable to her, if only the contract she had signed could now be revoked. This being impossible, she buckled down to duty and rendered brilliant account of herself. With Clara Schumann on the faculty, the Berlin Conservatory won its finest laurels.

Her position was privileged indeed, for in the middle of the winter she was allowed to scramble her teaching schedules in order to answer a concert summons from England. She played in London and Liverpool through the spring, returning to Berlin for what was left of the school term. It had been her plan to take a flat in a suburb called Zelten, where her sons Ferdinand and Felix were to join her. An unexpected development upset this scheme. Ferdinand, out of uniform and only twenty-three, surprised his mother with news of his engagement to a young lady named Antonie Deutsch. Since the prospective bridegroom and bride had neither fortune nor jobs it was understandable that Clara showed little enthusiasm on receiving the tidings. She put her foot down, but to no avail. Ferdinand found employment in a publishing firm at a pathetically low salary. On August 13, 1873, he and Antonie were married, and—with that month's pay—the pair spent a honeymoon weekend in Bonn.

Clara herself was well off financially that year. From a Leipzig society of Schumann adherents she received an unexpected donation of 3,500 *Thaler*, left over from a fund collected years ago to help Robert during his last illness. Also, during August of 1873 a three-day music festival took place at Bonn to raise money for erection of a monument on Robert Schumann's grave. Here Clara appeared as soloist, helping to bring the proceeds to 4,000 *Thaler*. Lastly another group of enthusiasts, this time admirers of her own, gathered 10,000 *Thaler* in Vienna as a spontaneous "tribute to an outstanding artist." Presentation of this lavish gift was made by a Princess Kinsky and the scientist-author Theodor Billroth.

That autumn Friedrich Wieck's long and productive life ended. Clara's diary reports:

> This month brought me great sorrow. My father passed away on October 6 after a short illness. A peaceful death. He was eighty-eight and had retained to the last his joy in nature and in art, always with the fresh passion of a young man. I am deeply shaken, for with him goes the last link to my youth. I loved him intensely and was often aware of this, but now the realization sweeps over me with special force. Even though we were not always in accord this never lessened my love, since I was bound by lifelong gratitude. How many years he devoted exclusively to me, how beautifully he directed me toward a useful existence, imparting maxims of wisdom and seeing to it that I followed

them! He was not narrow, but a man of scope. His most earnest concern was the discovery of talent, without thought of his own merit or reward. . . .

This final assessment of her martinet parent was eminently just. Beyond doubt, without Friedrich Wieck the famous Clara Schumann would not have achieved her present stature. Innate gifts can wither and die for lack of proper nurturing. The best of training, on the other hand, is wasted where there is no talent. Only the ideal combination of inborn genius and wise guidance win the crown. This had been the case between Clara and her father. When she went from him into the arms of Robert Schumann the embittered Wieck had tried to repeat the miracle with his remaining children. His most fanatic efforts were spent in forcing greatness upon them, but to no avail. The magical concatenation had been lost.

While Clara Schumann mourned her father she faced further troubles with her youngest son Felix, now nineteen. The boy was sent back to her from Heidelberg where he was deemed physically unfit to continue his studies. Apart from progressive tuberculosis he suffered attacks of asthma which prevented him from walking to classes. Now, in Berlin, the early winter brought on a severe pleurisy which put Felix on the brink of the grave. Even so, Clara went on a tour in November, leaving Marie in charge of household and sickroom. On the twenty-fourth she informed Brahms, from Hamburg:

> In Munich I had such a good time that it will hold me all winter, since in Berlin everything is mediocre save what comes from Joachim. I could not await the performance of *Genoveva* because Marie needs me at home. I can't describe how hard this renunciation was for me, and the children will scarcely guess what proof of love I have thereby given them. That which to us is noblest delight can be felt only by someone who is himself an artist in body and soul.

Returning to her son's bedside she found him propped amid pillows, writing poetry. Some time earlier Felix had submitted to Brahms a set of quatrains, opening with the line, "My love is green as the lilac bush." The rhythm lent itself excellently to musical adaptation, whereupon Johannes had asked for more. He would never know by how much this act of kindness prolonged the boy's slackening hold on life.

Preoccupied with Felix, Clara presently faced another emergency. Ludwig, the forgotten one, clamored at Colditz Asylum for release and permission to come home. A staff member at the institution urged the mother to pay a visit and calm her son. All through 1874 Clara did not manage this, but in May of 1875 her diary notes reveal:

> This month began badly for me. On the fourth I suffered dreadful pains in my arm, which continued for three weeks. Never in my life have I endured such torture. . . . The first and second days of Pentecost were sad. I cried all the time like a child, as I had so looked forward to the Düsseldorf Festival under Joachim's baton. . . . Decided to visit Ludwig before I go again to Kiel for my cure.

The meeting between mother and son proved unsatisfactory. The diary resumes:

> At last I saw my poor Ludwig again. . . . Inwardly I felt torn apart. He looked well, better than before, but in his glance there was that lost quality, mingled with tenderness. He was immensely happy to see me, hugging me desperately and begging to be taken away as he felt quite recovered. What agony to have to tell him that this could not be. It was all too awful for me! To see my child [Ludwig was now twenty-seven] virtually a prisoner. . . . His imploring eyes when I left—I shall never forget them!

Beyond question, it was all too awful for her.

There remains the surmise that things could have been hardly less awful for the unhappy Ludwig. He did not know it yet, but his thralldom would end only in death.

CHAPTER 26   Richard Wagner, or rather, the success of Richard Wagner, continued to be a thorn in Clara's side. On September 7, 1875, she took time out from concertizing to attend (with reluctance, yet impelled by irresistible curiosity!) a Munich performance of *Tristan und Isolde*. Her reaction could not have been more dismal. No time was lost in conveying this to a diary page the very next day:

> This is the most repulsive thing I have yet seen or heard in all my life. To have to listen all evening and witness such amorous delirium which offends one's moral sense, and then to observe that not the public alone but even the musicians are entranced, this is surely the saddest experience of my artistic career. I endured it to the end, wanting to have heard it all. Throughout the second act they alternately sleep and sing, while in the third act Tristan dies for forty full minutes, and that is called drama!!!
>
> Levi [Hermann Levi, conductor of the Munich Opera House] says that Wagner is a far better musician than was Gluck! . . . And Joachim? He hasn't the courage to stand up against others. Are they all imbeciles or am I one? . . . I found the theme so shabby: a love frenzy induced by a potion. Can anyone work up the slightest interest in the lovers, given such a premise? Here no emotion is involved, but a disease, a poisoning, with the protagonists literally tearing out their hearts, and the music wallowing in the most sensual tones! *Ach!* I could lament forever, crying oh and woe!

As for Clara's grudge against Levi, this rested on ignorance of the latter's true position. The thirty-six-year-old conductor was no hysterical Wagner addict but an enlightened musicologist with a grasp of past and future. After many debates he tried to explain his views to Clara:

> . . . Wagner again. It seems I shall not succeed in making myself understood with regard to this favorite subject of controversy; I can't prevent my opinions being considered paradoxical, in view of my past classic standards. And yet, it shouldn't be so difficult to separate a dramatist from a musician. Brahms certainly rates musically as high above Wagner as did Mozart over Gluck. Nevertheless did not Gluck have a place alongside Mozart?
>
> Wagner does not regard himself a musician in the classic sense. I find his purely instrumental compositions [concert numbers] tiresome and poor; if a student came to me with Wagner's *Albumblatt,* published by Schott, I would throw him out with my compliments. But when Wagner's music serves the theater he achieves effects like no one before him. Since, then, he differs so from all others in not being able to make music in the abstract but in being obsessed with the purpose of creating the German music-drama, I don't see why a sincere admiration of his works should not be compatible with an equally honest appreciation of Bach, Beethoven, and Brahms. For me, at least, the *Theme of Fate* and the *G-Major Sextet* lose no merit because I regard *Tristan und Isolde* as a great work of art.
>
> Here as in everything it is the fanatics, whether friends or foes, who cause the trouble. The rabid Wagnerians who simultaneously glorify that fake genius, Liszt, are as objectionable as the inveterate Wagner-haters. The latter irritate me with their ignorance, which unfortunately arouses in me an equally excessive defense [of Wagner] and the employment of not quite justifiable superlatives. . . .

The candor of these lines ought surely to have mellowed Clara's views, at least with regard to Levi's humanistic tolerance. But no. Her rancor over Wagner's success, when Robert Schumann's operatic attempts continued to meet with only mild response, smoldered on. She cooled toward Levi. He was just not the friend she had thought him to be.

Happily Brahms proffered her a much-needed service at this time. She was again undergoing severe pains in her right arm, which necessitated the striking of effective bravura numbers from her concert programs.

Knowing that she was a daring player who enjoyed sweeping an

audience off its feet, Johannes realized how she must bridle under
such enforced restraint. Consequently, without reference to her dis-
ability (she complained often about her ailment, but resented its mention by others) he transposed Bach's famous *Chaconne* into a brilliant
showpiece for the left hand. In mailing this to her he spoke of it as
a musical prank, indulged in merely for his own amusement. But he
well knew that Clara would pounce on it avidly. Here was just the
gala number she needed for placement in the exact middle of a recital,
to dazzle listeners with a fabulous *tour de force* while giving her right
arm an imperative rest. Since, to make matters worse, she had also
strained a tendon in the suffering hand (while forcing open a cabinet
drawer that was stuck), the Bach violin piece, transcribed for piano,
proved a true blessing. She assured Johannes of this in glowing words:

> What a marvelous salvation is the *Chaconne!* Only you are capable
> of such a feat; and what a strange sensation your piano effects give
> me, of still listening to a violin—what made you think of it? I find
> this so wonderful. My fingers of course don't quite hold out
> through the sustained low F's, I get paralyzed, and my right hand
> slips in to help out; apart from this I find no insurmountable diffi-
> culties, but only greatest pleasure.

In the same letter, written on July 6, 1877, Clara reported another
tragic event. Duaddo Marmorito, Julie's firstborn, had died suddenly
at Torino. The boy, gifted but of frail constitution, had resembled his
mother. Brahms had cherished the dream of one day furthering this
child's artistic development. That hope was shattered now, and another
bond with Julie broken.

Happier tidings came to Clara Schumann through her second eldest
daughter Elise. Already a spinsterish thirty-four, she had met a wealthy
American, Louis Sommerhoff, who was vacationing in Europe. The
couple became engaged and planned marriage for that same autumn
(Elise felt that she had not much time to lose). The Sommerhoffs
would of course live at the groom's home in New York.

On hearing the good news Brahms permitted himself a musical
prank. His present to the bride was a clock with a specially built-in
chime that played the opening measure of his famous *"Wiegenlied"*
("Lullaby"). Since subsequently Elise found herself with a well-
stocked nursery, the clock would be put to good use.

In 1878 Clara was invited to exchange her Berlin post for a similar one at the new Hoch Conservatory in Frankfurt-am-Main. The conditions were most tempting: Frau Schumann was to count on an assistant who would relieve her of routine duties such as the screening of untalented pupils. Also, she was to find a friend and colleague in the school's director, the Zurich-born composer Joachim Raff.

It was an excellent opportunity to escape the Berlin climate and the spiritual stagnation Clara ascribed to the northern city. She accepted eagerly. Frankfurt lay in the very heart of Germany, and of Europe for that matter, making it an ideal base for her recurrent travels. True, the Berlin Conservatory was left in the lurch, and grievously. But the contract signed by that institution had been all in Clara's favor, even permitting her to demit at will; thus her present action was entirely legal.

With her daughter Marie she visited Frankfurt during the summer to look for living quarters. A large house with well-tended garden was found at 32 Myliusstrasse. Painters and carpenters were hired to make a number of improvements and to put the place in readiness for occupancy by October 1. While this went on, Clara would spend the warm season at her favorite spas in turn: Berchtesgaden, Obersalzberg, and Baden-Baden. Since her son Felix was far too ill to accompany her to all these resorts she placed him in a sanatorium at Zurich. Here the boy was so unhappy that he left, on his own, to pay a surprise visit to his brother-in-law Marmorito in Italy.

During August of 1878, while passing through Munich, Clara stopped for a spell to have her portrait painted by the famous Franz von Lenbach. She commented, in her diary, on this undertaking:

> The children are so insistent on having a good picture of me, and Lenbach is a genius in achieving likenesses quite wonderfully. . . . The first sitting was peculiar: just a "looking-at," without canvas or palette! He wanted only to study my face before beginning. He opined that the portrait would take only a day, emerging at one try or not at all. I am very intrigued. It seems incomprehensible to me that in my old age [fifty-nine] I should sit for a painting. I certainly wouldn't be doing it for my own pleasure—what do I care about my time-marked face—but there is joy in having it done for the children. . . .

On August 12, three days after this entry, she received an alarming wire from Count Marmorito. Her pen reports:

Felix is so sick that Marmorito begs me to send for him as quickly as possible. I have almost no hope that we shall keep him alive. Thus one grows old in order to bury one's children.

And on the twenty-fourth:

In the evening Felix arrived. I found him just as I expected and can harbor absolutely no illusions regarding his condition. He is very ill, and in my opinion we can only ease his sufferings by good care at home—but there is no saving him. . . .

Even so, when autumn came, she did not take her son to the house in Frankfurt. A letter to Brahms, on September 17, explains her reasons:

Eugénie went with Felix to Falkenstein, an institution for the tubercular, only an hour's distance from here and said to be excellent. He wanted to remain with us so much, and we wanted it too, but with a house not yet in order and no servants we couldn't take him. And so I begged him to stay at Falkenstein for the time being. . . .

In the same letter the disciplined artist alternates with the distressed mother:

I have been here [Frankfurt] a few days now, but at the hotel; we can't move into our house before end of the month—that is, not for over night. But in the daytime I am able to practice there, in my beautiful music room, for the Hamburg recital; I have to work out some cadenzas—a terribly hard job in my present frame of mind. I've used some ideas of yours, with your permission, I hope? The pain in both my arms is severe, and I don't know how I shall manage playing in Hamburg! But one cancels such commitments only when it is impossible to do otherwise.

You will understand my low spirits; my heart is dejected as in the hardest days of my life. . . . To be old but healthy myself, and to see a son fade away in the flower of his years, this surely is one of the cruelest trials for a mother's heart, and a trial I am now undergoing with the third child. I could not bear it but for my love toward the remaining children, whom God may mercifully spare.

The Hamburg concert went brilliantly, cadenzas and all, as did a number of other engagements that fall. In October some honorary functions took place in Frankfurt and Leipzig to commemorate Clara's Golden Jubilee as a professional pianist. Now, in place of the modest flower bouquets she had received fifty years ago at her debut, she received from the Leipzig Philharmonic Orchestra and its directors a laurel wreath in solid gold, each leaf of which bore the engraved name of a composer whose works had figured in her programs throughout her long career. Soon after this Clara was also to be awarded, by King Ludwig II of Bavaria (friend and patron of Richard Wagner), the gold Medal for Achievement in Art.

Meanwhile, by the end of October, Felix at last was brought home from Falkenstein, bedridden and rapidly losing ground, yet touchingly grateful to be once more with his family. Marie and Eugénie took alternate turns in nursing him. Christmas came and a tree was trimmed. Felix sat up till ten o'clock of Holy Night, propped by pillows—at last a Christmas Eve not spent among strangers. Came January of 1879, and the following entry in Clara's diary:

> This month was rather full of events, some of which I took part in with heavy heart, but I did so because to remain active seems to me the only means of sustaining the spirit in time of trial. Besides, action is the essence of my profession and my life depends so upon the latter that I simply can't visualize myself in the everyday tracks of ordinary people. In addition, I knew that it pleased Felix to see me absorbed by the claims of art.

There is in these lines unquestionably a note of self-justification, as if the writer felt concern (all diary-keepers do, or they would not pen diaries) about the judgment of posterity. Certainly it was not amiss to clarify, especially for "ordinary people," the complexity of her position. The more so, as, a fortnight later, her youngest child lay dead. The diary narrates:

> On February 14 I played in the Museum Concert—a promise given long ago. It was very hard for me, and oh, I wish I hadn't done it. Had I known how near was the end of our sufferer, I wouldn't have done it. My heart bled when I said good-night to Felix before going to the concert. What a terrible contrast: all through the recital I saw only him, his emaciated body, the dim-

ming glance, the struggle for breath—it was awful! Yet I played with success, not missing a single note! In the night of the fifteenth to the sixteenth, Saturday to Sunday at three a.m., our Felix expired in Marie's arms; she did not call me. . . . He suffered dreadfully, a death struggle in the fullest sense of the word, and she wanted to spare me this hour—she, the always selfless and loving. . . . Thus I saw him in the morning, a corpse, ah, and I must confess that there came over me a feeling of relief [*Erlösung:* salvation or release] for which Heaven must be thanked. . . .

Yes, for almost a third of his existence (at the time of dying he was not yet twenty-five) Felix Schumann had been a living ghost. The knowledge that he would leave them had hung over his relatives from day to day.

When the parting finally came it had lost every element of surprise, and some of its sadness.

The grief that remained was the grief of anticlimax.

CHAPTER 27

In her sixtieth year Clara Schumann received what in modern parlance is called "fan mail" of extraordinary fervor. While her son Felix lay on his deathbed she had wound up a short concert tour of Switzerland (from the seventeenth to the thirtieth of January, 1879), from where an admirer—who signed himself merely as Dr. L.K.—sent her a glowing letter. Its text ran, in part:

Supremely celebrated, unforgettable artist!

The reward of a performing virtuoso lies in his satisfaction on finding public acclaim. This acclaim may be modest or stormy, but it can only feebly reveal the emotions and reactions of individuals in the crowd. The artist thus might be gratified to have a more specific tribute, and that is why I take this liberty to write these lines. My identity is a matter of complete indifference to you. Please regard me as an unauthorized interpreter or spokesman for hundreds.

When, a few weeks ago, the report circulated in our musical spheres that Clara Schumann was again to thrill us with her incomparable pianistic art everyone reacted with the most joyous excitement; this increased with publication of the program, and when Saturday and Sunday came there was purest bliss. I shall not talk about the overwhelming greatness and beauty of your playing. The most competent pens have for years used up all the superlatives for this. But I give voice to my most ardent thanks, with the assurance that the impression you caused will outlast any others that may come our way. One does not often in this world experience what is highest, perfection itself. And what all was involved as we considered the artist before us, with her long record: 1819—1840—1856—1878!

. . . May many more triumphs be yours; today's generation has need of such uplifting and sterling emotions to draw it away from

triviality. May you live many more happy years. Your memory
will remain, immortal, in the hearts of thousands, replete with
the wondrous music of Robert Schumann. My deepest reverence. . . .

To live many more happy years? She had for some time grasped
that longevity is paid for in accumulated pain. After her son's funeral
Clara had answered a message of condolence from Hermann Levi:

> It seems to me as if no ray of light can again pierce my soul. I
> struggle against this with all arguments of logic, telling myself
> that rich treasures remain to me still in my other children, my art,
> my friendships, yet every moment can rob me of all these. We
> grow old only to lose all, until we too are carried off, and then
> the snow and wind sweep over our graves while the world goes
> on as before.

No, she was by no means convinced that one ought to wish people
a ripe old age. The realization had yet to dawn upon her (sixty was
not, after all, senility!) that life's final years were mercifully accompanied by progressive sensory and emotional numbness. She herself,
with more than a decade and a half still to go, would find the "slings
and arrows of outrageous fortune" less wounding with each thrust.
The twilight of existence thus could be looked forward to without
dread.

At present Clara had no time for such reflections. In September of
1879 a buyer had been found for her Baden-Baden house. This caused
her another wrench, as the place held pleasant memories. Nor was the
sale advantageous; counting improvements, she had paid almost double
the price now obtained. But continuing deterioration and poor rentals
from transient holidayers would cause additional losses with each
passing year. It was as well to write the matter off without too much
regret.

Spells of melancholy assailed Clara for the rest of that year. On
October 10 the diary reports:

> Mozart's *D-Minor Concerto* at the Museum Hall; great enthusiasm.
> I played it well, too; I know this. Yet all evening I felt such an
> inner sadness. I don't know why I have been so depressed lately
> when appearing in public. I keep thinking it will soon be the
> last time. . . . In a way I've had enough of the world, but the

thought of all being over, and my having to leave the children makes me acutely unhappy! To give up public appearances would be hard for me insofar as I do play better now than ever. Still, I must curtail this, for the strain is too much. . . .

Much of her time was spent nowadays in revising her husband's manuscripts for the publishing firm of Breitkopf and Härtel, under whose aegis the collected works of Robert Schumann were soon to be issued. After this tedious job she was ready, in the summer of 1880, for a long holiday. With Marie and Eugénie she attended the Passion Play at Oberammergau during August and then visited the Carinthian lake region of Austria, stopping at Villach, Pörtschach, Klagenfurt, Aussee, and Ischl.

During this trip she received a letter from the wife of her son Ferdinand. It contained bad news. Ever since his war service, when he had lain in damp bivouac much of the time, Ferdinand suffered from joint inflammations. To combat the pain he resorted to drugs which, lately, were gaining too great a hold on him. Antonie reported that he must be treated for addiction. As the young family would have to disband to save expenses for Ferdinand's cure, could Clara take the couple's two elder children, Julie and Nand?

It was a request that could not be refused. In time, as Ferdinand's condition grew worse rather than better, Clara would have all four of his children on her hands. That is, she would clothe and educate them, but they would be "farmed out" among relatives and friends—as her own brood had been—in paid custody. Later, when the question of professional training arose, she decided against shouldering the cost of universities. Ferdinand's illness was swallowing up more than the share due him one day in inheritance. His children would have to be apprenticed in some practical trade so as to earn money as soon as possible. Thus, immediately after finishing grade school, the boy Nand became laboratory helper and errand runner for a Frankfurt apothecary; by way of pay he learned the chemist's craft.

Clara Schumann observed at this time an increasing disturbance in her ears. She suffered periods of faulty hearing, even complete deafness, which threw her into a panic. On confiding this to Brahms in a long and distressed letter she received a reply that held little comfort. He, too, though younger and in far more rugged health, was beginning to be similarly afflicted. It was the ailment dreaded by all musicians and for which—being self-induced—there was no cure. Beethoven had succumbed to it. Schumann's mental breakdown began with auditory aberrations. No microbe or canker could be made responsible. The hearing nerve, strained to excess, simply deteriorated into silence or went berserk and set up an acoustic pandemonium all its own. Johannes admitted being bothered with strange sounds inside his head. He blamed the matter on his having walked in the Vienna woods and stretched out carelessly on the damp grass.

But Clara knew that this was jejune evasion. The artist life did not come as a privilege, unearned and free. It was lived most often at the cost of precious faculties: eyesight, hearing, nerve-co-ordination. Even so, Clara struggled against fear. She experienced one of her most pleasurable satisfactions at a Frankfurt recital in the autumn of 1880. The diary speaks:

> I played most fortunately. Never have I done better with Beethoven's *E-Minor Concerto*. This spiritual dominance, the feeling of complete mastery thrilled me throughout the evening. There is something so exalting in the knowledge that, despite age, it is possible to continue going forward in one's inner life. At times I have suspected that I had grown cold inwardly, but today I am aware of the very opposite. Ah, if only the body's vigor could keep up with that of the soul!

Her observation that genius need not bow to the encroaching years found support in a performance of Verdi's *Aïda*, which Clara saw for the first time that November. It had been written by the composer ten years ago, as he approached sixty; he was now at work on *Otello*, to be followed by *Falstaff* (in his eightieth year). Nor did this mean mere potboiling repetition of earlier successes. On the contrary, Verdi's final operas showed a high degree of evolution from routine mechanics to the rich subtleties that would one day inspire such followers as Pietro Mascagni, Ruggiero Leoncavallo, and Giacomo Puccini.

In spite of herself Clara Schumann recognized that here and there Verdi showed Wagnerian leanings. He employed the leitmotiv or theme song not only vocally but as background music to accent the presence and importance of certain characters. Then again, he possessed a symphonic sweep fully as prodigal and grandiose as that of the master at Bayreuth.

Clara thought this regrettable. But on the whole she dealt justly with Verdi:

> . . . Extraordinary to see the old composer daring still to strike out along new paths. Much of his work decidedly pleased me, though there is also much of which I disapprove. The opera [*Aïda*] fills me nevertheless with respect for Verdi. It is indeed remarkable for a composer to change direction in his late years. And how great is the talent he has displayed in doing so!

In the spring of 1881 another summons came from England. Clara accepted eagerly, finding herself welcomed in London with a warmth that had already become habitual. Though she would never be a linguist, her English was now fluent enough to make the Channel crossings diverting as well as profitable.

During this season a new concept of Beethoven's *A-Major Sonata, Opus 101,* revealed itself to her. Even amateur pianists will find her comments reassuring:

> March 14, recital in Popular [London's so-called pop concerts]: *Opus 101.* I believe the Sonata went perfectly, as never before. . . . All the time I had to think of Mendelssohn who once told me, forty years ago, that at some later time I would play the first movement quite differently—whereas he praised, even then, my handling of the other portions, saying that *nobody* could play the second movement as did I. Regarding the first, I admit finding only recently a real grasp and the proper emotional warmth for its interpretation.

While in England, Clara was approached by a sixteen-year-old youth named Eugène d'Albert, born in Glasgow, of French and German descent. Highly gifted, the boy was preparing to play Schumann's *A-Minor Concerto* in London's Crystal Palace. Already a Mendelssohn scholar, he nevertheless begged humbly to be heard and criticized by the great Madame Schumann herself. She granted this and gave him sincere encouragement. Her diary states: "He is a pupil of Ernst Pauer, excellently trained, and I believe he will become a major pianist. . . . He also composes quite well." Actually d'Albert had studied also under Sir John Stainer, Ebenezer Prout, Sir Arthur Sullivan, Ernst Richter, and Franz Liszt. Because of his brilliant and limber technique the young man was already being hailed as another Karl Tausig (a Liszt pupil and noted virtuoso whose career was cut short by typhoid fever, in 1871, at the age of thirty).

Clara's interest in Eugène d'Albert was not to fade. A few years later he would fall in love with the sensational Venezuelan pianist Teresa Carreño, touring American and European capitals in 1889. This fiery lady, born in Caracas on December 22, 1853, already had two marriage failures behind her (with the violinist Émile Sauret, and a nonmusical Signor Giovanni Tagliapietra) when d'Albert wooed and won her.

The bride was eleven years older than the groom, and their union would endure for three stormy years. After the divorce, Teresa chose a former brother-in-law for her fourth husband.

Women pianists of stature were rare, hence Clara Schumann followed the Carreño career attentively. Trained by the Louisiana-born Louis Moreau Gottschalk, and later by Georges Mathias of Paris, the great Teresa was a showpiece in the Liszt tradition. Her tremendous technique made up for what she lacked in spirituality. Furthermore, she was musician enough to try her hand at composition. She wrote a passable quartet for strings and a number of piano "salon pieces."

Signora Tagliapietra would also leave behind a daughter, Teresita, who likewise trained for a pianist's career. In this undertaking the younger woman was sadly handicapped by her mother's success. There was to hang over the doubtless talented Teresita the same pall that inhibited the offspring of Robert and Clara Schumann.

The query poses itself: should genius not be satisfied to create, while leaving procreation to the less surcharged and more equably endowed population elements? An idle question, since the generation of life is not dependent upon reason.

The birthrate among the Schumanns showed no sign of abating. From New York came Clara's daughter Elise, with husband and two infants, for a family reunion (the first since Elise's marriage). The travelers joined Clara in London and, at the end of her concert season, returned to the Continent with her.

The ensuing summer proved a lesson in internationalism. Through her son-in-law Marmorito, Clara had acquired grandchildren who spoke only Italian. The little Sommerhoffs, though still in baby-talk stage, made strictly Yankee noises.

CHAPTER 28   The late nineteenth century represented a heyday for beards. Apart from members of the female sex, only schoolboys and the clergy braved the light of day barecheeked. Outside the latter two categories any unbearded male was considered not virile, retarded or queer.

Due to his zest for living Johannes Brahms had always appeared far younger than his years. Bushy-chinned cronies taunted him: "Are you planning, like Liszt, to become an *abbé?*"

This became tiresome. In 1881, at forty-eight, he put an end to it by letting his handsome face disappear behind a hirsute garnish which almost overnight made him look like Walt Whitman's twin. Clara, always sensitive about the difference in age between Johannes and herself, approved the change. At last people would stop saying, "Why, she's old enough to be his mother!" She had said this herself for years; but with Brahms having entered middle age she no longer liked to stress the point. Seeing him now in his shaggy disguise she felt suddenly younger. To look on this patriarch as a son was like wanting to mother the Apostle Peter.

Yes, Clara became touchy about age. She recalled a biting retort made by the waspish Bettina von Arnim, years ago, on hearing a woman sigh, "I hate to think of life at forty!" "Why?" the Baroness von Arnim queried sweetly. "What happened then, dear?"

Bettina's rapier tongue had delighted in malicious quips. A favorite piece of advice was, "If you don't want to grow old you must start early with the sloughing off of friends, else they will tell how long they've known you." And another, regarding the ability to make love: "If you don't use it, you lose it."

Poor Bettina had died, possibly unlamented, in 1859 (the year of Magenta and Solferino) at the age of seventy-four. Clara had heartily disliked her, yet nowadays she found much truth in the asperities so freely scattered by the Baroness. They found an echo in her own resentment of the piled-up years.

In this mood she became touchy and hypercritical of the slightest tactlessness, however accidental. During April of 1881 Brahms fell guilty of another *lapsus calami* which she took bitterly amiss. It happened in an ecstatic letter from Italy where he spent increasingly long holidays. He wrote to Clara from Rome:

> I think of you often, wishing that you might revel in the joys that the eye and the heart find here. If you could stand for an hour before the Siena cathedral, you would deem it enough reason to have made the trip. Then, on entering, you see not a patch of flooring in the entire church that does not fill you with delight. And tomorrow in Orvieto you exclaim that *its* cathedral is even lovelier. Finally you lose yourself in Rome, which is indescribable. I would never cease urging you to come, were I a better travel guide, and could I spare you the minor discomforts that women meet with. These, at your age—

There! It had happened again, and he had let the letter go off without noticing the slip. But Clara noticed.

At your age.

Only a truly ugly woman takes offense at being called ugly; she who is beautiful or even just passably fair can laugh it off. It is the old who resent the mention of birthdays (how skillfully they change the subject!) whereas the young celebrate them.

Clara's depression on receipt of the above letter was intensified by a concurrent note from the composer Ferdinand Hiller. With lugubrious humor the latter described the honors accorded him on reaching the age of seventy:

> . . . that kind of festivity is like the prologue to a funeral, people acting all the nicer because they will soon be rid of you. . . .

Wit was not one of her endowments, hence these words failed to amuse her. Herein she paralleled Queen Victoria. The latter too could not be blandished by irony or humor. Both women furthermore were pillars of fortitude, for whom fidelity-beyond-the-grave had taken on a quality of fetishism. Here the Widow of Windsor and the Widow of Bonn were one. And each embodied to perfection the world's most virtuous and unamusing era.

Perhaps impelled by the innocent tactlessness of Brahms, Clara drew up her last will and testament. She was well past sixty-two, an age which the nineteenth century looked upon as senile. She must provide for her dependents: Marie, Eugénie, the institutionalized Ludwig, the ailing Ferdinand and his wife and children. Elise, married to her rich American, presented no problem, anymore than did the remaining Marmorito grandchild. Carefully put in writing, the will was filed with a notary on January 24, 1882.

This duty behind her, Clara's spirits lifted enough to permit her attending some concerts. Charles Camille Saint-Saëns, celebrated since the triumph five years earlier of his opera *Samson et Dalila,* played at Frankfurt on January 25. Clara thought him an "eminent technician," but no artist. In her diary report:

> . . . He achieves his results through industry alone, and even technically he is only a circus rider, offering not a single instance of tonal beauty. His playing is all octaves, with interchanging hands, arpeggios over the whole keyboard (always blurring the finish), enormously powerful chords, trills in tierces [thirds] with two hands, etc. This really ceases to be piano-playing and becomes a tightrope-walking act.

The forty-one-year-old Peter Ilyitch Tchaikowsky (five years younger than Saint-Saëns) also toured the Continent following the 1879 première of his operatic masterpiece *Eugène Onegin.* English engagements lay still ahead of him, and a New York appearance for the inauguration of Carnegie Hall. Clara dealt more kindly with the composer of *Swan Lake, Francesca da Rimini,* and the dramatic *Symphonie Pathétique.* As with Chopin (Tchaikowsky also had French antecedents) the blend of Slav and Western accents cast a spell on her. "Much talent," she wrote, "adroitness, and interest due to the nationalistic accent—"

A few weeks after these events Clara was called again to England. During the peak years of her career she had followed the custom (current among top pianists in that day) of shipping her own instrument, a concert grand Steinweg of German manufacture and surpassing ease of action, wherever she was booked to appear. The fine firms leading the field in her youth, Érard, Pleyel, Stein, Bluethner, Bechstein, continued building high-class pianos of luxury woods and metals, but they were facing the competition of a onetime journeyman organ builder named Heinrich Engelhard Steinweg. This wizard, born at Wolfshagen in the Harz Mountains, in 1797, opened his first workshop at Seesen around 1820. Here, tinkering at night, he constructed his first piano in which he embodied the best features of all others that had come under his scrutiny.

Following the revolutionary violence of 1848, Steinweg emigrated to New York with four sons (Carl, Heinrich, Wilhelm, Albert), leaving a fifth (Theodor) at Seesen. After three years at odd jobs in America the father changed his name to an anglicized version and started his own firm of Steinway and Sons. This was in 1853. Theodor had meanwhile expanded and moved the Seesen shop to Braunschweig, then sold this in 1865 so as to join his brothers in partnership of what became the world's largest piano firm. The new owners of the original German factory were Grotrian, Helferich and Schulz, who recognized the value of the old name. They added to their signature the qualifying phrase *Theodor Steinwegs Nachfolger* (Successors to Theodor Steinweg) and tried meticulously to live up to the standard thus implied.

The preference shown by great pianists for a given brand of instrument was of incalculable value. Xaver Scharwenka took a Bluethner on tour, while Gustav Barth insisted on his Bechstein. Clara Schumann's Steinweg went everywhere with her, save to England where she was balked by an exceptional circumstance. The London firm of Broadwood, Britain's foremost piano makers, furnished her at all times with a practice room as well as a whole collection of "grands" anywhere in the United Kingdom; this included a piano onstage and another in her hotel room or at whatever private home she chose to stay.

In the face of such generosity she was defenseless. Already the invasion of the mellow Bluethners and Bechsteins had harmed English manufacturers. A Steinweg, which matched the rich low tones of these two while boasting an upper-register brilliance that no other piano has ever attained, would have put the Broadwood product still farther in the shadow. Gratitude thus forced upon Clara a paradoxical dilemma:

her best audiences were British, yet they never heard her at her best. That is, on the best of instruments. She put up with the finest that Broadwood could offer, and commented on a diary page dated March 5, 1882:

> The hard action and high pitch of this piano is again giving me trouble. I have been doing my practicing at Broadwood and Sons as always. The other day Scharwenka played on his Bluethner, and a year ago Barth brought a Bechstein, which has hurt the Broadwoods greatly. I simply haven't the heart therefore to insist on my Steinweg; but, oh, how happy I would be to have it, instead of torturing myself with this Broadwood.

A factor not to be discounted with regard to Clara Schumann's preference for an easy-action instrument was the form and structure of her hands. They were delicate, feminine, not at all enlarged or coarsened through a lifetime of playing. Repeatedly Brahms sent her transcriptions of his own works "adapted to the reach of your fragile fingers." It was evident then that Clara's performing magic lay in her velvet touch, though, when called for, she could display almost virile power. Naturally her noblest effects were achieved on a piano that responded to the slightest pressure or nuance. The Broadwood of the middle and late nineteenth century simply was not capable of this.

One person who rejoiced that no Steinweg had to be portaged across the Channel was Clara's overburdened daughter Marie. Now forty-one and withering fast, the eldest of the Schumann offspring never developed a life of her own. Her days were devoted to the furtherance of her famous mother's career. She managed all household problems, business correspondence (taking dictation), travel arrangements, and the carting to and fro of the precious Steinweg. To be spared the hazards of a Calais-Dover piano shipment was for Marie an infinite relief.

As always, Clara returned from England in buoyed-up spirits and with a handsome profit. So mellow was her mood that she decided once again to endure a Wagner performance, in case there "might be something to that fellow after all." On April 26, at Frankfurt, she attended *Das Rheingold,* the first of the *Ring* tetralogy. But, even in a favorable frame of mind, she could not conquer her antipathy. The diary bears witness:

All evening I felt as if I were wading in a morass. One good thing about this opera, it doesn't annihilate one with the brasses. But the boredom, it's awful! Every other moment the people on stage sink into a cataleptic stupor which lasts so long that you just can't look at them anymore. The ladies have barely a few measures to sing, they just stand around, and anyway everybody in the opera is some sloppy, rascally sort of god. How baffled our descendants will be by this lunacy which is spreading all over the world!

On May 9 she braced herself again for *Die Walküre,* with the following reaction:

Some of it interested me, though mostly it was tedious. . . . Those gods simply don't hold one's attention, they are all such bums [*Lumpen*], with Wotan the silliest of them all. . . . The orchestra members talk of the fascinating instrumentation. I suppose I'll have to suffer both operas again so as to pay special attention to this. . . .

She did. On May 16 her reaction is:

Went back to *Rheingold,* to listen to the orchestration. Yes, there are some lovely tonal effects, but they repeat themselves constantly. . . .

And on May 18, after a second visit to *Die Walküre,* her verdict was:

I wanted to follow the music more conscientiously, and really found some fine ringing passages in the first act, yet also a great deal that is reminiscent of Mendelssohn, Schumann, Marschner. . . .

If she was hard on Wagner, who irked her, Clara could also be severe with those she loved. On May 25 of that year she heard Mendelssohn's score to the Sophocles drama *Antigone.* The great Felix had, alas, no gift for opera. Wrote Clara:

Am disenchanted by the music to *Antigone,* which I hadn't heard for many years and had completely forgotten. It simply doesn't fit that superb subject. . . . How Mendelssohn can be the author of such a botchery is quite beyond me!

While on a critical rampage, she had something to say about the well-known conductor Hans von Bülow, ex-husband of Wagner's second wife Cosima. With unpardonable presumption, Clara thought, Bülow had recently undertaken the annotating, fingering, and marking of a new collective edition of Beethoven and Bach. Angrily Clara warned against these issues:

> [Bülow] modifies everything to such a degree that one hardly recognizes the texts, and he leaves students no room for imaginative personal interpretation. I have forbidden my pupils the use of these editions. Yet in the schools they are being adopted!

Bülow's publishers, Breitkopf and Härtel, were also preparing a reissue of Robert Schumann's works, for which Clara had been asked to make the same type of revisions. She declined, but with the suggestion that Johannes Brahms be entrusted with the task. Musically, to her mind, Brahms had no equal. He was *the* composer of his generation, and of generations yet to come. Under his hand no work of Schumann's would suffer.

With her accumulated British earnings Clara Schumann bought the Frankfurt house which up to 1882 she had occupied under lease. She explained her reasons to Brahms:

> . . . We have lived through an annoying time, retiring at night in fear of receiving notice the next day, as our landlord has been wanting to sell his property. Agents and buyers bothered us at all hours. After much thought, and finding no other lodgings to suit us, I decided on the purchase. After all, at my age, it is a nuisance to be moving every few years from one address to another.

At my age.

This time she had said it herself, in her sixty-third year! Johannes breathed a carefree sigh. No longer would he have to watch his tongue. Clara had come to face the inevitable truth.

Even so, and despite flood warnings from Italy, Clara went southward that fall on an extensive holiday. Her itinerary included Bellaggio in Lombardy, then Venice, Milano, and the St. Gotthard Pass, all this in the midst of catastrophic inundations prevailing below the Alps that year. While gliding along the Canale Grande she saw the Venetian Palazzo Vendramino where the septuagenarian Richard Wagner dwelled, already marked for death. She held her head high, taking barest notice. Some months later when German papers carried the news of his passing, on February 13, 1883, she felt a pang. Hauteur is not a pretty vice.

The return route from Italy permitted a detour through Austria and a stop in Vienna. Here Clara rejoiced once more in the cheerful company of Johannes, who had celebrated his forty-ninth birthday in May and was as brimful of *joie de vivre* as ever. She knew no one more appreciative of small pleasures: snow, rain, taking walks through a wood, talking to farmers, foresters, street urchins, or simply sitting down to breakfast at a window open to the morning sun. He loved life. Nay, he doted on it. No wonder then that there should be such felicity and radiance in his music.

"By their works ye shall know them. . . ." What greater truth could pertain to artists?

In one aspect nevertheless Brahms aroused Clara's chagrin. His piano-playing obviously was growing worse from day to day. Preoccupied with constant creation, he had—alas!—no time for practice. Besides, he never thought of himself as a virtuoso. Limelight and applause he gladly left to others. On the rare occasions when he did perform in public it was without formality or pretense, and Clara had to admit that he was hard to listen to. In a later diary passage, of December 29, 1883, she reaffirmed:

> Unfortunately Brahms plays more awfully all the time; he does nothing but bang the piano, cuff it, and grope for the keys. . . .

Her own musicianship during this period was still extraordinary. In her sixty-fifth year she had the following repertoire at her command:

Bach: *Italian Concerto*
    Prelude and Fugue in E-Minor, for organ
    Partita in G-Major
Beethoven: *Sonata, Opus 109,* E-Major
Brahms: *Hungarian Dances*
    Gavotte (Gluck)
    Variations on a Haydn Theme, Opus 56b, for two pianos
    Capriccio, Opus 76, A-Minor
    Intermezzo, Opus 76, A-Major

Quintet, Opus 34, F-Minor, for piano and strings
Sonata, Opus 78, G-Major, for piano and violin
Rhapsody, Opus 79, G-Minor
Hiller: *All Antico*
    Alla Polacca and *Intermezzo* (from *Suite Moderne*)
    Variations on Lützows Jagd (Weber) for two pianos
Mendelssohn: *Scherzo* (from *Midsummer Night's Dream*)
Mozart: *Sonata, E-Minor,* for piano and violin
    Concerto, E-Flat Major, for piano and orchestra
Schubert: *Sonata, A-Minor* (*Ländler* Dance, *Opus 171*)
    G-Major Phantasie, Opus 78
    Sonata, A-Major, for piano and cello
Scholz: *Concerto, A-Minor*
Schumann: *Blumenstück, Opus 19*
    Papillons, Opus 2
    Sonata, G-Minor, Opus 22
    Sonata, F-Minor Variations, Opus 14

In addition, though her opinion of women composers grew more intolerant over the years, Clara kept one of her own works in performing trim. This was her *Trio, Opus 17,* for piano and strings.

She played it, however, only on request.

CHAPTER 29

In February of 1884 Clara set out on her sixteenth concert tour of England.

Up to the last moment she had thought of canceling; the neuro-rheumatic pains plagued her more than ever and would only be aggravated by the Channel crossing. But the joy and stimulus that always attended her British sojourns overcame her pusillanimity.

After a stormy voyage she arrived in London with chest pains and a high fever. The breezy young doctor called in by Clara's hosts (the Burnand family) prescribed an unorthodox cure: a fine dinner doused with champagne. The prescription worked. In consequence Clara enjoyed her usual triumphant and profitable season which ran well into April. During one of her recitals an avalanche of flowers descended on the stage, something unheard-of in staid Albion. As the first bouquet came flying, Clara was terrified; only recently a bomb had been thrown at Queen Victoria in protest against British occupation of Egypt (during the nationalist uprising of Colonel Arabi Pasha to dethrone the khedive). Who could tell but that the posies tossed at Madame Schumann's concert did not contain a charge of dynamite, again as a terrorist gesture? But no. It was all harmless and genuine, a tribute from the audience's heart.

During May, back on the Continent, a tragedy in music circles gave Clara pause. Bedřich (Frederick) Smetana, the Czech pianist-composer (a pupil of Proksch and Liszt), died at sixty in a Prague insane asylum. His chief works lay outside Clara's field: *Prodaná Nevešta (The Bartered Bride)* of light opera fame; the symphonic *Ma Vlast (My Country)*, pervaded by folklore themes; and the *Moldava (Moldau River)* apotheosis. The sinister aspect of Smetana's end lay in the na-

15   225

ture of his illness. He had fallen prey to the musician's curse; deafness to exterior sounds (through a breakdown of the oversensitive tympanum) had set up a riot of dissonances within the composer's skull. These inner reverberations narrowed finally into the hammering of a single note. In despair Smetana had tried to ban his demons by building a composition upon that solitary percussive sound. The attempt drove him out of his mind.

For Clara Schumann this was alarming news. Her own increasing ear trouble was still periodic in character, but she too knew the anarchy of resonances that originated somewhere in the brain without outside stimuli. Would she likewise reach the stage of the single hammering note? Her days were overshadowed by this fear.

The ache in Clara's arms also continued to increase. By autumn of 1884 she had canceled engagements at Leipzig and Düsseldorf as well as in Frankfurt itself. Confined to her home (how she hated inactivity!) her attention turned to a task long postponed: the editing of Robert Schumann's correspondence for publication. In going through her husband's papers, especially the love-letters she had written him in her youth, Clara was deeply stirred. The diary reflects the emotion that beset her:

> An indescribable nostalgia is awakened by these letters, and the wound in my heart bleeds anew. How much have I possessed, and how much lost! Where did I find strength to live on for so much longer, and to keep working? Whence comes the courage of human beings? The children—and the artist life; it is their love and the compulsion of art that have borne me up. . . .

The following summer another familiar name appeared in the obituary columns. On July 31, 1886, Franz Liszt collapsed and died, at seventy-five, while attending a Bayreuth Festival. With him vanished the most brilliant and adored pianistic figure ever known to the musical world, and also an artist whose poorest works grew too popular while his solid achievements were lost sight of. It was Liszt's elegance and flair, plus his tremendous technique, that launched the modern concert-going vogue. Before him only a minority of listeners appeared at recitals, for they were drab and pedantic affairs unless sponsored by some royal court or princely patron. The handsome Hungarian (from Raiding, near Oedenburg) injected dash and glamour into what had been a starveling's profession. He was the matinee idol *par excellence*.

But this would be only a superficial appraisal were it not remembered that the exuberant Franz wrought miracles on the keyboard. That is, the piano with its conventional limitations was not enough for him. He was obsessed with turning it into a whole orchestra, a wonder of polyphonic and polychromatic magnificence. To do this he must have a rich repertoire, and there was none at his disposal. As yet too young to have composed what he needed, he therefore took unknown or seldom-heard works of other masters (as well as folk tunes and gypsy airs) which he expanded into dazzling concert numbers, making them and their original composers fashionable. At the time of his death the number of Liszt transcriptions had mounted to 371, a formidable treasure for the technical perfectionist to draw from.

In Clara Schumann's rejection of Liszt there was evident a conflict of opposite natures. Her plodding Germanic dogmatism could not abide the reckless sweep of his sophisticated and worldly fancy. Only in her childhood, when her own irrepressible instincts had still managed to burst the bonds of· discipline, did she—the sparkling Clara Wieck!—exclaim over Liszt and designate him "the wizard of the keyboard." This he never ceased to be. It was she who had changed. If she later accused him of showmanship (as she accused Wagner) there was more praise in her denunciation than blame, though Clara did not know it. The twentieth century lay just ahead: a century of such scientific and materialistic growth that "art for art's sake" would have a hard time surviving. With such manufactured marvels as the gramophone, the cinematograph, radio, and television—all quite outside the scope of Clara's imagination—the future concert artist was doomed to extinction unless he had precisely what Clara condemned: the dramatic qualities that drew people from their firesides to see and hear him in person. The world owed such artistic mountebanks as Liszt and his son-in-law Wagner a vote of thanks; their vibrant personal magnetism defied the coming age of the machine, and they triumphed (they are still triumphing!) over it.

These external aspects were not compatible with Clara Schumann's pure musicianship; moreover, Liszt the composer was largely unknown to her. The pyrotechnical Hungarian Rhapsodies, though spellbinding, could never be called great. But there were the Nocturnes (*Liebesträume*), the *Dante* and *Faust* symphonies, the *Sonata in B-Minor*, a *Missa Solemnis*, and twelve volumes of *Technical Studies*, which posterity need not disdain. All of this was of course not on a level with

Brahms. It will be a long time before anything ever is. But, though this be faint praise, Liszt's pen has managed to outlive that of his severest critic. Today's audiences do hear his works occasionally; those of Clara Schumann, never.

For the rest, she dedicated a diary page to his passing. It contained a sweet-sour tribute:

> . . . Again, an anyway rare person carried to his grave! How sad not to be able to grieve over this one out of the fullness of the heart. All the glitter around him obfuscates the image of the artist and the human being. He was an eminent virtuoso, but a dangerous example for the young. Almost all newer pianists have imitated him, though they lacked his *esprit*, his genius, and his charm, therefore they become only great technicians and freaks. . . .
>
> Apart from this, Liszt was a bad composer—and harmful to many, though not to the same extent, since his compositions lack the virtues he possessed as a performer; they are trivial, boring, and will surely vanish completely from the world after his death. He always beguiled people through his graciousness and brilliance, so that they performed his works. As a young man he was extremely captivating, but later so much coquetry blended with his scintillating charm that I often found him repellent.

Ah, the graciousness of Liszt! To the gruff and undemonstrative Saxons, not prodigal with amiability, he was indeed an abomination. Never would the waters of the Elbe or Rhine espouse connubially those of the Danube. Even politically the long preached German principle of *Anschluss* or union between Austria-Hungary and the Reich implied no love match; the idea was to bring a not altogether approved set of cousins (the Habsburg nations) into line under rule-bound Teuton preceptors. Franz Liszt and Clara Schumann, the outstanding pianists of the era, symbolized both musically and intellectually two worlds forever apart.

At Whitsuntide of 1886, while Europe learned with shock of the suicide drowning of Richard Wagner's royal patron, Ludwig II of Bavaria, the sculptor Adolf Hildebrand was working on a bust of Clara, which pleased her greatly. It proved a good likeness of her in the autumn of life: grave, matronly, overcast with a tired serenity. One sees here the regular features, familiar from early portraits of the small Clara Wieck, now enlarged and grown heavier with age. The head droops forward and the skin hangs limp under the chin. A faint smile plays on the firm lips, and there is certainly no trace of present or past coquetry. *That* Lisztian foible was something Clara Schumann would never, but never, have had any truck with.

Musically she began tapering off nowadays, though the English tours remained a must. In January of 1888 Clara crossed the Channel for the nineteenth time, dreading that it might be the last. In addition to the aggravated neuritic pains, her hearing had become so defective that she would soon curtail public appearances to a few isolated occasions. In case of indisposition, these could be canceled or postponed without causing too much of an upset. Calling off an entire season was a different matter.

On her return from London by the end of March, Clara found Germany mourning the death of the ninety-year-old Emperor Wilhelm I, and greatly disturbed over the health of his successor, Friedrich III, who had cancer of the throat. Friedrich's wife, a sister of England's future Edward VII, insisted on summoning a British surgeon to Berlin. The subsequent operation proved useless and brought bitter reproof upon the royal lady's head, though Friedrich was past saving even by Prussian knives.

In June (German history books would speak of this as *Das Drei-Kaiser Jahr*, the "Three-Emperor Year") the hapless Hohenzollern was laid to rest and his son Wilhelm II, aged twenty-nine, ascended the throne. With this event a new cycle of European history would be ushered in, beginning with the fall of Bismarck and the abandonment of his policy of Russo-German friendship. The genesis of two world wars, the fall of the Romanovs, and the sweep of Communism across half the globe, were consequences in the still unforeseeable future.

Few poets or musicians paused for a look at history. Clara's notebook for 1888 contains no reference at all to the change of emperors. Some months earlier, in November of 1887, she mentions playing for the Landgravine of Hesse, née Princess Anna of Prussia, who dropped a remark regarding the illness of the then Crown Prince Friedrich.

"Things look bad for the poor man," Clara noted at that time. "He will have to be operated on."

Immediately beneath this was a jotting that had touched her far more deeply; it concerned the death at Wynds Point, Malvern Wells in Worcestershire, of Jenny Lind, on November 2, 1887, at the age of sixty-seven.

With her there go some of my oldest and most beautiful memories. Her death makes me aware of my own age, since I too have one foot in the grave. Who—when we, her contemporaries, are buried —will think of Jenny Lind's great art, her genius?

A bitter thought rounded out this entry: "Such is the lot of every interpretive artist!"

She knew it would be her own as well, since mechanical recording was still in an experimental stage. Thomas Alva Edison had constructed his first phonograph only nine years earlier (its principle having been worked out by the Frenchman Charles Cros some months before that). By way of giving promotional aid to the new miracle, Queen Victoria had allowed her voice to be captured on wax, as had Sarah Bernhardt and other celebrities of the day, including Jenny Lind. A nineteen-year-old Neapolitan named Enrico Caruso would soon be doing the same. But the yelps and squeaks emerging from the mystery-machine sounded like nothing human. Clara Schumann was right: coming generations would never hear the true voice of her time.

Just before leaving for England in the spring of 1888 she realized that this was going to be a final farewell. Under a London heading, on March 26, the diary speaks:

> Last "Popular" [concert]. . . . I was again so nervous, but closed successfully with the *Carnaval*. I believe I have never played it as I did today, yet it is my decision that the England journeys must now end, which grieves me beyond measure. How hard it is to stop voluntarily, when one could still go on! But this resolution is surely right, as my health just won't resist the strain much longer. . . .

On reaching home she faced other perturbations to weigh down her spirit. Her son Ferdinand, interned in a clinic for morphinism, at Blankenburg in Brunswick, was growing worse. He suffered terrifying hallucinations and begged as pitifully as his insane brother Ludwig and the dying Felix had done, to be taken home.

This was of course impossible. But Clara negotiated with a sanatorium near Munich for transfer of the patient, whose muscular reflexes were so bad that he moved about on crutches. Learning of the Munich plans, Ferdinand fell into a state of panic. If his mother would not come for him, he preferred staying where he was rather than face yet another and perhaps more frightening environment.

A compromise was eventually arrived at. That is, Clara found a rustic health center at Köstritz in Saxony, where drug addiction and milder nervous ailments were treated in a homelike atmosphere. Escorted by her, Ferdinand allowed himself to be taken there.

Finding herself in Saxony, Clara stopped at Weimar for a visit to the small Goethe house, which had been turned into a museum. It filled her with strange emotion to enter the rooms where as a child of twelve she had faced the great man. She saw Goethe's piano, a Streicher, standing in the same spot it had occupied when she played for him in 1831.

Fifty-seven years, a lifetime, had passed since then.

She wrote to Brahms about Ferdinand's installation at Köstritz, and received a characteristically generous reply. She must be plagued with money worries, surmised Johannes, whereas mammon piled up in his coffers:

> I am swimming in coin, which gives me no pleasure. I can't and don't want to change my simple way of life. As for my relatives, it is silly to send them more than I already do, and any other dictates of my heart can be followed without causing me any loss.

In short, he begged Clara to accept from him a subsidy for the support of Ferdinand's wife and children. The sum, approximately 5,000 dollars, was lavish for those days. She was deeply touched, but did not agree to gift or loan. She promised, however, that in case of honest need Johannes would be the first to whom she turned for help.

For the present Clara had a different request to make. In the summer of 1888 there was published a book written by her stepsister Marie Wieck, born of Friedrich Wieck's second marriage. The volume dealt with their late father's life, and contained a quantity of notes, letters, and photographs left behind by Clara when she eloped with Robert Schumann. If consulted, she would never have consented to the publication of these.

No legal action could be taken in the matter, as the papers were the dead man's property and pertinent to his biography. But Clara became alarmed at the situation that might arise in case of her own death. In her vast correspondence the exchange of letters between herself and Johannes Brahms predominated. These, especially the early ones, contained passionate sentiments penned by his hand and (she had to admit this to herself) her own.

What would be the attitude of posterity if these things came to light?

She must take steps at once to destroy anything that might tarnish the record of her lifelong devotion to the one and only Robert. The incriminating *billets doux* (an appalling accumulation!) must disappear.

Writing to Brahms, she pointed out the danger involved, and requested the return of every scrap of paper that she had ever sent him. In exchange she would mail back all his own letters to her. There was no question but that each had saved the other's missives. The nineteenth century was a great era for hoarding.

Johannes acceded chivalrously. In his extreme modesty he doubted that his uneventful life (composing, composing, composing) would tempt any biographer. But he promised that, on obtaining from Clara the letters of which he himself was the author, he would consign them to a ceremonial fire in his chimney.

Now, with feminine inconsistency, Clara experienced a change of heart. Of the letters returned by Johannes she weeded out and burned the most effusive ones, allowing those of harmless tenor to survive. But when it came to surrendering what had been written by him, she paused. The ardent pages addressed to her in the first flush of adoration, more than a generation ago, pleased her still. A pity to let them be destroyed. Why should not the world learn that the widow of Robert Schumann, a matron with seven children, had been able to arouse so searing a passion? In short, the letters from Johannes to Clara were a tribute. But those from her to him might cast reflections on Clara's virtue. Sagely she brushed away the ashes of what could have become awkward evidence. Her reputation thus remained unblemished.

Brahms wrote a tongue-in-cheek reproach: "You aren't playing the game! I've sent your letters, but you are holding mine."

She temporized, sorting his epistles the while and tying them into neat chronological packets. Calmly she stored her treasure in an old trunk and tucked away the key.

Then she sent Brahms a glib reply to his comment. A lone bachelor, he might meet an abrupt end, whereupon strangers would invade his rooms and wreak all manner of mischief with papers never intended for public perusal. In Clara's own case no such danger obtained since her daughters Marie and Eugénie were models of discretion.

Johannes might have asked what was to happen when the two worthy spinsters lay also in their graves. But in his heart he understood the promptings of female vanity. Women were scalp-collectors, without exception. As for himself, he saw no reason for hiding from posterity the fact that Clara had been the great love of his life. Except for a brief sublimation of feeling directed toward her daughter Julie, he had allowed no other woman to take Clara's place.

Biographers have speculated on this aspect of his life. Some put forth theories regarding a glandular deficiency in Brahms, or a physical imperfection. But there were lighthearted flirtations to belie the former, and an eventual autopsy disproving the latter. As for his never marrying, he quipped with frequency:

"When I was young, I was too poor. By the time I had money, no girl would have me."

The truth lay elsewhere. It was he who wanted no girl. He wanted Clara.

Now, in their declining years, what did all this matter? The letters that bore witness to his lifelong passion also gave testimony to his failure. He bore this failure without shame. If Clara wished to expose it by preserving his letters, so be it.

He made no further request for their return.

As to the perfunctory analysis of his bachelorhood, propounded by Brahms himself, modern research was not to let the matter rest. For a time there were veiled allusions to homosexuality, based on testimony that in youth the composer was possessed of angelic, almost feminine beauty, and a high-pitched voice. Added to this, Brahms was shy and inhibited because of his short stature, a defect bothering him the more as his parents and other relatives were of average build. His stunted growth must be ascribed to the preschool years when the talented child earned money for his family's support, mostly during late hours when he should have been in bed. Loss of sleep and irregular eating habits left him frail, undersized. Nor could the prosperity of later years undo the damage altogether; when he grew rich enough to eat his fill he gained in sturdiness and girth, but not in height.

The shrill voice that characterized Johannes seems to have had a dual origin. The boy soprano, chanting in the pubs and alleys of Hamburg's waterfront, strained his vocal cords to cadge pennies from sailors on holiday and cabaret girls in their cups. On entering school, furthermore, Brahms was subjected to a prevailing discipline, the harsh insistence on "speaking up" during recitation. Many children of that day piped above their normal speaking level, with a crowing effect often observed in German statesmen, military figures, and orators, none of them less virile of mien than the Iron Chancelor or Martin Luther.

Since girls of his own age were invariably taller than he, Johannes shunned them in youth. During adolescence he played with smaller children or sighed for women twice his years. The fact that his mother had been seventeen years older than her husband also had a bearing on this. The growing boy unconsciously responded to the mother-image personified by fully matured girls.

The celibacy of Brahms nevertheless is not to be confused with chastity. His was a vigorous sex life, though on a crude and coldly rational plane. That is, he distinguished between what Titian called "Sacred and Profane Love," not from choice but necessity. Again the cause goes deep. When the child singer used to make his tavern rounds he was often lifted onto the lap of half-nude prostitutes who amused themselves by subjecting him to lascivious caresses. His innocence outraged and revolted (Clara Schumann's diary reports this), Johannes thenceforth dissociated body and soul, the sensual from the spiritual, mere instinct from emotion. The Hamburg underworld remained for him a symbol of all that was vulgar and base, a concept that also included the compulsions of sex. Having been initiated into the latter by trollops of lowest category he would be unable to turn for such needs to women of genteel upbringing and high station. His physical love life thus took place on a market level. He bought satisfaction, at home or abroad, in the bordellos best suited to his wants.

Sigmund Freud defines such cases (not infrequent among artists and intellectuals) as follows:

> Erotically these types are torn in two directions, classically labeled as celestial and bestial passion. Where they love they do not desire—where they desire they cannot love. The only defence against this dilemma consists in despising the object of one's sexual hunger while, conversely, adulating to excess the soul-mate that is often no more than an incest substitute (a parental or brother and sister reminiscence) . . .

The case of Johannes Brahms corroborates this theory. If, as most serious biographers believe, the composer's love for Schumann's wife (and widow) remained unconsummated on the physical plane, the virtue is not all Clara's. Brahms simply had placed her on so high a pedestal that she slipped out of his reach. Ideals are clothed in abstract beauty. Nothing so gross as the animal urge, or so grotesque as the mechanics of sex, seemed to Johannes compatible with his aesthetic creed. He thus worshiped Clara through the artifice of sublime music, while for earthier ecstasies he sought out alehouse wenches, servant girls, and professional whores.

At moments he recognized that he had chosen the harder way. "How I hate those who turned me against marriage!" he confessed to his friend (and later biographer) Joseph Victor Widmann. Yes, in a civilized society the institution of wedlock, despite all its demands and tribulations, gave man his most wholesome chance at happiness. It channeled his energies, nurtured his pride as parent and provider, and saved him the tiresome (in the long run) chase for a mate every time his hormone so dictated. In short, Brahms realized where lay the root of his personal tragedy. He had been taught too young, and in hideous fashion, a fatal half-truth regarding the cleavage between sex and love. The existence of each alone does not bar their ultimate oneness, where perception has not been distorted.

It is this oneness that Brahms could not bring to his music. While he composed, his two natures did battle. The *Lieder* he gave to the world are, textually and melodically, of the highest order. Yet through much of his work there runs a current of sudden revolt, a lapse in tempo and meter, the breaking off of a phrase as though through a wild groan wrung from tortured flesh (he wept at times, while at the piano). Some of his manuscripts bear startling witness to the conflicts raging within him: besides uncounted dedications to the supremely idealized Clara there are repeated title pages bearing the name of one or another trull from the roster of Vienna's more frequented bawdy-houses.

Another famous bachelor of the period, Friedrich Nietzsche, set himself a different rule. Said this haunted soul and desolate philosopher: "Chastity is the economy of one's creative force. The same energy is expended in conceiving a work of art as in the sex act. The impulses are identical . . ."

Johannes Brahms did not share that opinion. He loved above but lived below the belt.

CHAPTER 30　　　　　　　In 1889 Clara Schumann faced her seventieth birthday.

The year began on a tragic note. On January 30, at his hunting lodge of Mayerling the Austro-Hungarian crown prince, Archduke Rudolf, died in a suicide pact with his seventeen-year-old mistress, Baroness Maria Vetsera. The event stirred emotions throughout Europe but it was given no space in Clara's careful diary. She disapproved of people leading disorderly lives, and wasted no ink on them. Besides, her mind was on the unwelcome birthday ahead, and on the increased decrepitude it must bring. Why make any bones about it? She just didn't like growing old. With almost refreshing ill temper she rejected all embroidery of that bitter truth.

Always effacing themselves in subservience to the illustrious matriarch, Marie and Eugénie prepared to solemnize the great day. Clara was spending the summer at Baden-Baden, where a civic tribute was planned. Friends from near and far sent messages and flowers. The diary page for September 13, 1889, runs:

> At last it is here, the seventieth! Ought one to rejoice in it? A forlorn joy withal. Much love surrounds me, but of how much more I am already bereft. . . . How hard for an artist to reach senility! All the same, the day was made festive by the kindness of children and friends. . . . Masses of flowers; among the first gifts was a basket from the Grand Duchess of Baden. She also sent a personal messenger with a long and touching letter. . . . A happy surprise was the big Medal for Achievement in Art, from the Kaiser [Wilhelm II]. Telegrams all day long. . . . Letters *en masse*. At bedtime I had only one desire, one thought: that Heaven might allow me to enjoy the love of my children a few years longer, not in infirmity, but with the vigor that still stirs in my heart.

Brahms too had come for the celebration, bringing with him a pile of new music. The past decade had been one of his most productive periods, accounting for such compositions as the *D-Major Concerto*, two Rhapsodies, volumes III and IV of *Hungarian Dances*, the *B-Flat Major Concerto*, the *F-Major Quintet* for strings, the third and fourth symphonies, a large number of *Lieder*, some religious Motets, and the great *Sonata No. 3, Opus 108, in D-Minor*, for piano and violin.

Clara was entranced with all these works, particularly the sonata. Back in Frankfurt, her hands itched for the keyboard. She made a diary note on October 30:

> I am currently reveling in Brahms's Third Sonata, which I have started practicing for our quartet. To my vast sorrow it is a great strain for me to play. . . . Ah, how am I ever to live on, if I should have to give it up altogether?

Before the year ended she learned through a press article that another life, which for a time ran parallel to her own, had ceased: the widowed poet Robert Browning died at seventy-seven in Venice, at the Palazzo Rezzonico where he had resided with his son Robert Barrett Browning.

What memories the name evoked! Long ago England had been stirred by the conflict between the youthful lyricist from Camberwell and the despotic father of Elizabeth Barrett, just as in Germany public interest fixed on Robert Schumann's struggle against the inexorable Friedrich Wieck.

In both cases the lovers had eloped, to find idyllic bliss for an almost identical length of time. The Browning marriage ended after fifteen years with Elizabeth's passing. The Schumanns were parted one year earlier, through Robert's internment, though he lived on for another twenty-two months.

The curious interweaving of personalities extended farther. In their beardless and impassioned youth the two Roberts resembled each other most vividly. With equal courage they challenged the dragon of parental authority to liberate the maidens of their choice. Having achieved love's triumph, neither was to know a moment of regret.

Oddly, in later years there emerged a physical identity between Browning and Brahms: both were ruddy of complexion, stocky in build, sanguine, energetic, and—after middle age—unshaven. Their later portraits were practically interchangeable. One mental quirk nevertheless kept them apart: Browning had not much use for Germans, while Brahms was suspicious of Britons. But they coincided in an extravagant passion for Italy. With Browning, Brahms would have exclaimed:

Open my heart and you will see
Graved inside of it "Italy" . . .

Clara's frank preference for England, incidentally, bore fruit at this time. Among former London pupils there had been a talented youth named Leonard Borwick, from Walthamstow, who followed her to Frankfurt. By early 1890 she expected to have him ready for his debut with the London Philharmonic. To cap her joy, the young man was obsessed with Brahms, whose difficult music he mastered with ease.

With Borwick's accomplishments bringing her once again into the spotlight, Clara succumbed to a final temptation. The Frankfurt Museum requested her appearance in a recital on November 7, 1890, and she recklessly accepted.

No sooner had she done so than a nervous agitation befell her. A state of panic gripped both her daughters. Yet on the appointed date Clara sailed through her program with flying colors. The high spot of the evening, Chopin's *Second Concerto*, went superbly. A letter to Rosalie Leser nevertheless describes Clara's preliminary terror:

My frame of mind for eight long days prior to the concert was absolutely ghastly. First, from one hour to the next, the dread that something might happen to me on or off stage. Then there was the fear of performing badly. My thoughts, even at night, were constantly on the *Concerto*, backward, forward, even while people spoke to me; it was unbearable. In spite of this I played well, perhaps never better; I felt as carefree as though sitting at home, plus the inspiration of having an audience. Thank God, though, that it is over. It must be the last time! The children just can't stand the torment any more, Marie was dreadfully distressed for days. . . . What seems remarkable to me is that though I scorn the public from the depths of my soul, I am still dependent on that public and carried aloft by it when I sit there at the piano as in my young years. A secret sorrow grips me. Ah, how hard it is to say good-by forever!

In her diary the above lament is repeated:

> On November 8, I spent the entire day puzzling over the mental and physical agitation I get into nowadays before a concert. The struggle is too exhausting, and I have decided that this was the last big recital for me—but my heart bleeds at the thought that it may truly be the last. . . .

Already she was equivocating: not the last concert, but the last *big* concert. In fact, so long as she had survived it, why not brave the delicious terror anew?

Meanwhile her deafness progressed. That same year, while Brahms visited Frankfurt, Clara attended the theater with him. The play was *Die Ehre (Honor)* by the thirty-three-year-old dramatist Hermann Sudermann, whose realism shocked current German audiences. Happily Clara missed most of the dialogue. The plot, not yet grown hackneyed from overuse, was of the "never darken my door again" school wherein irate fathers drive pregnant daughters into opportune blizzards. Brahms, a placid bachelor in whose life no tempest raged, enjoyed the Sudermann saga.

"Of course," opined Clara's diary, "a man doesn't feel about Those Things as does a woman."

Shortly after this she saw, again without hearing, the soprano Marcella Sembrich in Mozart's *Le Nozze di Figaro.* This coloratura, born Praxede Marcelline Kochanska, at Wisnewszyk, Galicia (Sembrich was her mother's maiden name), had married her teacher Wilhelm Stengel. Just past thirty, she was embarking on a successful world tour with her husband. The Frankfurt engagement proved a triumphant steppingstone, but Clara Schumann had no share in the fanfare.

"Why do I go to the theater?" she wailed. "I enjoyed nothing; the magnificent music reached me only in snatches. I go because I am human, deluding myself with the thought that the next time maybe I shall hear something."

If she played ostrich thus with her own ailments, she did so the more where her son Ferdinand was concerned. Early in 1890 the doctors at Köstritz had notified Clara that Ferdinand was ready for discharge. Under careful supervision he might resume life in the family circle.

On his way to the Saxon town of Gera, where his wife Antonie was staying with relatives, Ferdinand passed through Frankfurt. "A thoroughly broken man," Clara found him, yet she did not suggest that he break his journey. Her own trunks were packed in readiness for the annual holiday at Franzensbad, Obersalzberg, and Baden-Baden, with side trips to Düsseldorf and Bonn.

The greater was her surprise when in the summer news came from Gera that Ferdinand had suffered a relapse and was again taking drugs. Two days later another message: Ferdinand had died suddenly on June 6, at nine o'clock in the morning.

She sent her daughter Marie to the funeral. The diary covers the event.

> *Baden-Baden, June 7.* I am deeply saddened, yet I must say it was a deliverance for the poor boy. What dreary years he has lived through. . . .
> *Monday, the 8th.* My students here have been so sympathetic. They didn't want to take their classes, but I thought it better to teach. I have all day, after all, to follow my sad thoughts. . . . Marie came back [from Gera] after two days. Quite by chance she met a helpful gentleman named Budy, a friend of Ferdinand's and a great admirer of Robert [Schumann]. . . .

Now she had one son left. Or rather, none at all, since Ludwig must be considered already removed from earth. Locked in his cell, mentally blacked out, he was (at forty-two, one year older than Ferdinand) a man buried alive.

What of her daughters? With Julie long dead, and Elise wrapped up in a family of her own, there remained only the eldest and the youngest of Clara's girls, Marie and Eugénie. Neither of these was likely to leave her in response to Cupid's call. Marie was almost fifty; Eugénie, thirty-nine. The pair, then, would be a solace and bulwark to Clara's old age.

Despite this comforting knowledge she faced the twilight years resentfully. Hers was the dilemma of all who want longevity, without grasping that it offers only an extension of the last portion of life, not of the first. To drag on into the nineties in no wise affects the brevity of youth. It merely prolongs the trials of age.

Clara took her hardships with ill grace, yet she could not make friends with the great liberator who alone brought respite: Death. She hated the falling darkness. More than that, she feared the certainty of night.

Her moods, always vehement, grew caustic during the last years.

She quarreled over trifles and fixed on imaginary wrongs. Her temper was vented often upon the faithful, always-forgiving Brahms. Their correspondence suffered interruptions, when it was not marred by an unwonted asperity on Clara's part. Johannes quoted Scripture to her, Proverbs 17, Verse 22: "A merry heart doeth good like medicine, but a broken spirit drieth the bones." She drew from this the wrong inference. Her bones were drying, that was it.

With passing time Brahms curtailed his Frankfurt visits. When he did come he encountered a web of petulance spun by Clara around herself, in which she sat as in a cocoon. Once, after a misunderstanding, he reminded her of a phrase of her husband's. It had occurred in a letter from Robert Schumann to the composer Julius Stern, with whom he had engaged in altercation:

"Let grass grow over it, my friend. Or better, flowers!"

During 1891 an issue arose over a question of copyright. Like most concert artists Clara had evolved a variety of cadenzas that added a special nuance to her program numbers. Such passages, often extemporaneous but later put to paper, were prized by lesser performers who lacked the inventiveness to create their own. The publishers Breitkopf and Härtel were eager to obtain from Clara, in manuscript, all such embellishments for which she had gained much notice.

She was proud to comply. When final proofs were submitted to her for correction, however, she discovered that a cadenza for the Mozart *D-Minor Concerto* contained some eight or ten bars borrowed by her— how many years ago?—from Johannes. It had happened with his permission, to be sure. But did that permission entail the right of publication? Ought she not add a credit line, or at least the initials J.B.?

With a punctilio bordering on the ridiculous she wrote to Vienna about the matter. The diary also bears witness to her scruples:

> How could I let such a thing happen! That cadenza has over the years become so much a part of me that I can't say which notes came from Brahms and which are my own, save for an exceptionally beautiful passage where I am determined to place his name.

Johannes, on the other hand, regarded it as a teapot tempest. Possessed of a better memory, he was able to point out to Clara what actually had happened. The cadenza was, in truth, her own. Long ago she had submitted it to him for criticism and he had added some

16

polishing touches. But these were negligible. On October 2, 1891, he reassured her:

> I beg you with all my heart to let the cadenza be printed over your name. Even the most inconspicuous J.B. would look queer. Besides, the whole thing is unimportant, as I can show you plenty of modern compositions that have "borrowed" from me more than a cadenza! Also, rightly, I should have to add to some of my best melodies, "actually by Clara Schumann"—because whenever I concentrated on *me* nothing clever or beautiful entered my mind. I am indebted to you for inspiring more tunes than you can ever snatch from me in the form of trimmings or the like. . . .

Here, as in all else, his modesty was unfailing. But the nineteenth century, with its plethora of great figures in art, could afford modesty. The Impressionist painter Paul Cézanne, now fifty-two, gave answer to a eulogy by his journalist friend Claude Roger-Marx: "I beg you not to write about me. What I accomplish, in any case, falls so short of what I want to do!"

Another Frenchman, the twenty-year-old Paul Valéry, was envisioning a poem called "Silence." An acceptable draft finally took form in 1896, but it did not satisfy its creator and he withheld it from publication. For more than forty years Valéry was to file and retouch his masterpiece, still castigating himself for its imperfections. Only after his death would "Silence" appear at last in print.

This principle could progress *ad absurdum.* The playwright Paul Claudel, three years older than Valéry; was similarly obsessed with giving only his best. After a dozen revisions of the play *Tête d'Or (Golden Head)* he went to his grave forbidding its presentation, ever.

Though of this self-critical brotherhood, Brahms did not go to such extremes. He wanted his work brought before the public regardless of condemnation. An earnest craftsman, he gave the best that was in him. This did not mean he thought his compositions past improvement. They might very well be improved upon, but not by him.

Regarding the cadenza he never harbored the faintest doubt as to who stood in the other's debt, himself or Clara. If the playing of his compositions had stimulated her toward certain refinements of her concert technique this was her merit surely, and not his.

He would not stoop to quibble. Over this as over all else, let there grow flowers.

CHAPTER 31 In her seventy-third year Clara fell ill of pneumonia. She was nursed by her daughters and made a fair recovery, but the incident led to distressing consequences in that the younger Fräulein Schumann, Eugénie, suffered a breakdown. This was attributed partly to the long night watches at Clara's bedside, in which the sisters alternated, but also to Eugénie's overwork in teaching piano by day. Doctors disclosed an additional cause: the same tubercular predisposition that had claimed Felix and Julie.

Arrangements were made for Eugénie to enter a Swiss clinic. After treatment and repose in Alpine sunshine a change came over the patient: she resolved not to return to Frankfurt, but to strike out on her own. Though her musical attainments were modest, the name Schumann was sure to gain her an instructor's job abroad. She chose England. With the Channel waters between her and the Continent, there was less chance for weakening and turning back.

The decision proved a wise one. London not only acclaimed her as teacher but, perhaps in deference to her famous progenitors, applauded Eugénie in recitals. Soon she was earning enough to permit annual holidays in Germany with her mother and sister. But her days of daughterly servitude were at an end.

At first offended, Clara learned to accept the change. In her heart she admired Eugénie's belated pluck, marveling only that the urge to take flight had not asserted itself sooner. This was after all the era of awakening feminism, a century adorned like no other in history by women touched with glory. George Eliot, George Sand, the Comtesse de Ségur (Sophie Rostopchina), Charlotte and Emily Brontë, the Comtesse de Noailles, Eugénie de Guérin and many others held Clara's admiration for their writings. She followed with interest the progress of Sonia Kovalewska and Marie Sklodowska (later Curie) in science. As for the arts, here women formed the proudest galaxy. Behind the footlights: Eleonora Duse, Elisa Felix Rachel, Sarah Bernhardt, Gabrielle Réjane, Ellen Terry, Adelaide Ristori. In painting: Rosa Bonheur, Marie Bashkirtseff, Paula Modersohn-Becker. And who could list the long train of nineteenth-century opera stars? At random: María Barrientos, Ilma di Murska, Rose Caron, Lucienne Bréval, Emma Calvé, Elvira de Hidalgo, Regina Pinkert, Emma Albani, Judice da Costa, Lilli Lehmann, Emma Eames, Etelka Gerster, Jenny Lind, Félia Litvina, Amalia Materna, La Malibran, Nellie Melba, Wilhelmine Schroeder-Devrient, Marcella Sembrich, Henriette Sontag, Milka Ternina, Luisa Tetrazzini, Pauline Viardot-García, Marie van Zandt.

Clara Schumann's pianistic field was less crowded. She had a quartet of competitors in Teresa Carreño, Emma Eissler, Marie Blahetka, and Faı ny Bloomfield-Zeisler. Also, there were some *Wunderkinder* coming to the fore: the Hungarian Yolanda Merö; the English Myra Hess, who seemed a re-embodiment of the child prodigy Clara Wieck not only in artistry but in physical appearance; and an American Miss Hickenlooper, to be known as Olga Samaroff and as Madame Leopold Stokowsky. Another infant virtuosa was being heard of, Wanda Landowska, whose specialty became the harpsichord.

Finally the century had produced a female composer, Cécile Chaminade, with a ballet and a symphony to her credit; and another, Julia Hanel von Cronenthal, who wrote twenty-two sonatas. The latter was married to the Marquis d'Héricourt de Valincourt, which enhanced her publicity. Though Clara Schumann held women composers (herself included) in low esteem, she allowed the last two names in her mental survey. She was proud of her sex. Even without aid from the suffragette leader Emmeline Pankhurst, currently rampant in England, women were learning to stand on their own feet.

A reactionary portion of mankind, both male and female, continued to invoke the adage that woman's place was in the home, unmindful of the fact that countless women had no home wherein a "place" beckoned to them. But adverse criticism of feminine advancements could also spring from envy. A Spanish nun, the poetess Juana Inés de la Cruz, wrote more than three centuries ago: "He who achieves greatness, makes others feel as though they have been robbed."

The more she thought about it the more Clara Schumann approved the rebel spirit. She realized now that she would have liked to see more of it in her daughters. Even while watching them wither in attendance upon her she had expected secretly, over the years, that they would break away. Julie alone had summoned up the courage while still young. Elise, already past the bloom, had attained marriage and motherhood in her eleventh hour. Eugénie was too late for life's banquet, though she picked up some crumbs.

It was Marie for whom nothing remained, not even crumbs. At Clara's death her eldest daughter would have money in the bank and a great empty house that echoed hollow footsteps. Like the house, Marie herself would be a shell, the husk of a woman wasted without having ever lived.

A house. Money in the bank. Indifferent to material possessions, Clara knew how little comfort rested in such things. In England she had picked up a line from the playwright, Sir James Barrie, which she liked to quote when birthdays or Christmastime approached: "Give me a kiss—then I won't have to dust it!" But for Marie nothing was left save things to dust, and dust itself.

Thoughts of death visited Clara often nowadays. She grew ever more aware of the cold presence. She had come to dread newspapers, yet every morning her eyes fixed with a kind of fascination on the obituary page. Familiar names appeared there in rapid succession: César Franck and Niels Gade in 1890, followed by Leo Delibes a year later, with Gounod and Tchaikowsky in 1893. During the same span there were some important births: Prokofieff, Honegger, Milhaud, Hindemith. But to these names the future had yet to lend significance.

The reading of death notices was hardly conducive to good cheer. Clara's writings reflected this. On December 21, the year of her daughter Eugénie's departure, the following diary entry occurred:

> . . . Bad nights, filled with gloomy broodings. I am so defeated, it hurts. My life is finished, with nothing more to look forward to, yet when a heart remains as sturdy as mine this is hard to bear. Marie has become everything to me, and to please her is my only joy. I also take comfort in the thought that Eugénie is enjoying her independence. . . .

Though the closing line appeared to smack of irony, Clara was sincere. *Au fond,* she applauded Eugénie's spunk. Yes, that was it. A measure of spunk had been required to walk out on Clara Schumann!

The old lady's days revolved now about a single pole, Marie, the first-born who became her last support. Marie wrote most of her mother's letters, received visitors, attended concerts which Clara's ears could no longer endure. Marie saw, listened, and reported.

Brahms came, as he had done so often through the years, at Christmas. Shortly after, another figure out of the past appeared in Frankfurt—Anton Rubinstein, sixty-three and still a sensation on the concert stage.

Marie went to Rubinstein's recital on February 10, 1893, then informed Clara that the keyboard wizard (he was a worthy follower of Liszt) displayed the same antics as of yore, hitting and missing with such gusto that the audience was ravished. Forty years earlier Clara had heard Rubinstein exclaim after one of his performances: "If I could pick up all the notes dropped under the piano I'd give a whole new concert!" The statement still held. But the fabulous Anton would never find time to carry out his boast regarding the debris under the piano. He died the year following his last Frankfurt appearance.

Clara felt the Dark Angel winging closer. A portion of her days was still spent in the music room where she tried out the piano part of three recent Brahms works, the *C-Minor Trio, Opus 101,* and the two Sonatas for violin, *A-major, Opus 100,* and *D-minor, Opus 108.* She also coached a few students. But there was a chill on her soul. The diary bears this out:

> It is doubly hard for an artist to grow old. I still have all my mental faculties, my finger agility; no technical difficulties exist for me. But my nerves have gone bad. What a bitter trial!

Even while penning the above she was troubled with knotty deformations of wrist and thumb joints. She ascribed this to gout, a revolting ailment beneath her scorn. A wholly different matter riled her soul:

> How often the thought besets me nowadays that I shall be forgotten even while still alive! That's the way it is with interpretive artists; once they leave the footlights they are remembered by no one save perhaps their contemporaries. The younger generation knows them not, and will only smile indulgently on hearing their names.

These conclusions were underscored when Eleonora Duse came to Frankfurt in January of 1894 for a performance of *Camille*. Since the great Italian, now thirty-five, was as renowned for her mimicry as for her speech, Clara thought it worthwhile to attend. She would see even if she did not hear. Her impression of Duse was preserved in graphic terms:

> . . . She is an extraordinary apparition, natural, refined, artistic, but the play was quite dreadful. The last act with the death-bed scene in its somber lighting, and the expiring woman there in the stillness—never shall I forget the horror; it was all so convincing that one cannot put it out of mind!

Yet who, in years to come, would be able to evoke Duse's masterful interpretation of Marguerite Gautier? The very next generation, never having seen Eleonora, would have no comprehension of her worth. Thus it was Dumas *fils* who would survive, and his play. But the actors and actresses who had helped build his glory faded into limbo. Of all the arts, that of the performer—the singer, the mime, the dancer, the instrumentalist—is the most ephemeral. Composers, writers, sculptors, painters, even architects, live on in their works. Again and again the aesthetic or emotional impact of their creation is felt by those coming after. This is the living essence of fame. The interpretive genius however is robbed by death of his reality. His name survives in faded records or the hollow ring of spoken recall, never regaining sensory form.

All this weighed heavily on Clara Schumann when Ferdinand's son Nand, now eighteen, broke away from the apothecary profession to which he had been apprenticed, and begged his grandmother to let him become a musician. She reasoned with the boy, pointing out the griefs of so hazardous a career. But the love of melody was in him, and he would not desist. So she took him under her wing as the last to be accepted in her long roster of pupils.

Everything she did nowadays would be so designated, for upon everything there lay an air of finality. In the summers of 1894 and 1895 she took her last trips, at least in so far as earthly travel was concerned. She had longed for one more visit to Paris. But France was in the throes of a military and political scandal: the treason judgment against Captain Alfred Dreyfus and his impending deportation to solitary confinement on Devil's Island. Sentence had been pronounced in 1894. Zola had yet to write "J'accuse," a defense of the doomed man, that would initiate the twelve-year battle ending in exoneration.

Again, these stirring events that so inflamed European consciences of the day found no place in Clara's diary. A reader of her faithful jottings, covering well-nigh eight decades of life, gains no panoramic view of the world and era in which she lived. Not even a clear picture of the Schumann family, the children in particular, emerges. The diary deals with music, and Clara. Seldom is the power of the one-track genius more forcibly exposed. Her single-mindedness was the secret of Clara's greatness, and its lack explains the failure of most mediocre and all amateur musicians.

For Clara Schumann never flagged until broken by age and failing health. She never knew the spasmodic surge and subsequent sloth that attacked spirits of lesser fortitude. Almost until the end she knew no arid periods, no single day when music was not her dominating passion. In this rested her special intransigence: she would not settle for less than perfection. An attitude such as hers might superficially be dismissed as egocentric. But it obeyed compulsions of a rare and complex order. The sculptor Auguste Rodin perhaps best defined the attributes of the great: "They are of necessity grim, harsh, exacting, overbearingly and unashamedly selfish."

In striking France from her holiday itinerary, Clara chose the Swiss resort of Interlaken, enclosed by the waters of Lake Thun and Lake Brienz. A wheelchair went with her on these journeys so that she might enjoy the beauties of nature without overtaxing her legs. She resented this concession to infirmity. On daily outings in the Bernese woodlands the wheelchair often was left under a tree while Clara hiked on with no aid other than a walking stick. On one such occasion she was overtaken by a rider on a runaway horse. To escape injury, Clara and her daughters (Eugénie had come on vacation from England) let themselves glide down a hillside. This proved a rough means of deliverance. With painful scratches and bruises, besides ripped clothing, the three ladies arrived back at their lodgings. Meekly Clara surrendered thenceforth to wheeled locomotion.

Her enforced inertia was somewhat eased by Eugénie's lively reportage on London happenings. A Dublin-born author, Oscar Wilde, had just finished a shocking play which was being published in French for Sarah Bernhardt. Another personage in the public eye was a clergyman's daughter from the isle of Jersey, Emily Charlotte Le Breton, now Mrs. Edward Langtry but known on the stage as Lillie Langtry or (because of her exquisite complexion) the Jersey Lily. This beauty, divorced and well past forty, was being wooed by a stripling twenty-five years her junior, Lord Hugo Gerald de Bathe (she would marry him a few summers later, when he came of age).

Clara Schumann was outraged. Her own renouncing of Johannes Brahms, with only a thirteen-year gap between them, seemed somehow turned into a mockery by this news. One could not but resent the Langtry woman for making Clara's sacrifice seem paltry. The old lady recalled a favorite opinion of her father's. An indifferent Latin scholar, Friedrich Wieck had enjoyed parading his cursory knowledge of the poet Juvenal, who once specialized in pillorying the vices of ancient Rome: *"Difficile est satiram non scribere."* The actions of human beings, even at their most serious, did lend themselves easily to satire.

CHAPTER 32 Toward the conclusion of the Interlaken days Clara again fell prey to melancholy. Her diary contains further carpings against the encroachments of age:

> Where shall I find the courage to live on? How long are the days without work! And even if I try working, what can I do that will not hurt my eyes or my back? I can't read for any length of time, or write, or play the piano, and the outdoors makes my neuritis more painful. Thus my whole concern is to ease the burden for my dear Marie, who lives solely and completely for me. . . .

The closing sentence above held poignant truth. Marie had indeed assumed a pseudo-mother role, denied her in real life. For years now, though neither of them realized it, Clara had become Marie's child.

In this too a vagary of genius was revealed. When need so dictated, genius remained childlike, helpless, demanding. Even in hungry squalor the artist of immortal endowments may show himself irresponsible, world-removed, disdainful of misfortune, and seldom raising a finger to pull out of it. With olympian matter-of-factness and the most perfunctory gratitude, he leans on others.

This could hardly be otherwise, since the genius is in essence godlike, a fragmentary image of the Supreme Creator, and an end unto himself. From what we know of cosmic law, self-purpose leads to self-destruction, though obeying the phoenix pattern of the timeless infant always awaiting rebirth.

Clara Schumann was such a one, sweeping meteor-like across the firmament. Eight times a mother, she was herself the "timeless infant" to whom in varying degree all her children had been sacrificed. Elise suffered the least, escaping barely in time into a foreign marriage. The rest succumbed even if, like the two spinster daughters and the immured Ludwig, they survived the meteor that had scorched their wings. Nor was this altogether Clara's fault. The uncommon cannot be judged by common standards. And for their uncommonness they pay a price: while still on earth, theirs is a special heaven which to the rest of humankind would seem an isolation ward.

With travel having now become a hardship and an impossibility, Clara's distractions grew even more limited. Moments of delight occurred, such as the passing through Frankfurt of the best of the *Lieder* composers, the thirty-five-year-old Austrian, Hugo Wolff. Apart from turning out a plenitude of songs, Wolff was trying his hand at opera, one of his unsuccessful attempts being *Der Corregidor,* based on Pedro de Alarcón's *Sombrero de Tres Picos (The Three-Cornered Hat).* Like Robert Schumann, whom he regarded his model, the Austrian *Lied* master worked under pressure, as though he knew his time was running out. Like Schumann, he was in love with language, often building a whole composition on a single mellifluous word. This led him occasionally into deep waters. On an English visit he glanced at a novel by Sir Walter Scott, wherein appeared the term *usquebaugh.* So exotic did this strike him that he was well along with the fashioning of a compatible tune when he learned that the lovely syllables labeled a famed whisky.

"Ah well," said he as he recalled this mishap to Clara, "since I could not sing it, I drank it!"

They had a little laugh together, happily unaware that Hugo Wolff would die seven years later, deaf and insane like Robert Schumann, his model.

Wanda Landowska also came to Frankfurt with her harpsichord, and Clara saw without being able to hear.

"She will go far," was her verdict. The dark, lean, oval-faced girl reminded Clara of her own youth.

This was, to be sure, not yet the full-blown Landowska of the caustic tongue, capable of disconcerting a select dinner party by screeching at a long absent friend: "Tell me, dear, are you still a virgin?" But, in potential, she was already the prodigious artist foreseen by Clara Schumann. In Landowska's playing there emerged that rhythmic balance which is not unrelated to the mystic delight inherent in higher mathematics. At moments the secrets of harmony allow a glimpse of what astronomers call the Music of the Spheres.

Early in 1896 Clara lost her appetite. Sylphlike in adolescence, she had grown sturdy with maturity. Now she turned suddenly haggard, shrunken. The diary notes her condition:

> *March 21st.* My evenings are dreadful. I am so faint that I can hardly sit up, and something is terribly wrong with my stomach.

Two days later:

> . . . Another dreadful evening. I feel as if I were dying. Poor Marie nurses me day and night—oh!—and weeps with me when I am depressed. . . . Who knows how soon I must leave my children; this thought troubles me all the time. How awful that Eugénie should be coming right now [from London], with a vacation in mind, and then to find me in this miserable state. . . .

March 25, 1896, was a Wednesday. Clara lifted her pen that morning for only a short jotting:

> Yesterday a letter from Dr. Wilkinson [an English friend] from Rome, who writes—

Here the diary broke off. It would be Marie Schumann, the dedicated vestal, who took over. She wrote to Brahms that Clara was now mostly confined to bed, save for brief carriage rides on sunny afternoons.

On one such outing Marie noticed her mother's face change expression and grow ashen. Fearing a fainting spell, she ordered the coachman to turn back. At home Clara recovered quickly, but her tongue became heavy and her speech blurred. Later in the day she sat before her desk and tried to autograph a picture for an admirer. In setting hand to paper she started with a wrong initial. She shook her head disconsolately and closed the inkwell. The doctor diagnosed a mild stroke.

April went by in anxious suspense. Brahms informed Marie that he had canceled an engagement at Merano and was standing by for further news. If Clara's condition grew more alarming he would leave at once for Frankfurt.

In May he received a birthday greeting, badly garbled but in Clara's so dear script. It reached him a day late, and he answered in terms strangely suggestive of Robert Browning:

What's Last is Best! Never have I found this more true than today, with arrival of the words I deem most precious—yours!

Always and always Clara would remain to Johannes "the Last, for which the First was made," and the thought of her loss was inconceivable. In these days of overhanging dread he composed the group of musical poems called *Ernste Gesänge (Solemn Songs)* that would, to his sorrow, become her dirge.

The news from Marie continued hopeful. On May 9, after being wheeled through the garden for a view of its springtime glory, Clara sat in the parlor to watch her grandson Nand at the piano. He was talented after all. Though she heard almost nothing, her eyes took in the sureness of attack and manner with which he played the Schumann *Intermezzi* and the *F-Sharp Major Romance*. Speech came hard, so she thanked him with a nod.

There was another week of seeming improvement. Then, at dawn of May 10, 1896, a change. Emaciated despite forced feedings, the frail body flagged under the weight of nearly four score years. In September, Clara would have been seventy-seven.

A wire was sent to Brahms, and the hours went by in nervous waiting. Afternoon came, with the Angel of Death winging nearer. At sunset the spark of life, already so feeble as to be almost undetectable, faded out.

When Brahms arrived, the eyes of her whom he called *"diese herrliche Frau"* ("this magnificent woman") were closed forever. He could accompany only her earthly remains to Bonn. Here they were laid to rest beside the husband to whom she had remained true through forty years of widowhood.

After the Bonn exequies were over, Johannes returned to Vienna. He tried to pick up the threads of his existence. But they were so irreparably interlaced with her whom he had loved first, last, and always, that there was no untangling them.

He vegetated through the summer, listless, lost, a shadow of his normal vibrant self. Occasionally his gift for banter reasserted itself, as when a young student asked what was the first requisite for the would-be pianist. Remembering his years of poverty, Johannes answered:

"A small appetite, my boy!"

But the days of salty repartee were over. Almost hourly Brahms was seen failing in health. A visit to Carlsbad in October elicited the medical verdict that his liver was going bad.

So it was.

He had no doubt about it, and cared less.

On March 7, 1897, Brahms pulled himself together and gave his last recital. It happened in Vienna. His playing, long flayed by Clara, was lamentable. But listeners found the music, all of it his own, sublime. The audience clamored for encores, though he did not seem to hear. He went home quietly and was not again seen in public.

Less than a month later, at dawn on April 3 Johannes Brahms died intestate. In life he had repeatedly spoken of leaving his quite considerable fortune to indigent musicians, under administrative control by the Vienna Society of Music Friends. But he had never got around to putting this in writing. The drawing up of a last will and testament appeared to him, as to many people, somewhat ominous. Thoughts of death meant the conjuring and inviting of death. His buoyant, life-affirming ego would never issue such an invitation. Thus time ran out, and his intended dispositions did not come to be executed. The money that might have done such general good fell into the hands of distant relatives whom Johannes had seen seldom and heartily disliked.

He reached the age of sixty-four—a slight man, but in spirit a Titan of joyous and inexhaustible resources. Joyous they had to be, since he lacked any tendency toward doldrums. Inexhaustible they remained while there was love. All radiance vanished for him, however, with her in whom his love reposed. He did not survive Clara Schumann by a single year.

The feel of death is in the heart.

The End

The Works of
Robert Schumann, Clara (Wieck) Schumann, and *Johannes Brahms*
in Chronological Order

NOTE: Opus numbers may not appear in proper sequence because composers, in common with other artists, often put one task aside in order to pursue another. Thus long periods can elapse before a fragmentary manuscript is again picked up and completed, its number having meanwhile dropped out of line.

Similarly, any date given here marks the year a work was finished and (in some instances, though not always) published.

Robert Schumann

YEAR	OPUS	
1828	1.	*Abegg Variations*
1830	2.	*Papillons*
1831	8.	*Allegro,* B-minor
1832	3.	*Six Concert Etudes* based on Paganini's *Capricci,* Vol. I
	4.	*Intermezzi:* A-major, E-minor, A-minor, C-major, D-minor, B-minor
1833	5.	*Impromptus on a theme by Clara Wieck*
	7.	*Toccata,* C-major
1834	10.	*Six Concert Etudes* based on Paganini's *Capricci,* Vol. II
1835	9.	*Carnaval:* Préambule, Pierrot, Arlequin, Valse Noble, Eusebius, Florestan, Coquette, Réplique, Sphinxes, Papillons, ASCH-SCHA (Lettres Dansantes), Chiarina, Chopin, Estrella, Reconnaissance, Pantalon et Colombine, Valse Allemande, Intermezzo-Paganini, Aveu, Promenade, Pause, Marche des Davidsbündler contre les Philistins
	11.	*Sonata No. 1,* F-sharp minor
	13.	*Twelve Symphonic Études*

YEAR	OPUS	
1836	17.	*Phantasie,* C-major
1837	12.	*Phantasiestücke:* Des Abends—Aufschwung—Warum?—Grillen—In der Nacht—Fabel—Traumes Wirren—Ende vom Lied
	6.	*Davidsbündler Dances:* G-major, B-minor, G-major, B-minor, D-major, D-minor, G-minor, C-minor, C-major, D-minor, D-major, E-minor, B-minor and major, E-flat major, B-flat major, G-major and B-minor, B-major and minor, C-major
1838	14.	*Sonata No. 3,* F-minor (also known as Grand Sonata for Concert)
	15.	*Childhood Scenes (Kinderszenen):* Von fremden Ländern und Menschen—Curiose Geschichte—Hasche-Mann—Bittendes Kind—Glückes genug—Wichtige Begebenheit—Träumerei—Am Kamin—Ritter vom Steckenpferd—Fast zu ernst—Fürchtenmachen—Kind im Einschlummern—Der Dichter spricht
	16.	*Kreisleriana Phantasies:* D-minor, B-flat major, G-minor, B-flat major, G-minor, B-flat major, G-minor with E-flat major, G-minor
	21.	*Novelettes:* F-major, D-major, D-major, D-major, D-major, A-major, E-major, F-sharp minor with D-major
	22.	*Sonata No. 2,* G-minor
	32.	*Four Piano Pieces:* Scherzo, Gigue, Romance, Fughetta
1839	18.	*Arabesque,* C-major
	19.	*Blumenstück,* D-flat major
	20.	*Humoresque,* B-flat major
	23.	*Nachtstücke:* C-major, F-major, D-flat major, F-major
	26.	*Faschings-Schwank aus Wien (Pre-Lent in Vienna):* Allegro, Romance, Scherzino, Intermezzo, Finale
	28.	*Three Romances:* B-flat minor, F-sharp minor, B-major
1840	25.	*Myrthen* cycle for voice and piano: Widmung (Friedrich Rückert)—Freisinn (Goethe)—Der Nussbaum (Julius Mosen)—Someone (Robert Burns)—Sitz' ich allein (Goethe)—Setze mir nicht (Goethe)—Die Lotosblume (Heine)—Talismane (Goethe)—Lieder der Suleika (Goethe)—The Highland Widow (Burns)—Mutter, Mutter! (Rückert)—Lass' mich ihm am Busen hangen (Rückert)—Highlander's Farewell (Burns)—Highland Lullaby (Burns)—My heart is heavy (Byron)—Riddle (Byron)—Softly rowing (Moore)—When through the piazza (Moore)—The Captain's Wife (Burns)—Far, far (Burns)—Was will die einsame Träne (Heine)—Nobody (Burns) In the West (Burns)—Du bist wie eine Blume (Heine)—Aus den östlichen Rosen (Rückert)—Zum Schluss (Rückert)
	24.	*Liederkreis* (Heine cycle): Morgens steh' ich auf—Es treibt mich—Ich wandelte unter den Bäumen—Lieb' Liebchen

—Schöne Wiege meiner Leiden—Warte, warte, wilder
Schiffmann—Berg' und Burgen schau'n herunter—An
Rosen

27. *Lieder und Gesänge,* Vol. I: Sag' an, o lieber Vogel mein
(Friedrich Hebbel)—My luve's like a red, red rose
(Burns)—Was soll ich sagen (Adalbert von Chamisso)—
Jasminen Strauch (Rückert)—Nur ein lächelnder Blick
(Johann Georg Zimmermann)

34. Four Duets

30. *Drei Gedichte* (three poems by Emmanuel Geibel): Der
Knabe mit dem Wunderhorn—Der Page—Der Hidalgo

31. *Drei Gesänge* (three chants by Chamisso): Die Löwenbraut
—Die Kartenlegerin (Chamisso-transcribed text of Pierre
Jean de Béranger)—Die rote Hanne (Chamisso-Béranger)

33. *Sechs Lieder,* six a-capella songs for male voices: Der
träumende See (Mosen)—Die Minnesänger (Heine)—
Die Lotosblume (Heine)—Der Zecher als Doctrinair
(Mosen)—Rastlose Liebe (Goethe)—Frühlingsglocken
(Robert Reinick)

35. *Zwölf Gedichte* (twelve poems by Justinus Kerner): Lust
der Sturmnacht—Stirb, Lieb' und Freud'—Wanderlust—
Erstes Grün—Sehnsucht nach der Waldgegend—Auf das
Trinkglas eines verstorbenen Freundes—Wanderung—
Stille Liebe—Frage—Stille Tränen—Wer machte dich so
krank?—Alte Laute

36. *Sechs Gedichte* (Reinick): Sonntag am Rhein—Ständchen—
Nichts schöneres—An den Sonnenschein—Dichters Gen-
esung—Liebesbotschaft

37. *Zwölf Gedichte* Liebesfrühling (Rückert): Der Himmel hat
eine Träne geweint—Er ist gekommen (in collaboration
with Clara Schumann)—O ihr Herren—Liebst du um
Schönheit (with Clara Schumann)—Ich hab' in mich
gesogen—Liebste, was kann dies uns scheiden—Schön ist
das Fest des Lenzes—Flügel! Flügel! um zu fliegen—
Rose, Meer und Sonne—O Sonn', o Meer, o Rose!—Warum
willst du andre fragen (with Clara Schumann)—So wahr
die Sonne scheinet

29. *Drei Gedichte* (Geibel) for male quartet, with piano:
Ländliches Lied (duo)—Lied (trio)—Zigeunerleben
(quartet)

39. *Liederkreis* (Joseph von Eichendorff): In der Fremde—In-
termezzo—Waldesgespräch—Die Stille—Mondnacht—
Schöne Fremde—Auf einer Burg—Wehmut—Zwielicht—
Im Walde—Frühlingsnacht

40. *Fünf Lieder* (four texts by Andersen, fifth by Chamisso):
Märzveilchen—Muttertraum—Der Soldat—Der Spielmann
Verratene Liebe

Second Parts: B-flat major, G-minor, B-flat major (Camp Scene), E-flat major

70. *Adagio-Allegro,* horn or violin or cello, piano, A-flat major

1846   55. *Five Lieder* (Burns) a capella: Highland Maid—Toothache —I Long for the Village—The Good Old Days—Highland Lad

61. *Symphony No. 2,* C-major

59. *Vier Gesänge* mixed chorus, a capella: Nord oder Süd (Lappe)—Am Bodensee (Karl-August von Platen)— Jägerlied (Eduard Mörike)—Gute Nacht (Rückert)

1847   63. *Trio, No. 1* (piano, violin, cello), D-minor

80. *Trio, No. 2* (piano, violin, cello), F-major

62. *Drei Lieder,* male chorus, a capella: Der Eidgenossen Nacht- wache (Eichendorff)—Freiheitslied (Rückert)—Schlacht- gesang (Friedrich Gottlieb Klopstock)

64. *Romanzen und Balladen,* Vol. IV: Die Soldatenbraut (Mörike) — Das verlassene Mägdelein (Mörike) — Tragödie (Heine): Entflieh' mit mir; Es fiel ein Reif; Auf ihrem Grab (duo)

65. *Ritornelle* (Rückert) roundelay in canon form for male quartet: Die Rose stand im Tau—Lasst Lautenspiel und Becherklang—Blüth' oder Schnee—Gebt mir zu trinken!— Zürne nicht des Herbstes Wind—In Sonnentagen—In Meeres Mitten

84. *Beim Abschied zu singen* ("Farewell") for chorus and wind instruments, text by Feuchtersleben

66. *Bilder aus dem Osten,* six impromptus for four hands: B-flat minor, D-flat major, D-flat major, B-flat minor, F-minor, B-flat minor and major

73. *Phantasiestücke,* clarinet or violin or cello; piano

1848   68. *Youth Album,* piano pieces
Part I, for smaller children: Melodie—Soldatenmarsch— Trällerliedchen—Ein Choral—Stückchen—Armes Waisen- kind — Jägerliedchen — Wilder Reiter — Volksliedchen — Fröhlicher Landmann—Sicilianisch—Knecht Ruprecht— Mai, lieber Mai—Kleine Studie—Frühlingsgesang—Erster Verlust—Kleiner Morgenwanderer—Schnitter Liedchen
Part II, for older children: Kleine Romanze—Ländliches Lied —(nameless)—Rundgesang—Reiterstück—Ernteliedchen —Nachklänge aus dem Theater—(nameless)—Canon- isches Liedchen—Erinnerung—Fremder Mann—(name- less)—Kriegslied—Scheherazade—Weinlesezeit, fröhliche Zeit!—Thema—Mignon—Lied italienischer Marinari— Matrosenlied — Winterszeit 1. — Winterszeit 2. — Kleine Fuge Nordisches Lied (Gruss an G.)—Figurierter Choral —Sylvesterlied

81. *Genoveva* (opera with text by Tieck, Hebbel, Schumann)

YEAR	OPUS	
	82.	*Waldscenen,* piano pieces: Eintritt—Jäger auf der Lauer—Einsame Blumen—Verrufene Stelle—Freundliche Landschaft—Herberge—Vogel als Prophet—Jagdlied—Abschied
	71.	*Adventlied* (Rückert), soprano solo, choir, and orchestra
1849	115.	*Manfred* (overture and incidental music based on Byron epic)
	76.	*Four Marches,* piano
	85.	*Zwölf Klavierstücke,* twelve four-handed piano pieces for small and big children: Geburtstagsmarsch—Bärentanz—Gartenmelodie—Beim Kränzewinden—Kroatenmarsch—Trauer—Turniermarsch—Reigen—Am Springbrunnen—Verstecken—Gespenstermärchen—Abendlied
	92.	*Introduction and Allegro Appassionato,* for piano and orchestra, G-major
	132.	*Märchenerzählungen,* piano, clarinet or violin, viola; *Andante and Variations,* two pianos, two cellos, horn (original version of Opus 46)
	74.	*Spanisches Liederspiel,* quartets, duos, and solos from the Spanish, with piano: Erste Begegnung—Intermezzo—Liebesgram—In der Nacht—Es ist verraten—Melancholie—Geständnis—Botschaft—Ich bin geliebt—Der Contrabandiste
	138.	*Spanische Liebeslieder,* as above, with two pianos: Vorspiel—Lied—Lied—Duet—Romanze—Intermezzo—Lied—Lied—Duet—Quartet
	67.	*Romanzen und Balladen,* chorus a capella, Vol. I: Der König von Thule (Goethe)—Schön Rohtraut (Mörike)—Heidenröslein (Goethe)—Ungewitter (Chamisso)—John Anderson (Burns)
	75.	*Romanzen und Balladen,* chorus a capella, Vol. II: Schnitter Tod (old German folksong)—Im Walde (Eichendorff)—Der traurige Jäger (Eichendorff)—The Recruit (Burns)—Vor verwundeten Knaben (old German ballad)
	78.	*Four Duos,* piano, soprano, tenor: Tanzlied (Rückert)—Er und sie (Kerner)—Ich denke dein (Goethe)—Wiegenlied (Hebbel)
	124.	*Albumblätter,* piano: Impromptu—Leides Ahnung—Scherzino—Walzer—Phantasie Tanz—Wiegenliedchen—Ländler—Leid ohne Ende—Impromptu—Walzer—Romanze—Burla—Larghetto—Vision—Walzer—Schlummerlied—Elfe—Botschaft—Phantasie Stück—Canon
	79.	*Liederalbum für die Jugend:* Der Abendstern (anon.)—Schmetterling (anon.)—Frühlingsbotschaft (anon.)—Frühlingsgruss (anon.)—Vom Schlaraffenland (anon.)—Sonntag (anon.)—Zigeunerliedchen (Geibel)—Des Knaben Berglied (Johann Ludwig Uhland)—Mailied (anon.)—Käuzlein (from anthology *Des Knaben Wunderhorn*)—

Hinaus in's Freie! (Hoffmann von Fallersleben)—Der Sandmann (Kletke)—Marienwürmchen (*Wunderhorn*)—Die Waise (Fallersleben)—Das Glück (Hebbel)—Weihnachtslied (Andersen)—Die wandelnde Glocke (Goethe)—Frühlingsankunft (Fallersleben)—Die Schwalben (anon.)—Kinderwacht (anon.)—Des Sennen Abschied (Schiller)—Er ist's (Mörike)—Spinnelied (anon.)—Des Budenschützen Lied (Schiller) Schneeglöckchen (Rückert—Lied Lynceus des Türmers (Goethe)—Mignon (Goethe)

86. *Concerto,* four horns and orchestra, F-major
69. *Romanzen,* women's chorus and piano, Vol. I:
Tamburinschlägerin (Eichendorff)—Waldmädchen (Eichendorff)—Klosterfräulein (Kerner)—Soldatenbraut (Mörike)—Meerfey (Eichendorff)—Die Kapelle (Uhland)

91. *Romanzen,* women's chorus and piano, Vol. II:
Rosmarin (old German folksong)—Jäger Wohlgemut (*Wunderhorn*)—Der Wassermann (Kerner)—Das verlassene Mägdelein (Mörike)—Der Bleicherin Nachtlied (Reinick)—In Meeres Mitten (Rückert)

93. *Verzweifle nicht* (Rückert) motet, double male chorus, organ
94. *Drei Romanzen,* oboe or violin or clarinet; piano
97. *Symphony No. 3* ("Rhineland"), E-flat major
95. *Drei Gesänge* (Byron; Hebrew songs), with piano or harp:
The Daughter of Jephtha—To the Moon—To the Hero

77. *Lieder und Gesänge,* Vol. III: Der frohe Wandersmann (Eichendorff)—Mein Garten (Fallersleben)—Geisternähe (Baron Joseph Münch-Bellinghausen, pseud. Friedrich Halm)—Stiller Vorwurf (anon.)—Aufträge (L'Egru)

96. *Lieder und Gesänge,* Vol. IV: Nachtlied (Goethe)—Schneeglöckchen (anon.)—Ihre Stimme (Platen)—Gesungen (Wilfried von der Neun)—Himmel und Erde (old German folksong)

98. *Lieder und Gesänge aus "Wilhelm Meister"* (Goethe): Kennst du das Land?—Ballade des Harfners—Nur wer die Sehnsucht kennt—Wer nie sein Brod mit Tränen—Heiss' mich nicht reden—Wer sich der Einsamkeit—Singet nicht in Trauertönen—An die Türen will ich schleichen—So lasst mich scheiden
Requiem für Mignon from *"Wilhelm Meister"* (Goethe), solos, chorus, orchestra

99. *Bunte Blätter,* piano: Drei Stücklein—Fünf Album Blätter—Novelette—Praeludium—Marsch—Abendmusik—Scherzo—Geschwindmarsch

101. *Minnespiel* (Rückert), solos, duets, quartets, with piano:
Lied—Gesang—Duet—Lied—Quartet—Lied—Duet—Quartet

YEAR	OPUS	
	102.	*Fünf Stücke im Volkston* for piano and violin, or cello
	103.	*Mädchenlieder* (Elisabeth Kulmann), duets with piano: Mailied Frühlingslied—An die Nachtigall—An den Abendstern

Sommer Ruf (Schad), duet with piano

108. *Nachtlied* (Hebbel), chorus and orchestra
106. *Schön Hedwig* (Hebbel), piano accompaniment to recitation
137. *Jagdlieder* (Laube), five hunting songs, chorus, with horns
131. *Phantasie*, violin and orchestra, C-major
141. *Vier Gesänge*, double chorus, a capella: An die Sterne (Rückert)—Ungewisses Licht (Joseph Christian von Zedlitz)—Zuversicht (Zedlitz)—Talismane (Goethe)
144. *Neujahrslied* (Rückert), for chorus and orchestra
145. *Romanzen und Balladen*, chorus, a capella, Vol. III:
Der Schmidt (Uhland)—Die Nonne (anon.)—Der Sänger (Uhland)—John Anderson (Burns)—Romanze vom Gänsebuben (Malsburg)
146. *Romanzen und Balladen*, chorus, a capella, Vol. IV:
Brautgesang (Uhland)—Streetsinger Willie (Burns)—Der Traum (Uhland) Sommerlied (Rückert)—Das Schifflein (Uhland) *ad lib.* flute and horn

Der deutsche Rhein, solo, chorus, piano

1850 83. *Drei Gesänge*, with voice and piano: Resignation (anon.)—Die Blume der Ergebung (Rückert)—Der Einsiedler (Eichendorff)

87. *Ballade: Der Handschuh* (Schiller), voice and piano
89. *Sechs Gesänge* (Neun), voice and piano: Es stürmet am Abendhimmel—Heimliches Verschwinden—Herbstlied—Abschied vom Walde—In's Freie—Röselein, Röselein
90. *Sechs Gedichte* (Lenau), voice and piano:
Lied eines Schmiedes—Meine Rose—Kommen und Scheiden—Die Sennerin—Einsamkeit—Der schwere Abend—Requiem

129. *Concerto*, for cello and orchestra, A-minor
100. *Overture, Braut von Messina* (Schiller)

1851 120. *Symphony No. 4*, D-minor

110. *Trio No. 3*, piano, violin, cello; G-minor
105. *Sonata No. 1*, violin and piano, A-minor
121. *Sonata No. 2*, violin and piano, D-minor

Accompaniment, piano, for six violin Sonatas of Bach

128. *Overture, Julius Caesar* (Shakespeare), F-minor
136. *Overture, Hermann und Dorothea* (Goethe), B-minor
104. *Sieben Lieder* (Kulmann), voice and piano: Mond, meiner Seele Liebling—Viel Glück zur Reise—Du nennst mich armes Mädchen—Der Zeisig—Reich' mir die Hand—Die letzten Blumen starben—Gekämpft hat meine Barke
117. *Vier Husarenlieder* (Lenau) for voice and piano: Der Husar,

YEAR OPUS

123. *Overture* on the "Rheinwein Lied"
126. *Sieben Clavierstücke in Fughettenform:* A-minor, D-minor,
     A-major, F-sharp minor, F-major, A-minor
118. *Drei Clavier Sonaten für die Jugend:* G-major, D-major,
     C-major
130. *Kinder Ball,* six easy dances, for four hands: Polonaise—
     Walzer—Menuett—Ecossaise—Française—Ringelreihe
133. *Gesänge der Frühe,* piano: D-major, D-major, A-major, F-
     sharp minor, D-major
     Canon "To Alexis," A-flat major
     Scherzo and Presto Appassionato (an abandoned scherzo
     from the Sonata, Opus 1, and the original finale of the
     Sonata, Opus 22)
     Five Variations (discarded from Opus 13)
     Theme, E-flat major (supposed by Schumann, already very
     ill, to be a spirit message from Schubert and Mendelssohn)
134. *Concerto* (Allegro and Introduction), D-minor and major,
     for piano and orchestra

Compositions by Clara Wieck (in childhood and girlhood; dates uncertain)

FOR PIANO

OPUS

1. *Quatre Polonaises*
2. *Caprices* en forme de Valse
3. *Romance Varié*
4. *Valse Romantique*
5. *Quatre Pieces Caracteristiques*
6. *Soirées Musicales:* Toccatina, Ballade, Nocturne, Polonaise, Deux Mazurkas
7. *Premier Concert,* with orchestra
8. *Variations de Concert* (on Bellini's "Pirate's Cavatine")
9. *Souvenir de Vienne* (Impromptu)
10. *Scherzo*
11. *Trois Romances*

Compositions by Clara Schumann (during marriage and widowhood)

12. *Liebesfrühling* (Nos. 2, 4, 11) for piano
13. *Sechs Lieder,* voice and piano: Ich stand in dunklen Träumen (Heine)
    —Sie liebten sich beide (Heine)—Der Mond kommt still gegangen

Johannes Brahms

YEAR	OPUS	
1862	17.	*Lieder* (female chorus, two horns, and harp): Es tönt ein voller Harfenklang (Ruperti)—Twelfth Night (Shakespeare) Der Gärtner (Eichendorff)—Song from "Fingal" (Ossian)
	19.	*Fünf Gedichte* (voice and piano): Der Kuss (Hölty)—*Scheiden und Meiden* (Uhland)—In der Ferne (Uhland)—Der Schmied (Uhland)—An eine Aeols Harfe (Mörike)
	22.	*Marienlieder* (four-voiced mixed chorus): Part I. Der englische Gruss—Maria's Kirchgang—Maria's Wallfahrt; Part II. Der Jäger—Ruf zur Maria—Magdalena—Maria's Lob
	24.	*Variations and Fugue on a Handel Theme* (piano)
1863	23.	*Variations on a Robert Schumann Theme* (two pianos)
1864	34.	*Sonata for Two Pianos,* F-minor (also written as a string and piano quintet)
1865	40.	*Trio* (piano with violin and horn or cello and viola), E-flat major: Andante—Scherzo—Adagio—Allegro
1866	45.	*German Requiem* (chorus, solos, orchestra), organ *ad lib.*
	51.	*Two String Quartets:* I. C-minor Allegro—Romanza—Allegretto—Un poco più animato —Allegro II. A-minor Allegro—Andante—Quasi Minuetto—Allegretto—Allegro
	35.	*Variations on a Paganini Theme* (etudes, 2 vols.)
	36.	*Sextet No. 2,* G-major (strings): Allegro—Scherzo—Poco Adagio—Poco Allegro
	37.	*Three Sacred Chorales* (female voices, a capella): O bone Jesu—Adoramus te—Regina Coeli
	38.	*Sonata No. 1* (cello and piano), E-minor: Allegro—Allegretto —Allegro
1867	39.	*Waltzes for Two Pianos*
	41.	*Soldatenlieder* (male choir, a capella): Ich schwing mein Horn (old folksong)—Freiwillige her! (Carl Lemcke)— Geleit (Lemcke)—Gebt Acht (Lemcke)
1868	50.	*Cantata "Rinaldo"* (Goethe) for chorus, tenor solo, and orchestra
	33.	*Fifteen Romances of Magelone* (Ludwig Tieck), voice and piano: Book I. Keinen hat es noch gereut—Traun! Bogen und Pfeil—Sind es Schmerzen, sind es Freuden Book II. Liebe kam aus fernen Landen—So willst du des Armen—Wie soll ich die Freude Book III. War es dir—Wir müssen uns trennen—Ruhe, Süssliebchen

Book IV. So tönet denn—Wie schnell verschwindet—Muss es eine Trennung geben?

Book V. Geliebter, wo zaudert dein irrender Fuss—Wie froh und frisch—Treue Liebe dauert lange

43. *Vier Lieder* (voice and piano): Von ewiger Liebe (Joseph Wenzig)—Die Mainacht (Hölty)—Ich schell' mein Horn (old folksong)—Das Lied vom Herrn von Falkenstein

46. *Vier Lieder* (voice and piano): Die Kränze (Daumer)—Magyarisch (Daumer)—Die Schale der Vergessenheit (Hölty)—An die Nachtigall (Hölty)

47. *Fünf Lieder* (voice and piano): Botschaft (Daumer-Hafiz)—Liebesglut (Daumer-Hafiz)—Sonntag (Uhland)—O liebliche Wangen (Paul Flemming)—Die Liebende schreibt (Goethe)

48. *Sieben Lieder* (voice and piano): Der Gang zum Liebchen (Bohemian ballad)—Der Uberläufer (from anthology *Des Knaben Wunderhorn*)—Liebesklage des Mädchens (*Wunderhorn*)—Gold überwiegt die Liebe (Bohemian ballad)—Trost der Tränen (Goethe)—Vergangen ist mir Glück (German folksong)—Herbstgefühl (Count Adolf Friedrich von Schack)

49. *Fünf Lieder* (voice and piano): Am Sonntag Morgen (Paul Heyse)—An ein Veilchen (Hölty)—Sehnsucht (Bohemian ballad)—Wiegenlied (Brahms)—Abend Dämmerung (Schack)

42. *Transcriptions of German Folksongs* (seven volumes) *Drei Lieder* for male chorus (six voices a capella): Abend Ständchen (Clemens Brentano)—Vignette (Wilhelm Müller)—Darthula's Burial Song (Ossian, translated by Johann Gottfried von Herder)

44. *Zwölf Lieder und Romanzen* for female chorus (a capella or with piano): Part I. Minnelied (Johann Heinrich Voss)—Der Bräutigam (Eichendorff)—Barcarole (Italian folksong)—Die Müllerin (Chamisso)—Die Nonne (Uhland) Part II. Nun steh'n die Rosen (Heyse)—Die Berge sind spitz (Brahms)—Am Wildbach die Weiden (Brahms)—Und gehst du über den Kirchhof (Brahms)—Die Braut (Müller)—Märznacht (Uhland)

1869 52. *Liebeslieder* (Brahms) for mixed voices, two pianos *Liebeslieder* for string quartet, two pianos

65. *New Liebeslieder Waltzes* (Brahms) for mixed voices, two Hungarian Dances, Vols. I, II, for two pianos; also Vols. III, IV, completed and published in 1880

1870 53. The "*Alto Rhapsody,*" contralto solo, male chorus, orchestra

1871 55. *Triumphlied,* chorale for eight voices, orchestra (and organ, ad lib.)

YEAR	OPUS	
	54.	*Schicksalslied* for mixed chorus and orchestra
	57.	*Acht Lieder* (Daumer) for voice and piano:

      Vol. I.   Von waldbekränzter Höhe—Wenn du nur zuweilen
—Es träumte mich—Ach, wende diesen Blick

      Vol. II. In meiner Nächte Sehnen—Strahlt zuweilen auch
ein mildes Licht—Die Schnur, die Perl an Perlen—
Unbewegte laue Luft

   58. *Acht Lieder* for voice and piano:

      Vol. I.   Blinde Kuh (August Kopisch)—Während des Regens (Kopisch)—Die Spröde (folksong from Calabria)—O komme holde Sommernacht (Grohe)

      Vol. II. Schwermut (Carl Candidus)—In der Gasse (Hebbel)—Vorüber (Hebbel)—Serenade (Schack)

1872		Nothing published
1873	56A	*Eight Variations on a Haydn Theme* for orchestra
	56B	The same for two pianos
	59.	*Acht Lieder* for voice and piano:

      Vol. I.   Dämm'rung senkte sich von oben (Goethe)—Auf
dem See (Carl Simrock)—Regenlied (Klaus Groth)
—Nachklänge (Groth)

      Vol. II. Agnes (Mörike)—Gute Nacht (Daumer)—Mein
wundes Herz (Groth)—Dein blaues Auge (Groth)

| 1874 | 60. | *Quartet No. 3*, C-minor (piano and strings): Allegro—Scherzo —Andante—Allegro |
| | 63. | *Neun Lieder* for voice and piano: |

      Vol. I.   Frühlingstrost (Max von Schenkendorf)—Erinnerung *(ditto)*—An ein Bild *(ditto)*—An die Tauben
(ditto)

      Vol. II. Junge Liebe 1. *(ditto)*—Junge Liebe 2. *(ditto)*—
Heimweh 1. (Groth)—Heimweh 2. (Schenkendorf)
—Heimweh 3. *(ditto)*

   64. *For Vocal Quartets* with solo parts (mixed) and piano: An
die Heimat (Carl Otto Sternau)—Der Abend (Schiller)—
Fragen (Daumer)

   61. *Four Duets* (soprano and contralto, with piano): Die Schwestern (Mörike)—Klosterfräulein (Kerner)—Phänomen
(Goethe "Westöstlicher Divan")—Die Boten der Liebe
(Josef Wenzig)

   62. *Sieben Lieder* (mixed chorus a capella): Rosemarin (from
anthology *Des Knaben Wunderbuch*)—Von alten Liebesliedern (*Wunderbuch*)—Waldesnacht (Heyse)—Dein
Herzlein mild (Heyse)—All' meine Herzengedanken
(Heyse)—Es geht ein Wehen (Heyse)—Vergangen ist mir
Glück und Heil (old folksong)

| 1875 | 68. | *Symphony No. 1*, C-minor: Un poco sostenuto—Andante— Un poco allegretto—Adagio |
| 1876 | 67. | *Quartet for Strings No. 3*, B-flat major: Vivace—Andante— Agitato—Allegretto con variazioni—Doppio Movimento |

YEAR	OPUS	
	85.	*Sechs Lieder* for voice and piano: Sommerabend (Heine)— Mondenschein *(ditto)* — Mädchenlied (Kapper) — Ade *(ditto)*—Frühlingslied (Geibel)—Todessehnen (Schenkendorf)
1883	90.	*Symphony No. 3,* F-major: Allegro—Andante—Allegretto— Allegro
1884	91.	*Contralto Lieder* (with viola and piano): Gestillte Sehnsucht (Rückert)—Geistliches Wiegenlied (Geibel-Lope de Vega)
	92.	*Mixed Quartets* (solo voices and piano): O schöne Nacht (Daumer)—Spätherbst (Hermann Allmers)—Abendlied (Hebbel)—Warum? (Goethe)
	93.	*Lieder und Romanzen* (four voices, a capella choir): Part I. Der bucklichte Fiedler (folksong)—Das Mädchen (Kapper)—O süsser Mai (Louis Achim von Arnim)— Fahr' wohl (Rückert)—Der Falke (Kapper)—Beherzigung (Goethe) Part II. *Tafellied* (Eichendorff), six voices, piano *ad lib.*
	94.	*Fünf Lieder* (for low voice and piano): Mit vierzig Jahren (Rückert)—Steigt auf, geliebte Schatten (Halm)—Mein Herz ist schwer (Geibel)—Sapphische Ode (Schmidt) Kein Haus, keine Heimat (Halm)
	95.	*Sieben Lieder* (for voice and piano): Das Mädchen (Kapper) Bei dir sind meine Gedanken (Halm)—Beim Abschied *(ditto)*—Der Jäger *(ditto)*—Vorschneller Schwur (Kapper) —Mädchenlied (Heyse)—Schön war, das ich dir weihte (Halm)
1885	98.	*Symphony No. 4,* E-minor: Allegro—Andante—Allegretto— Allegro
1886	99.	*Sonata No. 2 for Piano and Cello,* F-major: Allegro—Adagio —Allegro Appassionato—Allegro
	100.	*Sonata No. 2 for Piano and Cello,* F-major: Allegro—Andante —Vivace—Allegretto
	101.	*Trio No. 3 for Piano, Violin, Cello,* C-minor: Allegro—Presto —Andante—Allegro
	96.	*Vier Lieder* (voice and piano): Der Tod, das ist die kühle Nacht (Heine)—Wir wandelten (Daumer)—Es schauen die Blumen (Heine)—Meerfahrt *(ditto)*
	97.	*Sechs Lieder* (voice and piano): Nachtigall (Carl Reinhold) —Auf dem Schiffe *(ditto)*—Entführung (Alexis)—Dort in den Weiden (folksong)—Komm bald (Groth)—Trennung (folksong)
1887	102.	*Concerto for Violin, Cello, Orchestra,* A-minor: Allegro—Andante—Vivace
	103.	*Zigeuner Lieder* (four voices and piano): He, Zigeuner, greife in die Saiten—Hochgetürmte Rimafluth—Wisst ihr, war mein Kindchen—Lieber Gott, du weisst—Brauner Bursche, führt zum Tanze—Kommt dir manchmal in den Sinn

YEAR	OPUS	
1888	108.	*Sonata No. 3 for Piano and Violin,* D-minor: Allegro—Adagio Un poco presto—Presto Agitato
1889	110.	Three Motets (four to eight voices, mixed choir a capella): Doch ich bin arm—Du, arme Welt—Wenn wir in tiefem Leid
1890	111.	*Quintet for Strings No. 2,* G-major: Allegretto—Un poco Allegretto—Vivace
1891	114.	*Trio for Piano, Violin, Clarinet* (or Viola), A-minor: Allegro —Adagio—Andantino—Allegro
	115.	*Quintet for Clarinet and Strings,* B-minor: Allegro—Adagio— Andantino—Con Moto
1892	116.	*Phantasien* (for piano):

Vol. I.   Capriccios: D-minor, G-minor, Intermezzo in A-minor

Vol. II.   Intermezzos: E-minor, E-minor and E-major, Capriccio in D-minor

| | 117. | *Three Intermezzos* (for piano): E-flat major, B-flat minor, C-sharp minor |
| 1893 | 118. | *Sechs Clavierstücke:* |

Intermezzos: A-minor, A-major, F-minor, E-flat minor
Ballade G-minor, Romanze F-major

| | 119. | *Vier Clavierstücke:* Intermezzos in B-minor, E-major, C-major, Rhapsody in E-Flat major |

Etude (after Chopin), F-minor
Etude (after Weber), D-major (Rondo)
Presto for violin solo (after Bach)
Presto for piano, left-hand solo (after Bach)
Chaconne for piano, left-hand solo (after Bach), D-minor
Gavotte, A-major (Gluck, "Paride et Elena")
Fifty-one Exercises and Etudes in two vols.
Abendregen from "Blätter für Hausmusik"

| 1894 | 120. | *Two Sonatas* for piano and clarinet (or viola): |

1. F-minor: Allegro—Andante—Allegretto—Vivace
2. E-flat major: Allegro—Allegro appassionato—Andante

Movement in C-Minor for a sonata (piano and violin) cowritten by Brahms, Schumann, and Dietrich
Six Volumes of German Folksongs (transcribed) for voice and piano
One Volume of German Folksongs (transcribed) for solo voice and piano

| 1895 | | No composing, due to worry over last illness of Clara Schumann |
| 1896 | 121. | *Vier ernste Gesänge* (voice and piano, with Biblical text): Denn es gehet dem Menschen—Ich wandte mich und sahe —O Tod, wie bitter—Wenn ich mit Menschen und mit Engelszungen |

Brahms Works of Uncertain Date

OPUS

29. *Two Motets* for mixed chorus (five voices, a capella):
    1. Es ist ein Heil uns kommen her
    2. Schaffe in mir, Gott, ein reines Herz
30. *Sacred Song* for mixed choir, four voices, organ or piano (text by Paul Fleming): Lass' dich nur nichts dauern
8. *Trio No. 1* (for piano, violin, cello), B-major: Allegro—Scherzo—Adagio—Allegro
13. *Funeral Hymn* (mixed choir and wind instruments)
5. *Sonata No. 3*, F-minor (piano): Allegro—Intermezzo—Andante—Allegro
9. *Variations* on a theme by Schumann
10. *Four Ballades:* D-minor, D-major, B-major, B-minor
    1. Variations on an original theme
    2. Variations on an Hungarian theme
122. *Eleven Choral Preludes* (for organ)
    Fugue, A-flat minor
    O Traurigkeit, A-minor: Prelude—Chorale—Fugue (for organ)
104. *Fünf Lieder* (mixed voices, a capella):
    1. Nachtwache—"Leise Töne der Brust"
    2. Nachtwache—"Ruh'n sie? ruft das Horn"
    3. Letztes Glück—"Leblos gleitet Blatt um Blatt"
    4. Verlorene Jugend—"Brausten alle Berge"
    5. Im Herbst—"Ernst ist der Herbst"
109. *Deutsche Fest-und-Gedenksprüche* (Thanksgiving Service)
112. *Six Gypsy Songs* (four voices, a capella):
    1. Sehnsucht
    2. Nächtens
    3-6. Four Gypsy rhythms
113. *Thirteen Canons* (female voices, piano)
3. *Sechs Lieder* (tenor or soprano, and piano):
    1. Liebestreu (Reinick)
    2. Liebe und Frühling, I (Fallersleben)
    3. Liebe und Frühling, II (Fallersleben)
    4. Lied aus dem Gedicht "Ivan" (Friedrich Martin von Bodenstedt)
    5. In der Fremde (Eichendorff)
    6. Lied (Eichendorff)
6. *Fünf Lieder* (soprano or tenor, and piano):
    1. Spanisches Lied (Heyse)
    2. Der Frühling (Jean Baptiste Rousseau)
    3. Nachwirkung (Alfred Meissiner)
    4. Wie die Wolke nach der Sonne (Fallersleben)
    5. Nachtigallen schwingen *(ditto)*
7. *Sechs Lieder* (voice and piano):
    1. Treue Liebe (Count Claude Ferrand)
    2. Parole (Eichendorff)

OPUS

OPUS

      4. Meine Lieder (Adolf Frey)
      5. Ein Wanderer (Reinhold)
107. *Fünf Lieder* (voice and piano):
      1. An die Stolze (Flemming)
      2. Salamander (Lemcke)
      3. Das Mädchen spricht (Otto Friedrich Gruppe)
      4. Maienkätzchen (Liliencron)
      5. Mädchenlied (Heyse)

Brahms Works without Opus Number

Vierzehn deutsche Volkslieder (chorus in four voices) presumably composed in 1862 and 1863 while Brahms directed the Singakademie of Hamburg and Vienna.

Vol. I.   1. Von edler Art
          2. Mit Lust tät ich ausreiten
          3. Bei nächtlicher Weil
          4. Vom heiligen Märtyrer Emmerano, Bischoff von Regensburg
          5. Täublein weiss
          6. Ach lieber Herre Jesu Christ
          7. Sankt Raphael

Vol. II. 1. In stiller Nacht
          2. Abschiedslied
          3. Der tote Knabe
          4. Die Wollust in dem Mayen
          5. Morgengesang
          6. Schnitter Tod
          7. Der englische Jäger

Vierzehn Kinderlieder (for children's voices and piano):
      1. Dornröschen
      2. Die Nachtigall
      3. Die Henne
      4. Sandmännchen
      5. Der Mann
      6. Haidenröslein
      7. Das Schlaraffenland
      8. Beim Ritt auf dem Knie
      9. Der Jäger im Walde
    10. Das Mädchen und die Hasen
    11. Wiegenlied
    12. (missing)
    13. Marienwürmchen
    14. Dem Schutzengel

Mondnacht ("Es war, als hätt' der Himmel") for high voice and piano (Eichendorff)

BIBLIOGRAPHY

Ambros, A. W. *Robert Schumann Tage und Werke*. Leipzig: 1890.
Audley, A. *Frederic Chopin, Sa Vie et ses Oeuvres*. Paris: 1880.
Baker, Theo. *Franz Schubert*. New York. 1897.
Basch, V. *La Vie Douloureuse de Schumann*. Paris: 1928.
Beaufils, M. *Schumann*. Paris: 1932.
Bedford, Herbert. *Schumann*. London: 1933.
Benassis, J. *La Folie de Schumann*. Paris: 1931.
Bie, Oscar. *History of Pianoforte and Pianoforte Players*. London: 1899.
Boetticher, Wolfgang. *Robert Schumann: Persönlichkeit und Werk*. Berlin: 1941.
Browne, P. A. *Brahms: The Symphonies*. New York: 1933.
Calvocoressi, M. *Schumann*. Paris: 1912.
Casella, Alfredo. *El Piano*. Buenos Aires: 1942.
Chantavoine, Jean. *Musiciens et Poètes*. Paris: 1912.
Charles, M. *Zeitgenössische Tondichter*. Leipzig: 1888.
Colles, H. C. *Brahms*. London: 1908.
Colling, A. *La Vie de Robert Schumann*. Paris: 1931.
Cortot, Alfred. *Aspects de Chopin*. Paris: 1949.
Dahms, Walther. *Robert Schumann*. Berlin: 1916.
David, E. *Les Mendelssohn-Bartholdy et Robert Schumann*. Paris: 1886.
Delacroix, Eugène. *Journal*. Paris: 1929. Vol. III.
Duval, Georges. *Les Amours (du poète) de Robert Schumann*. Paris: 1901.
Erb, J. Lawrence. *Brahms*. Translated by Eugenio Ingster. Buenos Aires: 1952.
Erler, Hermann. *Robert Schumann: Aus Seinen Briefen*. Berlin: 1887. 2 Vols.
Ernest, Gustave. *Johannes Brahms: Persönlichkeit, Leben und Schaffen*. Berlin: 1930.
Ernouf, Baron. *Les Compositeurs Célèbres*. Paris: 1888.
Fuller-Maitland, J. A. *Masters of German Music*. London: 1894.
_____. *Robert Schumann*. London: 1884.
_____. *Schumann's Pianoforte Works*. London: 1927.
Füllöp-Miller, René. *Beethoven*. Munich: 1924.
Guedalla, Philip. *The Second Empire*. New York: 1922.
Hadow, W. H. *Studies in Modern Music*. London: 1926.

Herbert, May. *The Life of Robert Schumann Told in His Letters*. London: 1890.

Hueffer, F. *Die Poesie in der Musik*. Leipzig: 1874.

Huneker, James. *Chopin*. New York: 1916.

Jansen, F. G. *Die Davidsbündler: Aus Robert Schumanns Sturm und Drang Periode*. Leipzig: 1883.

Julien, Adolphe. "Johannes Brahms," *Revue Internationale de Musique*. Paris: 1898.

Kalbeck, Max. "Robert Schumann in Wien," *Wiener Allgemeine Zeitung*. Vienna: Sept.-Oct., 1880.

Karenin, Wladimir. *George Sand, Sa Vie et Ses Oeuvres*. Paris: 1899-1926. 4 Vols.

Keller, Otto. *Wolfgang Amadeus Mozart: Bibliographie und Ikonographie*. Berlin and Leipzig: 1927.

Krehbiel, H. E. *Johannes Brahms and His Songs*. New York: 1902.

Lee, E. Markham. *Brahms' Orchestral Works*. New York: 1931.

Litzmann, Berthold. *Clara Schumann: Ein Künsterleben*. Leipzig: 1925. 3 Vols.

_____. *Clara Schumann, Johannes Brahms: Briefe*. Leipzig: 1927. 2 Vols.

MacMaster, Henry. *La Folie de Robert Schumann*. Paris: 1928.

Marmontel, Antoine Françoise. *Les Pianistes Célèbres*. Paris: 1878.

Marsop, P. *Musikalische Essays*. Berlin: 1899.

Maubel, Henri. *Préfaces pour les Musiciens*. Paris: 1895.

Mary, Florence. *The Life of Johannes Brahms*. London: 1928. 2 Vols.

Moebius, P. J. *Ueber Robert Schumanns Krankheit*. 1906.

Murdoch, William. *Brahms: With an Analytical Study of the Complete Pianoforte Works*. London: 1933.

Niecks, Frederick. *Robert Schumann: A Supplementary and Corrective Biography*. London: 1925.

Niemann, Walter. *Brahms*. Translated by Catherine Alison Phillips. New York: 1931.

_____. "Johannes Brahms als Klavier-Komponist," *Die Musik*. Berlin: 1904. Vol. II.

_____. *Mendelssohn's Lieder ohne Worte*. Leipzig: 1916.

Ninck, V. *Schumann und die Romantik*. Heidelberg: 1929.

Nottebohm, Gustav. *Mozartiana*. Leipzig: 1880.

Pascal, J. "Les Maladies Mentales de Schumann," *Journal de Psychologie*. Paris: March, 1908.

Patterson, Annie W. *Schumann*. Translated by Ingster. Buenos Aires: 1952.

Pitrou, Robert. *La Vie Intérieure de Robert Schumann*. Paris: 1925.

Pohl, Richard. "Erinnerungen an Robert Schumann," *Deutsche Revue*. Berlin: 1878.

Pulver, Jeffrey. *Brahms*. London: 1926.

Riemann, Hugo. *Johannes Brahms*. Berlin: 1899.

Reinecke, C. *Schumann*. Berlin: 1902.

Reissmann, August. *Robert Schumann, Seine Leben und Seine Werke*. Leipzig: 1879.

Sand, George. *Un Hiver à Majorque*. Paris: 1843.

Schoene, A. *Ueber Musikerbriefe*. Leipzig: 1886.

Schumann, Clara. *Robert Schumanns Jugendbriefe.* Leipzig: 1886.

Schumann, Eugénie. *Robert Schumann.* Paris: 1937.

Schumann, Robert. *Briefe: Neue Folge.* Edited by F. G. Jansen. Leipzig: 1904.

————. *Ecrits sur la Musique et les Musiciens.* Translated by Henri de Curzon. Paris: 1898.

————. *Gesammelte Schriften.* Leipzig: 1914.

Schwarz, W. *Robert Schumann und die Variation.* Koenigsberg: 1931.

Specht, Richard. *Johannes Brahms.* Translated by Eric Blom. London: 1930.

Spitta, Phillipp. "Schumann," *Grove's Dictionary of Music and Musicians.* London: 1928.

Tessmer, H. *Robert Schumann.* Stuttgart: 1930.

Turner, Walter James. *Mozart: The Man and His Works.* New York: 1938.

Vogel, B. *Robert Schumanns Klavierton-Poesie.* Leipzig: 1887.

Wasielewski, W. J., von. *Robert Schumann: Eine Biographie.* Bonn: 1880.

Weingartner, Felix. *Symphony Writers since Beethoven.* Translated by A. Bles. New York: 1933.

INDEX

Because the whole of this book is the story of Robert Schumann and Clara (Wieck) Schumann, their names have not been included in the following index.